THE SHADOWS

THE SHADOWS

THE DEFINITIVE STORY

BOB STANLEY

new modern

new modern

First published in the UK in 2026 by New Modern
An imprint of Putman Publishing
Mermaid House, Puddle Dock, Blackfriars, London, EC4V 3DB

@newmodernbooks
@newmodern_books

Hardback ISBN: 978-1-917923-87-3
eBook ISBN: 978-1-917923-88-0

A CIP catalogue record for this book is available in the British Library.

Publishing and editorial: Pete Selby, James Lilford and Eleanor Porter
Typesetting: Marie Doherty

1 3 5 7 9 10 8 6 4 2

New Modern is an imprint of Putman Publishing

www.newmodernbooks.co.uk
www.putmanpublishing.co.uk

FSC www.fsc.org
MIX
Paper | Supporting responsible forestry
FSC® C018072

Printed and bound in Great Britain
by Clays Ltd, Elcograf S.p.A.

For my Dad,

David 'Wolf' Shukman

CONTENTS

FOREWORD

Hank and Bruce had been playing at the then 2i's coffee bar in Soho, London, where I had also been playing, but who would have thought a few months later I would have my first record 'Move It' climbing our British charts? With the success of the record came an invitation to join the Kalin Twins, who were about to tour the UK. I asked Hank and Bruce to join me and they did.

We became a new group overnight. Jet Harris became our bass player, with Tony Meehan playing drums. We played together, toured together and recorded together. We were family. But we soon had competition, and loads of it.

We loved what we did and I can only look back and sometimes wonder… *Would I have made it without the Shads?* Maybe not.

I will always be grateful for the support I had from one of the greatest bands that rock 'n' roll ever gave birth to.

Sir Cliff Richard, 2026

INTRODUCTION

The first time I heard the Shadows was at my grandmother's. She had that *Shadows' Greatest Hits* LP, the original one on Columbia, with the great cover. I used to listen to it at her house – it was a terraced house in a long-since demolished part of Sheffield in Darnell, two-up two-down houses with the shared backyard and shared outside toilet. Those streets were actually dangerous places to live in the early '70s when I was a boy because the cement had completely gone to dust between the bricks – it was only gravity that was holding them all upright.

My dad was always either in the steelworks or working in bands, and mum was a nurse, so I was looked after quite a lot by my grandparents on both sides. My dad's mum was a single mum, which was quite unique in the '50s – she was into really great music. That's how I discovered Fats Domino, too, amongst many others; she used to sing his 'Wait and See' to me and say that things were going to get better for us. And they did, through music. But she used to play the Shadows all the time.

Dad never really admitted to liking them, but he grudgingly thought that Hank was great, and a lot of those hard rockers were like that. I think it's a real shame, the begrudging way he's talked about by some guitarists – I believe that he deserves a great deal more respect than he's got. Jeff Beck definitely – if you watched him do his thing – took a shitload from Hank.

Hank's almost like the face that launched a thousand ships; he was the guitar player that launched a thousand careers. Everybody who heard the Velvet Underground formed a band, that's the tagline, because they sold no records at the time. Obviously, the Shadows sold millions of records, but they inspired so many guitar players that went on to achieve radically different things, myself included.

And I love their sound. Another beautiful thing about them was that it was a very British sound. I think they probably tried to copy American artists like Duane Eddy, but they didn't succeed. It was like the way the Rolling Stones were trying to copy the blues, and they failed massively, but they invented something completely new by trying, which is always the nature of everything that we do. We fail hugely to copy exactly, but maybe by accident rather than design we create a different shade or a hue from the prism of it all.

Hank is not only a great guitar player but he's also a great engineer, or like a skilled machinist and boss technician of guitar playing because the Fender Stratocaster is a very complicated instrument to play if you want to master it. The control that he has over what he's doing on the fretboard, plus the tremolo arm, and the volume and tone controls, it's like somebody flying an exhibition-level starship to me. Like the Red Arrows, but in space. Because if you actually understand anything at all about playing that particular guitar, to do what he's doing technically, it's not just about fingers and thumbs and plectrums and stuff like that, it's something else far more elaborate and precise. If you get it even slightly wrong, it sounds hideous.

I had the great fortune to work with him. Apart from being a wonderful, inspirational, unique, years-ahead-of-his-time guitar player, his name has entered the English language as a rhyme for being very, very hungry. I wonder how many people who use that phrase every day are actually aware of who he is and his music? I hope they are.

Anyway, I'd got this piece of music. My manager heard it and said, 'You should record that, it's beautiful.' I said, 'No, it's too close to a pastiche of the Shadows, I can't do it.' It was over the line – it wasn't like a tribute, it could have actually been a Shadows song. So I said, 'I'll do it if Hank Marvin plays on it.' I thought, *that'll shut him up!* But my manager's an extremely tenacious human being – he sent a demo to Hank, who miraculously got back to him – he loved it.

When it came to a title, I could only think of 'I'm Absolutely Hank Marvin' because of the irony, where I am actually not Hank Marvin but I'm having him play on the record. If you listen to it, with his volume swells, and the bends, and the tremolo… it's so beautiful. Even though I know I wrote it, it's like a showcase for Hank, for what he does. I'm very proud that happened.

I think it's an interesting arc. From me listening to Hank as a little boy – in that terraced house which, when they came to knock it all down, they literally touched it with the wrecking ball and the whole street just collapsed – from that humble kind of place to me actually working with him, that was wonderful. We never met, we still haven't… we did that track over the internet, but he's friends with people I know from Sheffield who now live in Australia. Wheels within wheels.

At the end of it, he sent a handwritten note, something along the lines of, 'I've done this in a couple of takes. Use what you like, ditch what you don't. I hope you like it and I've done my best, kind regards, Hank.' And then he's written, 'PS I don't do refunds!'

I kept it, and I framed it.

Richard Hawley, 2026

PREFACE

In April 1974 at Leeds Crown Court, T. Dan Smith, the former city council boss of Newcastle-upon-Tyne, was jailed for five years. The John Poulson affair was a scandal that had involved large-scale bribery in the post-war redevelopment of Britain. It had brought down home secretary Reginald Maudling; it destroyed T. Dan Smith. Palms had been greased, no question, but Smith would always claim he was made a scapegoat.

Smith's legacy – or his crime – was a physical wrenching of Newcastle, from a decaying Victorian backwater into the modern age. Born in Wallsend, he thought his hometown could be another Milan, an Athens even. In a few short years, he tore down the slums, restored the parks, cleaned up the river, built new homes, shopping centres and a civic centre; he'd made it a destination. Leaving rivals Sunderland and Middlesbrough eating dust, Newcastle became the unquestioned capital of the north east. Smith believed the whole of the north could rise again and counter London's dominance. It was simply a matter of will and determination.

Among the grimy, decrepit houses to be demolished in this grand rebuilding of Newcastle-upon-Tyne were the homes of one Brian Rankin and his rhythm guitar-playing sidekick Bruce Welch.

Thomas Dan Smith gave himself a Hollywood-styled name – T. Dan – in the style of a visionary movie director. Brian Rankin would likewise be reborn, aged sixteen, as Hank B. Marvin, a brave move for a stick-thin Geordie with milk-bottle spectacles and spots. But Hank B. Marvin and T. Dan Smith were great modernisers; both had a concept to change Britain.

As the country's first rock group at the turn of the 1960s, the Shadows would provide mental escape for British teenagers still ground down by national service, bowing down to their elders, keeping up appearances and working on lathes at the age of sixteen. Hank Marvin, in particular, would become a lightning rod for liberation from monochrome post-war England. Listening to the thunder of the Shadows, you were transported to Dakota, or the High Sierra, or further into the beyond to Atlantis – away from 'the Frightened City'. If you got yourself a red Fender Stratocaster and learned how to play, you too could be this free. The Shadows – two guitars, bass and drums – became the original blueprint for a youthquake. They would revolutionise and rebuild British popular music.

T. Dan Smith was a radical agitator – and a successful one. Hank Marvin, though, would not be followed around by MI5; he kept his politics to himself. He started a revolution without intending a band of followers to spray-paint HANK MARVIN IS GOD on back-alley walls.

It's tempting to say that, had he been born into a slightly later age, Hank would have known how to play the game of the guitar hero a little more cutely. Maybe he wouldn't have organised a bed-in, but he might have been there at Grosvenor Square and he might have said he'd written the scything 'Throw Down a Line' about the confusion and violence of 1968. Or maybe he'd have been in San Francisco, writing paeans for the peaceniks, such as 'The Dreams I Dream'.

It's tempting to say this because it's easy to mistake the Shadows as being of an earlier generation than the Beatles. This is not the case.

They were exactly the same age. The main difference between the formative Shadows and Beatles was that Hank Marvin and Bruce Welch escaped their upbringing in the industrial north sooner, trying their hands in London aged just sixteen. John Lennon, Paul McCartney and George Harrison (then the Quarrymen) made their first recording in the exact same month as Hank and Bruce (then the Chesternuts). But John and George wanted to go to art college, so they stayed in Liverpool which – in 1958 – meant they may as well have been living in Greenland as far as the British music industry was concerned.

Hank Marvin moved from Newcastle to London where, quite quickly, people realised he was the best guitarist in town. He played clean, single notes with extraordinary power and versatility. He owned the first-ever Fender Stratocaster in Britain, meaning he could bend notes and sound like a prophet from the future. Or, at least, from California. Before 'Apache', no one before had been able to make records that sounded both authentically American and shot through with an Anglo originality. What's more, Hank wrote his own songs with his grouchy lieutenant, Bruce. This was equally unheard of. In the first half of the 1960s, they were a national soundtrack, cajoling a country to emerge from the rubble, bright primary colours spinning out of singles – made with and without their singer Cliff Richard – like 'Summer Holiday', 'Foot Tapper', 'The Young Ones' and 'Kon-Tiki'.

T. Dan Smith did the public relations work for Peterlee – the kind of post-war dreamscape that the Shadows would soundtrack with 'Wonderful Land' – a brand-new community, unspoiled by bombsites and class divides, where there would be jobs for women, clean housing, public art and green spaces. The reality of Peterlee, Stevenage, Crawley and Glenrothes proved to be rather different, and the melancholic edge to later singles like 'Atlantis' and 'A Place in the Sun' would echo the illusory perfection of the new towns.

Objectively, the Shadows were huge. Unquestionably the most influential British group before the Beatles, they had twelve number-one singles in the early '60s: seven with Cliff and five instrumental. They were also one of the most influential groups in the world. Their style was adored and mimicked in Scandinavia, Yugoslavia, Spain, France, Australia and New Zealand, Brazil and Argentina and Mexico, the Far East and Canada. In fact, the only country that seemed immune to them was the US, which was more down to bad luck than bad judgment, as we'll discover later on.

Different eras and different situations affect our judgment and bend our understanding. Everything that has come since the '60s – whether it's Hank goofing around on Cliff's TV show, or their Eurovision entry in 1975, or the TV-advertised albums in the '90s that were essentially MOR instrumental albums of songs by Foreigner or Mike Oldfield – will, of course, shape how we think of the Shadows. They stuck around, and stuck around, and sometimes they were their own worst enemies. But then my pet theory is that if John Lennon had lived long enough, he'd have got the Beatles back together for Live Aid; he'd have been glad-handing with Bob Geldof and Midge Ure, possibly wearing a similar suit to Phil Collins, and we'd likewise be unable to shake that image from our heads. (I appreciate some people might think this would be a good look for John Lennon, but not me.)

What we can hear in the Shadows' '60s records, though, especially with the original quartet of Hank B. Marvin, Bruce Welch, Jet Harris and Tony Meehan, becomes indestructible with context: the rawness of the guitar break on 'FBI', the insanely fast rhythm guitar on 'The Savage', the fat R&B backbeat on 'The Rise and Fall of Flingel Bunt'. These records, and the group's image, defined the look, sound and feel of a British beat group as early as 1960. They are completely intertwined with what came after, with the Beatles, the Who, Fleetwood Mac, Queen, Dire Straits, the Smiths, Blur – the complete British rock and pop lineage. Outside of the UK, you can throw in Neil Young, too, who wrote 'From Hank to Hendrix' about his primary influences.

I won't be talking at great length in this book about guitar tone, or specific guitars and pedals. There are other books available that have already done a fine job of this.

My aim instead is to give context to the Shadows' music and shine a light on their legacy, to strip away the decades of moss and lichen and uncover the machinery underneath, the original sound, the original fury. I want to talk about how and where and why the Shadows' records were made, in the '60s and the '70s (the latter a considerably more unsettled decade for the group, but often just as rewarding).

I also wanted to talk about the Shadows' extended, though compact, family and how the original members unintentionally guided a generation of great pop songwriters and producers in the '70s and '80s, as well as becoming the source material for some of the most influential American music of the twenty-first century.

The Shadows kept their circle small, but the members were completely trusted.

'All you need is ten good people and you can do anything,' said T. Dan Smith. 'You don't even have to know what you're going to do. You can achieve anything, if you have the conviction. Between you, you have the ability to organise, then to publicise, and then to get across to ordinary people.'

Hank Marvin and Bruce Welch had to find eight more people. They didn't know them when they were in Newcastle; they would find them in London and Lincolnshire and Leeds. The other members of this elite were Jet Harris, Tony Meehan, Cliff Richard, Brian Bennett, John Rostill, Brian Locking, Alan Hawkshaw and – over in Australia – John Farrar. Just ten people.

Also in Australia were Alan Tarney, Trevor Spencer and Terry Britten while, crossing the oceans from Sydney to London in the same year as Newcastle's world-class international air terminal opened, was Olivia Newton-John. Then, hiding in the shadows of the Shadows, there would be Peter Gormley, Norrie Paramor and Peter Vince, the engineers who could produce, publicise and amplify the Shadows so they could shape and re-shape what was possible for kids in post-industrial Britain, and then in post-war Europe.

But once you take power, you get your hands dirty.

My aim is also to tell the story of the Shadows individually as well as collectively, which is often one of deep sadness in spite of their smiling public image – the missed opportunities, the deep depressions, the stupidly intense work rate, the mistakes they made so that the Beatles and others of their generation wouldn't have to. I've also been driven by Paul Morley's quote that 'a group called the Shadows should have been better and stranger than the group called the Shadows actually were'. I wanted to write this book to explain why the Shadows was actually the perfect name for the Shadows, and hopefully I will also help to pull their reputation from the shady corner it has been hiding in.

Viva los Shads!

Bob Stanley
West Yorkshire, March 2026

1

DIRTY OLD TOWN

Brian Rankin grew up in a two-bedroom flat, at 138 Stanhope Street, in the west end of Newcastle-upon-Tyne, with his mum and dad and little brother Joe. Newcastle was involved in a three-way tie – along with Glasgow and Liverpool – for the title of hardest city in post-war Britain. 'Violent fights between our back lane and an alliance of the other neighbouring back lanes was a major feature in my life for a while,' remembered Brian. 'We'd fight with stones, half-bricks, broom handles, whatever came to hand. I don't think we were naturally violent. Because we'd seen local gangs having a go at each other, we assumed that's how life's meant to be.' Aged eight, he ended up in Newcastle infirmary after being hit on the head with a brick.

One way out of getting brained by your neighbours was sport. Cricket in the alley, with the wicket painted on a dustbin, could just as easily lead to scraps, but football was different. The law of the jungle dictated an age-related hierarchy among the kids on his street, though being a decent footballer could make you an exemption: 'You respected the guys who could dribble a ball like Jackie Milburn.' Milburn was

'Wor Jackie', who had been a teenage pit worker in Ashington, Northumberland, until he took a wild chance and wrote to Newcastle United asking them for a trial. On Bonfire Night 1946, he led them to a 13–0 defeat of Newport County. He was a shining example – there *was* a life away from the shipyards and the back-to-backs; you just had to know when and how to take your chance. The kid Rankin also looked forward to the annual fair – the Hoppings – on the town moor where he would spend all his money on the dodgems. 'The whole idea of travelling around from town to town with no routine was really appealing.'

Routine was built into working-class Newcastle life. If you didn't want to work in the shipyard, there was always Richardson's leatherworks in Elswick, where raw, untreated animal hides were brought in and fine leather came out the other end (you didn't really want to know about the processes in between; that was men's business). On washing day, mothers would load up the pram and go to Bond Street baths and washhouse where, for a small fee, they had access to a sink, a bench and a dryer. Pubs were out of bounds for unaccompanied women, so the washhouse became the source of local news. No one had any money.

Nothing seemed to phase Brian Rankin, ever. Poverty at home didn't bother him – his dad didn't drink or gamble so, compared to some of his mates, Brian thought of them as relatively blessed financially. He was also developing a fascination with the family's wireless radio. How did it work? What *was* that noise? He thought the orchestra was somehow inside it, which was cute, but he also loved the weird noises you could get from twiddling the dial, which would be the first sign that Brian Rankin might turn out to have an ear for unusual sounds.

*

Bruce Cripps was an illegitimate child, something that hardly means a thing in the twenty-first century, but in post-war England it meant you were a 'bastard'. He didn't find out until he was seventeen and would feel deeply uncomfortable about it for decades, as if it meant he was sub-standard and always had something to prove. It also led to bouts of depression; finding out that his parents weren't married led to him suffering from what he described as an 'almost obsessive desire for perfection'.

The Cripps lad would grow up with no recollection of Grace Welch, his mother, who died when he was only five years old. She had married William 'Topper' Meehan in Ferryhill, County Durham, a pit village surrounded by nothing more than other pit villages. It was such a difficult marriage that Grace left Meehan and moved to Bognor on the south coast, a grey seaside town so desperate to improve its image – and its ugly name – that it was rechristened Bognor Regis in 1929 after King George V had spent a few weeks there on his sick bed, gulping in healthy sea air.

Age twenty-seven, Grace took her mother and sister Sadie with her to Bognor and found work at the Royal Norfolk Hotel, where she met Stan Cripps. One thing led to another and Bruce was born on 2 November 1941. Grace was still married to William Meehan; the rest of the Welch family in Ferryhill were not informed of Bruce's arrival.*

* In the early '60s, at the peak of the Shadows' fame, Bruce would get into his Rolls-Royce and drive over to the genteel suburb of Whickham, to see his Aunt Sadie at the bungalow he had bought for her. The Shadows were going to play at Newcastle

Soon after Bruce was born, the family all moved back to County Durham, leaving Stan Cripps in Bognor. They went to the tidy town of Chester-le-Street and a semi-detached house on Broadwood View. Bruce grew up to be a big, square-jawed lad who spent his time at the Palace cinema and fell in love with the romance of cowboy movies – Roy Rogers, Gene Autry, Hopalong Cassidy. Music was also starting to sink in. At home, Sunday roast was eaten to the strains of *Two-Way Family Favourites* on the BBC Light Programme, with Cliff Michelmore and Jean Metcalfe introducing the likes of Teresa Brewer's 'Music! Music! Music!', Patti Page's 'Tennessee Waltz' and Guy Mitchell's 'My Heart Cries For You'. It was light, undemanding stuff that eased Britain through the post-war era and its collective post-traumatic stress.

The idyll of Chester-le-Street was short-lived. Grace caught TB and died aged thirty-two. Bruce, just five years old, remained in the house on Broadwood View with Aunt Sadie. When his grandmother died in 1950, Sadie sold the house and moved in with her boyfriend, Nazam Din, in Newcastle, some eight miles to the north. It wasn't Chester-le-Street. Bruce remembered early '50s Newcastle as being 'almost devoid of colour'.

Machine shops, industrial terraces, the Dunston engine works, the Elswick ship yard... The city would soon be rebuilt by the city planners, but 'for the time being at least, the falling-down buildings and

---

City Hall that night, and Bruce must have been feeling on top of the world. Aunt Sadie decided this was the right time to tell Bruce that, when he was born, his uncle Jimmy had been best friends with Topper Meehan, so none of that side of the family had ever been told where his mother had escaped to. Even in the '60s, they weren't aware of Bruce's existence.

city slums I passed each day had to remain,' Bruce remembered. 'They fostered hopelessness, depravity and bitterness.'

They lived above Nazam's fish and chip shop on Elswick Road, a run-down thoroughfare west of the city centre. A few doors down from the chippy was the Crown Hotel, a pub that was always the first port of call for men who had just come out of prison, as it was opposite the dole office. A hundred yards away was Scotswood Road where the names of the pubs unceremoniously reflected the industries of Elswick: the Gun, the Hydraulic Crane, the Forge Hammer, the Vulcan, the Blast Furnace, the Rifle Hotel, the Mechanics Arms. Bruce had moved to Elswick Road just as the area was sinking into terminal industrial decline. Its dark brick terraces were at the end of their lives, their purposes outgrown. Hopelessness, depravity… the streets of Elswick would be where the pre-teen Mary Bell went on to notoriously kill two small boys in the late '60s.

*

> 'The houses down here were falling apart. No inside water. All along Scotswood Road, there was no water. If [T. Dan] Smith didn't do something, these slums were going to be here forever. It wasn't as civilised as people think. About ten years after the war, it got like if you turned 'round they pinched your bootlaces.'
>
> Jimmy Forsyth, photographer

Aged eleven, Brian Rankin and Bruce Cripps were both sent to Rutherford Grammar School after passing the eleven-plus. This dirty old part of the city, where the sun refused to shine, was a crumbling relic. Eighteen months later, the boys were moved to a new, purpose-built school at Westgate. Bruce remembered there was 'room to breathe, as Newcastle started the first stages of its post-war redevelopment'.

Brian earned a nickname, Hank, on account of his bow legs which meant he walked like a cowboy. On top of his bandy legs, it turned out his eyesight was terrible and he was given an inch-thick pair of NHS glasses after he managed to throw a dart into his brother's leg rather than at a dartboard. Still, he appeared to have remained incredibly carefree. Instead of his nickname and his NHS specs getting him down, he ran with them, adopting the nickname and dressing in a blue duffle coat and brightly coloured scarf, cutting a dash like a fourteen-year-old Parisian jazzer. 'I had this image of myself as being kind of bohemian, with the duffle coat and the school scarf, and the hair slightly longer than normal – not long hair by any stretch of the imagination. Just a little longer, so the fringe hung down a bit, sideburns… But I couldn't afford to be more bohemian. You needed money to be a beatnik.'

Bruce, on the other hand, would turn up at school angry and half asleep after having to gut fish and peel potatoes for Nazam every evening and scrambling to do his homework every morning on the bus. At weekends he'd be loading, unloading and selling wares on one of Nazam's market stalls across Tyneside. All this work was unpaid. He had no time for himself, not even for homework. One teacher caught him nodding off and shouted 'Cripps! Your mother must have dragged you up to have such appalling manners.' Bruce was already on the rugby team, already a fighter, a good fighter; when he didn't have time to do his homework on the bus he'd copy some other kid's and they never argued. Now his dead mother's name was being used in vain and that was too much. He walked to the front of the class and smacked the teacher in the face.

In 1955, Bruce got to see *Blackboard Jungle* at the Regal cinema in the Newcastle suburb of Kenton. It was an X, meaning you had to be eighteen to get into the theatre and Bruce was just fourteen. No matter. He had an eighteen-year-old friend who wanted to see it; his mate bought a ticket, made like he was heading for the toilet and, instead, opened the exit doors to let Bruce in. Once the film started, with Bill Haley's 'Rock Around the Clock', Bruce remembered how 'everyone in the cinema stood up and cheered. It was so different from what anyone expected.' When he came home from school one day with his hair greased back in a quiff, Sadie tried to literally pull his hair out – she was convinced he'd joined a local gang. She didn't understand. Most parents didn't understand. That was half the appeal.

Bruce found fairgrounds, with like-minded souls dressed up to the nines, to be the place to hear rock 'n' roll loud and unfiltered – and it sounded even better from a carousel or a big wheel. You didn't have to wait for the annual Hoppings. Spanish City was a permanent funfair at nearby Whitley Bay, six miles up the coast. The smell of diesel and candy floss, the multi-coloured lights, the girls... Bruce heard Buddy Holly, the Everly Brothers, Johnnie Ray's forgotten rocker 'Yes Tonight Josephine', Gene Vincent's barely controlled 'Be-Bop-a-Lula'. This was the life he wanted.

*

Hank discovered jazz. His schoolfriend Brian White (nicknamed Jim; none of the Brians at Rutherford Grammar seemed to be called Brian) gave Hank a wind-up gramophone and the first record he bought to play on it was Earl Bostic's 'Flamingo'. He started reading *Melody Maker* and would cut out the jazz columns, gluing them into a school exercise book, alongside tickets for shows he had been to by George Melly and Lionel Hampton. Their French teacher, James Moody, took a shine to Hank. He brought his five-string Windsor G banjo into school one day and Hank cheekily asked if he wanted to sell it. So Mr Moody sold him the banjo, which Hank paid for in weekly instalments of half a crown. He bought a tutor book and practised long and hard. He saw Chris Barber's Jazz Band, the greatest in the land, play Newcastle City Hall and got all of their autographs (signed, even then, 'to Hank'). Johnny Duncan was their banjo player, having replaced Lonnie Donegan who was by then a solo star; Duncan himself would leave soon after and have his own rollicking solo hit with the frenetic 'Last Train to San Fernando'. Hank tried to imagine being a good-enough banjo player to play with Barber. He tried to imagine having his own record deal, his name printed on the maroon Nixa or green Columbia labels.

In 1956, Hank started to hang out at the Vieux Carré, a club in a condemned building on Melbourne Street near the Tyne. It was run by Big Pete Deuchar, another banjo player, who had been to Tabley House public school but now lived in a caravan. Born in 1933, Pete was the heir to Newcastle's James Deuchar brewery business and his obsessions were cycling and New Orleans jazz. His wealthy upbringing provided him with an admirable nerve and after he heard that banjo player Diz Disley had left the Ken Colyer band, he wrote to British jazz hero Colyer. 'I received a letter from Pete Deuchar,' wrote Colyer in his autobiography, *When Dreams are in the Dust*, 'saying he was second only to [New Orleans player, Lawrence] Marrero and would like to join us. He came down and he was useless. We sent him home.'

Once back in Newcastle, Deuchar co-founded the Vieux Carré Jazzmen with trumpeter Peter Gascoigne and set up the club. He wore his run-in with Colyer like a badge, telling a local paper: 'He has scolded and derided me until now I can play with him whenever I like in London. And that is always a great thrill.'

Possibly through Deuchar's family connections, the Vieux Carré had a drinks licence, despite the state of the property. 'It was pretty rough at times,' recalled Peter Gascoigne in 1969, but he also reckoned 'it had an atmosphere like nowhere else – rain coming in, snow coming in. We had to stand on beer crates to get out of the water ... I think on one occasion we had umbrellas up, but the audience still came.'

For '50s British youth, after swing had swung its last, jazz was subdivided into three distinct areas: traditional – or trad – jazz (the earliest ensemble-based work, for the hardcore who thought it all went horribly wrong after Louis Armstrong quit New Orleans); revivalist jazz (post-Storyville jazz, with its main protagonists now in Chicago, which allowed space for solos and improv); and modern jazz, the post-war sound, fully alive and blossoming in the 1950s but hard to dance to. When the Vieux Carré opened, Chris Barber was at the heart of the revivalist scene to which Hank was drawn.*

Hank was a regular at the club and would chat to Big Pete about Ken Colyer, the world of jazz, his favourite players and the London clubs. Hank squinted, blurred the scene, and imagined he was in New Orleans talking to some jazz legend or other, rather than a beery bloke on Tyneside who could have been his uncle.

Apart from the banjo, Hank was also drawn to the clarinet 'for its fluidity, agility and tone'. He idolised Benny Goodman, Sidney Bechet and Monty Sunshine of Chris Barber's band. Unfortunately, Hank couldn't afford one. What's more – although no one in 1957 could have known – its days as one of the lead instruments in jazz were numbered. Then he heard something on the radio which turned his world around, as it would for thousands of British kids.

'When I was around fourteen, I got very much into listening to New Orleans and Chicago jazz and folk blues music,' Hank later told the BBC. 'Purely by chance, someone mentioned something about skiffle, which I'd never heard of, and they mentioned this track "Rock Island Line". I then heard it on the radio and thought, *Wow*. Lonnie [Donegan] had a marvellous ability to put energy and excitement into a track, and one thing that used to really grab me about this song is the way it builds up speed like a train, gradually – it's very rhythmic, and it gets more and more exciting. I was hooked when I heard that

---

* The trad jazz boom would come later, between 1959 and 1962, spearheaded by clarinet player Acker Bilk and then a host of lesser lights like Kenny Ball, who would survive as TV regulars until the 1980s, playing Beatles songs in a Dixieland style. Big Pete Deuchar was not too principled to ride this wave.

track and suddenly I wanted to be playing this sort of music. Lonnie was kind of instrumental of getting me into the stringed instrument area rather than a woodwind.'

Hank's school exercise books were soon covered with drawings of banjos, trumpets, clarinets, guitars and washboards; nothing electric, not yet. He also drew a plan of his first-ever group, the Riverside Skiffle Group made up of schoolmates and Vieux Carré comrades: John Tate and Derek Johnson were on guitars, Howard Muir on washboard, the wonderfully named Mal Malarky on mandolin and Hank's kid brother Joe would be the bassist. Willing it into life, variations on this line-up played in an old hall next door to the original Rutherford Grammar School building. Realising a Riverside Skiffle Group already existed, they became the Crescent City Skiffle Group to give themselves a bit of New Orleans weight. Hank was cool, but self-deprecating. 'I was pretty impressive in those days. You'd get a lot of admiration from people who could see you playing two different instruments. They thought somehow you were multi-talented – I mean, I was struggling to play either.

'We used to stagger around on a Friday night to all the local youth clubs and I'd walk in and say, "Look, we have a skiffle group – can we play for you?" And all the kids loved it, and they give us a cup of tea and a biscuit. We thought it was fantastic.'

By May of 1957, the Crescent City outfit felt confident enough to enter a skiffle contest run by the South Shields Jazz Club in the town's Pier Pavilion. They were up against the likes of the Team Valley Skiffle Group, Peter Bond Skiffle Group, Brian Vainbridge Skiffle Group, the Rumjunglers and the Black Cats. They performed 'Stagger Lee', with

Hank playing a banjo solo, an idea he'd got from watching Big Pete Deuchar and Ken Colyer at the Vieux Carré; Deuchar also happened to be on the panel of judges in South Shields. Undoubtedly impressed by this teenage prodigy in front of them, the judges awarded first prize to the Crescent Skiffle Group.

*

Hank and Bruce knew each other at school, but only became friends when Bruce brought his American-built, steel-bodied National guitar to school. He had been bought it for Christmas by Aunt Sadie, probably after she'd done a deal with another market stallholder. This was also – presumably without Nazam's knowledge – how she'd acquired a wind-up gramophone for Bruce, on which he played Lonnie Donegan and Chris Barber 78s while eating his favourite snack, sugar sandwiches. So, unsurprisingly, it was guitars that eventually brought them together – Hank the duffle-coated beatnik, scarf flying out at a jaunty angle, and Bruce the thick-set, would-be rocker, with a quiff that Sadie had literally tried to tear off his head. Hank was the scholar, exploring the origins of American music, an ethnologist; Bruce was happy just to make some noise.

Bruce had picked up the fundamentals quickly and put together his own group called the Railroaders, with his mate George Williams on guitar and schoolfriend Jim Simmons on washboard. It was 1956, when hundreds of skiffle groups were being put together in a hurry, all in the wake of Lonnie Donegan's breakthrough hits 'Rock Island Line', 'Lost John', 'Dead or Alive' and 'Bring a Little

Water, Sylvie'. The Railroaders would meet in a café at Newcastle Central station.

'It was the only place open all night,' said Bruce. 'It was for the railway workers, you know, so if we were doing pub gigs or whatever – I'm talking about eleven o'clock in the '50s – everywhere was closed. I mean, everywhere's open late now, but in the '50s it wasn't. We could go there to the station and get a steaming mug of tea and a sandwich at twelve, one o'clock, whatever. Great stuff. So we named ourselves the Railroaders after the café.'

Bruce dug into the catalogues of Leadbelly, Woody Guthrie, Lonnie Johnson, Big Bill Broonzy, Josh White and Muddy Waters for new songs to play, all on Lonnie Donegan's recommendation; it seemed like every other skiffle staple ('Rock Island Line', 'Streamline Train', 'Freight Train') was about railways. The Railroaders had the confidence to enter local pub competitions called Go As You Please, where cash prizes were available. It definitely beat gutting fish in the Elswick Road backyard in mid-January.

Rutherford must have turned a blind eye to the official rule that you couldn't take musical instruments to school. Regularly, Hank brought his banjo in and Bruce his guitar, and they would play most breaktimes. 'Music was my escape,' said Bruce, and he had to put the hours in just to master three basic chords. He began bunking off school, first the odd day and then whole weeks at a time. He would play guitar in the morning and go to the cinema in the afternoon. He felt rotten when the school inspectors knocked on the door and told Aunt Sadie what had been going on.

Inevitably, in the summer of 1957, Bruce asked Hank to join the

Railroaders, since the Crescent City group's appetite for skiffle had melted away after their South Shields success. 'The Crescent City Skiffle Group was just a bit of fun,' remembered Hank, 'a lot of obscure stuff which I enjoyed doing. We'd pull up outside a youth club hall, knock on the door and they'd say "Yeah! Yeah!" The Railroaders was much more a business operation. George Williams, the bass player, ran the group, a go-getter sort of a guy, and he wanted to earn money. It was more commercial material that people knew through the Vipers and Lonnie. Bruce and George sang lead. They got me in because they needed another guitarist.' Soon the Railroaders were playing two or three nights a week in socials and working men's clubs, and making real money.

Skiffle was on the wane and rock 'n' roll had captured Bruce's heart. He'd even seen Tommy Steele's first show outside of London at the Sunderland Empire, seen the sold-out theatre, seen the screaming girls, felt the real excitement. And this was a working-class kid from Bermondsey in south London on the stage. Tommy Steele helped Bruce to understand the possibilities of British rock 'n' roll.

After he caught Nazam hitting his Aunt Sadie one night, Bruce intervened, throwing Nazam down the stairs and shouting 'If you hit her again, I'll kill you.' Nazam didn't throw him out, but Bruce moved into one of the flats he rented out on Westmoreland Road. He could suddenly do whatever he wanted. He played Elvis records loud, and louder, in his new flat. He ate bacon and eggs and black pudding for breakfast. He had a short, intense, physical relationship with the daughter of one of the other lodgers. He was still only fifteen, but his independence gave him confidence.

For Hank's sixteenth birthday, his dad bought him a guitar 'which coincidentally cost sixteen guineas, a Hofner Congress. It wasn't very good. It had a very high action, which means the strings were quite high above the fingerboard, and not easy to play, but to me it was an absolute joy because I could lock myself in the box room and start playing. I used to take a bucket in there, put it on its side and sing into the bucket, because it gave this kind of echo – like singing in an echo chamber.'

The Railroaders started to include Elvis Presley's 'Paralyzed' and Fats Domino songs in their set, alongside traditional songs like 'O Mary Don't You Weep'. Soon, Eddie Silver joined as a singer and second guitarist with his black American Vega guitar. George Williams switched to bass and Hank retired the banjo. This line-up played Newcastle University on Bonfire Night 1957, a real red-letter day, as Monty Sunshine – clarinet player with the Chris Barber Band – sat in with them for a few numbers. Hank celebrated by drinking large amounts of cider and waking up the following morning on the floor of the university hall with a dozen other victims.

*

Jim Dale played at the Newcastle Empire in October 1957 and Bruce went along. Like Tommy Steele, Dale was another new British teen idol up from London, who'd just had a number-two hit with 'Be My Girl' on the Columbia label, on which his basic but echo-smothered guitar solo was the highlight. He was also compere for the National Skiffle Contest. The girls screamed for him. The atmosphere was electric. One man and a guitar – Jim Dale seemed to have it all sewn up. Bruce's mind was blown.

The Jim Dale show convinced Bruce to make a recce to the 2i's on Old Compton Street in Soho, the coffee bar where stars were being discovered on a seemingly weekly basis. He stayed at the YMCA on Tottenham Court Road. The neon lights of Soho reminded him of the fairgrounds in Newcastle. The pubs never seemed to close. The coffee bars had a tangible teenage glamour. Music came out of every door.

Just before Christmas 1957, George Williams noticed an ad for a talent contest in London. Bruce, desperate to escape monochrome Newcastle, convinced the other Railroaders that they could do it. There would be stiffer competition than on Tyneside, yeah, but what the hell, they knew they were good. The talent contest was to be held at the Granada cinema in Edmonton. On a damp Friday evening, the Railroaders took the LNER train south from Newcastle Central. 'London seemed so vast compared to Newcastle,' recalled Hank. 'Even King's Cross, where we were staying, seemed major. We went to a club called the Nucleus [on Endell Street]. And it was bohemian – it was dark, it was open late and the people there looked *interesting*. They looked like they didn't work! Drinking coffee and that kind of thing. And there was a transvestite there called Angel. Then Ewan MacColl came in and did a song, and we were like *Wow!* because we'd seen him on TV. Very far-out surroundings ... the whole thing was definitely food for thought. We decided to stay down and try to crack it.'

The following day, they played two songs in Edmonton and made it through to the semi-finals. These would be in January 1958, only a few weeks later, but long enough for skiffle to have died in Britain. In that semi-final, George Williams would play a real double bass, Jim Simmons upgraded his washboard to a drum kit and Bruce swapped his National for a Framus acoustic. They walked it. To celebrate, they spent the evening at Chiquito, a real-life London coffee bar on Hanway Street, with a cappuccino machine and a jukebox. This was the stuff of their dreams.

Bruce had left Rutherford Grammar at Christmas, both parties relieved to see the back of each other. Hank would follow his lead a couple of months later. Neither sat their O levels; they were too impatient. On 6 April 1958, it was the final of the talent contest. Hank and Bruce would never go back to Newcastle. 'We were fifteen, it's true,' Hank told Nick Owen in 2002, 'but I don't think we saw any real dangers. We were pretty naïve.'

2

TEACH YOU TO ROCK

The Railroaders came third in the final, behind a jazz band and a Malayan opera singer. They fell apart overnight. Drummer Jim Simmons needed to get back home for his mining shift, while George Williams abandoned his bass and decided he would become singer Eddie Silver's manager. Hank had been confident that the Railroaders would win the talent contest, but third was admirable, good enough, and better than any other rock 'n' roll or skiffle group in the contest. Third was enough to persuade Hank and Bruce to keep trying their luck in London.

Eddie Silver stayed down too, with his newly appointed manager George, but he ditched Hank and Bruce. 'He thought we were just a couple of kids,' remembered Bruce 'and he had no further use for us. Eddie was a bit older than us – late twenties, old enough to be my dad – and had a good ballad voice. He got a contract with Philips. George became his manager and negotiated his contract. He put out a couple of records, but nothing happened.'

Hank and Bruce had no prize money, no money at all, and nowhere to stay. The manager of the venue where the final had taken place, the Granada in Edmonton, took a shine to the Geordie teenagers and made a telephone call to a landlady he knew; he found digs for the Railroaders with a Geordie woman called Mrs Bowman. Her house was next to the Holly Park estate, between Crouch End and Finsbury Park, a neat piece of municipal design that had been built in 1952 on the site of Park House, a former World War One military hospital. Brimming with post-war purpose and the tangible energy of 1951's Festival of Britain, it felt like a good base to start a new life; Mrs Bowman would be Bruce and Hank's landlady for nine months. She had an attic room for them, complete with a gas fire.

Mrs Bowman's place was a large Victorian house full of showbiz people who weren't quite *there* yet, rooms for theatrical types and impoverished musicians. One of the other lodgers, who Hank remembered wearing 'fancy embroidered American shirts and snazzy black and white shoes', had a collection of Sun 78s he had brought back from the US – Elvis Presley, Jerry Lee Lewis, Johnny Cash and Carl Perkins. The motherlode. This was American rock 'n' roll at its newest and its most primal, the intersection of country and rhythm and blues that had been partially engineered by Sun Studios owner Sam Phillips and then spread like a virus across the wider world by Presley, Lewis, Cash and Perkins.

*

The switch from skiffle to rock 'n' roll had happened in Britain almost overnight. There had been rockers coming through in 1957, co-existing with the bigger skiffle names like Lonnie Donegan, the Vipers Skiffle Group and Johnny Duncan, but from New Year's Day 1958 onwards, the word skiffle was completely expunged from pop's lingo. Even the Vipers Skiffle Group now became the Vipers, releasing a version of Dickie Bishop's hypnotic, slinky 'No Other Baby' in January '58.

Rock 'n' roll had been treated like a passing fad by the British media ever since Bill Haley had reached number one with 'Rock Around the Clock' in December 1955. The previous fad they had clocked was mambo (Perry Como's 'Papa Loves Mambo', Rosemary Clooney's 'Mambo Italiano', et al) in 1954. Rock 'n' roll was expected to crash and burn by 1957; according to these seers, Harry Belafonte was set to replace Presley and Donegan in teenage hearts. The sound of '58 was gonna be calypso, baby!

Quickie cash-in movies were evidence for the ages: Tommy Steele, an important figure, was squeezed into *The Tommy Steele Story* (which featured some decent home-grown rockers, like 'Elevator Rock') and *The Duke Wore Jeans* (which didn't), both in cinemas in 1957; the soundtracks to both became number-one albums. There was clearly an appetite for this stuff which extended beyond Tommy's all-hair-and-teeth cartoon appeal. Dry as they were, at least those two movies included a charismatic star. *Rock You Sinners* also reached British screens in 1957 and was the point at which the British establishment thought they had rock 'n' roll canned and processed. It starred Tony Crombie and his Rockets, Art Baxter and his Rockin' Sinners, Joan Small, Dickie Bennett, Rory Blackwell and the Blackjacks, Curly Pat Barry and – in an acting role – future novelist Jackie Collins.

One of its featured tunes was Joan Small's improbable 'You Can't Say I Love You To a Rock 'n' Roll Tune'. Another was 'You've Gotta Get the Message Now', sung by actor Colin Croft, which included a brace of drug references that sneaked past censors who can't have known what the terms meant: 'One for the message / Two for the blow / Three for the Benzedrine / And then you go man go!'

The song, like the film, wasn't any good, though. Other lines like 'rockin' in a clip joint, dislocate your spine' and 'up in Siberia, rock 'n' roll hysteria' gave away the cynicism of the whole project.

Z-list British rockers like Joan Small and the barely-teenage Curly Pat Barry were incredibly lucky to be immortalised on celluloid, but a couple of other acts in *Rock You Sinners* were a considerably bigger deal. Tony Crombie had been a jazz drummer and would end up working on film scores, but in 1956 he had been one of the few people in Britain to spot which way the wind was blowing. Singles like 'Teach You To Rock' – a top-thirty hit in October '56 – were perky tributes to Bill Haley and his Comets, and they really moved. His bass drum bore the legend 'Tony R'n'R Crombie'; he wasn't a part-timer.

Sadly not pictured on screen in *Rock You Sinners* was Crombie's teenage double-bass player, a gaunt figure with hooded eyes and high cheekbones called Terry 'Jet' Harris.

*

Hank and Bruce ended up staying in Holly Park for a year. They had no means of income and relied on Mrs Bowman's generosity, plus the odd tenner from Aunt Sadie back home in Newcastle. Once they were so hungry they survived for two days on a single apple pinched from the garden; when they were feeling brave enough, or convinced that her dogs were fast asleep, they'd pinch a bottle of milk from Mrs Bowman's fridge.

During rehearsals for the talent contest, they'd got to hang out with some of the other contestants. There was Errol Hollis and the Velvets from Palmers Green, with a drummer whose style reminded Hank and Bruce of the Crickets' Jerry Allison; his name was Brian Bennett. Another drummer was Pete Chester, who led his own outfit, the Chesternuts. He was the son of radio personality Charlie Chester and lived in the plush area of Hampstead Garden Suburb. Hank and Bruce stayed in touch and, within a few weeks, became full-time members of the Chesternuts. 'It was a great name,' laughed Hank. 'The nuts bit was right, I can tell you. We wrote a few songs together. Pete wasn't a bad writer at all. He was very enthusiastic. He was full of zeal. We enthused each other.'

Trainee chemist and singer Gerry Furst played harmonica, Neil Johnson was on bass and Pete Chester handled the drums. They were a little older than Hank and Bruce, and had all passed their driving tests – Gerry would turn up to rehearsals in his dad's Ford Consul, Neil had a Wolseley and Pete had an Austin convertible. The Chesternuts felt like a step up. What's more, rehearsing at the Chester home in Hampstead Garden Suburb meant large plates of egg and chips for the Geordies, gratis, so they went there almost every day. Hank was sure Pete's mum was giving them extra-large portions as it must have been obvious to her that they weren't eating properly. 'She would look at us kindly and she could see we hadn't eaten for a couple of days. "Would you two like something to eat?" And she'd whack a couple of poached eggs on toast for us. That really helped us out, to keep us sustained.'

In Newcastle, Hank and Bruce had both made easy money in the pubs and clubs. The Chesternuts, presumably because the other three didn't have an urgent need for money, hardly played live at all, preferring to rehearse and write their own material. In the meantime, Hank and Bruce had become obsessed with Buddy Holly and the Crickets. Like Chuck Berry before him, Holly was a singer-songwriter with a guitar. In 1958, they were a rare breed. What's more, Holly didn't look like Elvis. He didn't look like much at all, all angularity and crooked teeth, with a pair of wire spectacles to top off this unique look. He was the first pop anti-star and Hank couldn't have been happier that it was now clearly okay to look like a bespectacled streak of nothing.

The opening guitar line on the Crickets' 'That'll Be the Day' gave Bruce chills every time he heard it. They began to write songs by playing a Holly record several times, then seeing what it inspired. They rehearsed and rehearsed. With a sympatico Pete Chester, they soon had a handful of songs to call their own.

The Chesternuts did manage to escape from the garden suburb once in a while. There was a charity concert at Stoke Newington town hall and, probably through Charlie Chester's connections, the Chesternuts were to be the backing group for comedian Benny Hill. Bruce played the show through gritted teeth. Was this his rock 'n' roll dream? What if Benny Hill wanted to take them on tour? He couldn't have turned the money down. He slept badly that night.

Benny Hill didn't stay in touch, but Leslie Conn did. He was an impresario and plugger who had been tasked with running the UK branch of Carlton Records, an American label that had just broken big with slow-eyed Michigan rock 'n' roller Jack Scott. Conn helped Scott's beat ballad 'My True Love' into the UK top ten. He was also aware that Scott, like Buddy Holly, wrote his own songs; when he found out the unknown Chesternuts did likewise, he saw potential down the line. Bruce reckoned that 'Leslie was seriously hoping that we would emerge as a British version of the Crickets'. Conn paid for a £40 session at the Philips studio, behind Marble Arch on Stanhope Place, and the terrified teenagers spent several hours trying to get two songs down on a one-track tape recorder. In their heads, they had tonal perfection, the ultimate harmonies, just like the Everly Brothers. When they heard the results, Hank and Bruce were hugely disappointed.

Carlton turned the Chesternuts down, but Conn was persistent. In July 1958, his employers said that he was free to shop the tracks to a British record label, so he asked his friend Norman Newell – a recording manager for Columbia Records, part of EMI – for advice. To his surprise, Newell said he'd release the tracks exactly as they were and, within days, 'Teenage Love' (b/w Jean Dorothy, Columbia Records DB 4165) was in the shops as both a 45 and a 78. A brief *Melody Maker* piece referred to the Chesternuts as 'teenage jazzmen' – it also named Brian Rankin as one of the singers, suggesting Hank hadn't quite settled on his new name.

'Teenage Love', a Chester/Rankin number according to the label, was credited to the Five Chesternuts, though it's surprising to learn that there are more than three people on the record. Bruce plays a functional rhythm part and Hank's single notes are buried in the mix, but a battery of Latin percussion – presumably found after raiding a school music room – manages to lift a song that sounds like an exercise in teen lyric minimalism: love, turtle dove, bird on the wing, makes you sing. The harmonies are high and naïve, the Everlys with the fog from the Tyne affecting their nasality. Looking back, Hank was entirely dismissive.

'We recorded a thing called "Jean Dorothy", which sounded more like "Jean Darthy" because we were trying to sound American. It was kind of a raggedy, err… it was a shocking record. It needed more rehearsal for a start, more discipline. The thing was in those days you needed to sing and play at the same time, you didn't have the facility of a backing track. You just did it – three or four takes, and then they said "Yeah, that's all right… next one."

'It also needed someone who knew what they were doing. A producer who could have given us a bit of direction. Leslie Conn was not a record producer. It was a bit amateur night with sixteen-year-olds – that's all we were. It had plenty of passion and enthusiasm, but that was it.'

Still, he acknowledged that 'it was fun. We were *doing* something.'

The single had a dizziness, a sense of delight at the mere matter of being in a studio, and its slapdash energy was engaging, no matter the DIY nature of the recording. It didn't sound like a hit in a million years. Still, Hank and Bruce had a record out on the Columbia label, just like Paul Anka, Jim Dale and – as Hank had dreamt just a year earlier – banjo player Johnny Duncan. On that level, just for a moment, they were all equals. Whatever happened next, no one could take that away from them. What's more, Leslie Conn had not only got the record released, he'd got them on TV. On 12 July 1958, the

Chesternuts had played 'Teenage Love' on BBC TV show *Six-Five Special*, which showed just how influential both Norman Newell and Leslie Conn were.

While the Geordie Boys were finding the benefits of living in London, where the spotlight might randomly hit you if you showed your face, a Liverpool group called the Quarrymen also paid their first visit to a studio in June 1958. They were the same age as Hank and Bruce, and similarly obsessed with the Crickets – one of the two songs they cut that day was 'That'll Be The Day' – but they also took Holly's lead in writing their own material. Sixteen-year-old Paul McCartney and fifteen-year-old George Harrison took the writing credit for the second song, 'In Spite of All the Danger'. But there were no record companies based in Liverpool and the Quarrymen's single was only pressed as a solitary acetate, with no chance of anyone hearing it who might have booked them for *Six-Five Special*. Still, it showed promise.

The Chesternuts also had a full-page feature in one of the weekly music papers. The *New Musical Express*'s 8 August 1958 edition wrote that 'Hank and Marvin (sic) by the way are the two members responsible for the harmony. They came to London from their native Newcastle to appear in the National Skiffle Contest and stayed on … How does the Chester family react to the latest star in their midst? Says Peter himself, "When Dad was a lad, his parents tried to stop him entering the business – and he left home!" And Charlie says enthusiastically "Jolly good luck to him!"'

Maybe if the Chesternuts had been shuttled into Abbey Road by Norman Newell, 'Teenage Love' would have been given a sheen, even a string arrangement, then become a hit and this story would have headed in a very different direction. Instead, the endearingly messy, decidedly DIY single sold next to nothing.

*

Jet Harris was a jazzer. Before that, he was a blitz baby called Terry. His dad would come home to Willesden and tell his family that the café where he'd had lunch had been machine-gunned by German planes. He had calmly put his cutlery down, he said, then ducked under the table until the planes had flown over. Then he'd got back up and finished his lunch. Terry Harris's dad was cool, but his son was cooler.

Music was always on the radio at home. Young Terry loved Frankie Laine's 1952 single 'Cry of the Wild Goose' – spooked, urgent and exotic. He also picked up on pop-country singer Tennessee Ernie Ford's 'River of No Return' and Trinidad-born pianist Winifred Atwell, who played boogie-woogie straight and became a major star in early '50s Britain.

At school, Terry Harris was a decent athlete – he represented Middlesex as a runner – and so his friends nicknamed him Jet. He left school at fifteen and started working with his dad at a company called Dairy Supply in the sheet metal department. Wrenches, grinders and wheel dollies were less fun than hanging out at the Mapleton Club, in the basement of the Mapleton Hotel, on Coventry Street, where he was now spending his evenings. Jet was fascinated by both the music and the atmosphere, and he saved up for a deposit on a clarinet. But it didn't take him long to find out that the clarinet wasn't the instrument for him – around four months, which was just long enough for him to realise that the instrument he *really* wanted to play was the double bass. He now understood that he'd mostly liked Winifred Atwell's records for what she was doing with her left hand. And so Jet Harris traded in his clarinet for a double bass.

All dreams of a cool jazz lifestyle were put on hold, aged fifteen, when Jet's hair started falling out. He was a hit with the girls! This couldn't be happening! He went to the doctor who told him that he was losing his hair because of stress. The only possible reason for this, Jet figured, was that he was so desperate to become part of the jazz scene that spending all his days working in a factory was driving him round the twist. He took the doctor's advice and decided the best cure would be to spend more time at the Mapleton Club.

His favourite group was the Allan Ganley Quartet, modernists with a slow, smoky feel that suited the post-war landscape of London. Their bassist was Sammy Stokes. One night, Jet asked Stokes if he would teach him how to play the bass. He said no. The next night, Jet asked again. Stokes figured that this fifteen-year-old would soon get bored of asking, but Jet was persistent, and charming, and eventually Stokes relented when he saw how genuine his enthusiasm was. Stokes asked for nothing more than a packet of cigarettes for each lesson. 'If it hadn't been for Sammy Stokes, I'd probably be a bald-headed sheet metal worker now,' wrote Jet in the 1961 book *The Shadows By Themselves*. 'After a couple of months, I was learning gradually and had some idea of what I was playing. I liked all sorts of music by then – skiffle, Bill Haley, jazz, the lot.' Jet formed his own modern jazz band called the Delinquents, who were good enough to play at the Mapleton for two pounds ten shillings a night – not much once the money got divided. Luckily for Jet, his tastes had broadened and the rock 'n' roll scene emerging in the coffee bars of Soho had piqued his interest too.

When Sammy Stokes was offered a job playing bass in the Dene Aces, the backing group for Bermondsey rock 'n' roller Terry Dene, he turned it down, but offered the job to Jet, who jumped at the opportunity. Dene's manager Paul Lincoln – who also ran the 2i's – offered him £30 a week, untold riches for a teenage factory worker on £8 a week. Dene had been the first British rock 'n' roller to breakthrough after Tommy Steele. His cover of Marty Robbins's 'A White Sport Coat (And a Pink Carnation)' was gentler than Steele's early singles, but his live show was something else.

'My stage debut with him was in variety for a week at Middlesbrough. Terry went down a bomb, the kids loved him. This was my first time away from home, but I didn't have time to feel homesick. I took enough clothes with me for the week, so I didn't have to worry about laundry. At the end of the week, I took my dirty clothes back for mum to wash.'

Jet was good, but not yet good enough. The Dene Aces played a further week in London at the Astor Club, then another week's residency in Hull, before he was told it wasn't working. Paul Lincoln knew that Jet had given up his job at Dairy Supply to go on tour, so he offered him work at the 2i's, dispensing Coca-Cola and orange juice. If he was lucky, he might get to sit in with the band onstage in the tiny room downstairs.

*

Soho in the '50s oozed with wide boys, beatniks, down-and-outs, journalists, art students from St Martins, musicians from Ken Colyer's Studio 51 club, Teddy Boys, modernists, pissed intellectuals stumbling out of the Colony Room, call girls left right and centre, and villains with names like Jack Spot and Billy Hill, Greeks, Italians, Poles, Jamaicans, Americans... All were caged in by four circuses – Oxford, Cambridge, Piccadilly and St Giles. Outside this hot-housed UN safe haven, London got on with being a grimy, bombsite-ridden city still recovering from the war and still viciously suspicious of foreigners. Racism was rife. Seventy-three-year-old Teresa Lubienska, a heroine of the Polish resistance, was stabbed to death on the platform of Gloucester Road tube station in 1957 just because she talked funny; her last words were 'Bandits! Bandits!' and her killers were never caught.

Soho was quite unlike the rest of England in the 1950s. Sitting on the roof of the Moulin Rouge restaurant on Shaftesbury Avenue, just to the south of Old Compton Street, was eight-year-old Steven Georgiou, surveying the mad tapestry of Soho in his own quiet bubble. He had a Greek dad and a Swedish mum, and used to help wash the dishes when he got home from school. He was a true product of mid-century Soho. In another ten years, he'd go through the first of several metamorphoses and change his name to Cat Stevens.

The appeal of the place was its difference – somewhere to experiment, somewhere for British youth to find their own way across the border from childhood into adult life. Some people wanted to pop in and gawp, or maybe they wanted to stay and check out some jazz. Either way, they'd need refreshments, their own café society. Coffee bars, wrote George Melly, were 'the first exclusive teenage meeting places. A nationwide network of cells where, above the fierce gurgling and hissing of the Gaggia machine, the secret codes and passwords were formulated.' By the mid-'50s, coffee bars proliferated.

*

For a mere coffee bar, the 2i's played an extraordinary role in the development of British rock 'n' roll and so, in turn, all of British rock. The place was named after the building's original owners – two brothers called Irani – and had been taken over in April 1956 by a couple of Australian wrestlers: Paul Lincoln, otherwise known as Doctor Death, and 'Rebel' Ray Hunter. The cellar featured live music to pull people in off the street. The Vipers, one of the leading skiffle acts in the country, began playing there in July 1956, just a few weeks after it opened; they attracted both customers and would-be musicians down the stairs. It quickly acquired a reputation as a breeding ground for new talent. The thrown-together nature of skiffle made it easy for visitors to sit in with whoever was playing that day.

In the daytime, the 2i's was like any other Soho coffee bar. It specialised in cappuccinos, but also served apple strudels, toasted cheese sandwiches and goulash. No hard drinks – just orange juice and Coca-Cola. By night, though, its basement had become a focal point, first for skiffle and then for nascent rock 'n' roll. Songwriter Lionel Bart visited the basement with his writing partner Mike Pratt and thought it looked a little drab. They talked to Paul Lincoln and came to an agreement: for a few free beers and membership for life, they'd paint the place. Wally Whyton, leader of the Vipers Skiffle Group, described Bart and Pratt's artwork as 'a sort of abstract cubist thing in bright colours' behind the stage, while on the side walls, Bart painted series of huge eyes, Cleopatra-style, as a pun on the venue's name. Either the basement was too damp for it to dry properly or Bart had brought the wrong kind of paint with him, but unlucky punters would find traces of it on their clothes as a souvenir the following morning.

Like the other players at the 2i's, Jet Harris would soon become a floating member of ad hoc bands backing rock 'n' roll singers: a week here with Don Lang, another there with Larry Page, 'the Teenage Rage'. Wee Willie Harris had been the resident pianist at the 2i's before he took up singing. A former worker at the Peek Freans biscuit factory in Bermondsey, he was possibly the first pop singer in the world to get attention for dying his hair wild colours; it didn't take much to make a name for yourself in mid-'50s Britain. In late 1957, Wee Willie headlined a full six-month nationwide tour called Rockin' At The 2i's, on which he was joined by the Most Brothers, plus former jazzer Tony Crombie, who had asked Jet to become the bassist with his Rockets. Crombie's group had their own spot, as well as providing backing for Wee Willie and the Most Brothers. On that tour, Jet also managed to acquire Mickie Most's pet monkey, Mostie. These shows were part of the dying days of variety theatre; at some venues, the bills were a bizarre mixture of rock 'n' rollers, dancing troops, acrobats, ventriloquists and performing animals. Crombie and Jet drank together, shunned the animal trainers, talked about jazz, and got on pretty well.

One day, after the Wee Willie Harris tour was over, Jet and Crombie were walking down Charing Cross Road when they saw an electric bass guitar in a shop window. Neither had ever seen one before. *You should get it*, said Crombie. *You'll be the only bassist in town who has one.* Up until this point, Jet, a gaunt, skeletal lad, had been carrying his double bass home to Willesden by tube every night. One time, too tired, he'd lost his grip and dropped it down the escalator – it bounced all the way to the bottom with Jet running down the stairs after it, hoping to hell that it hadn't broken. To his relief, it had a slight crack but nothing worse. He thought about this while he looked in the shop window at this electric bass guitar. He bought it on the spot.

People began to notice Jet and this space-age instrument, which was as thunderous as his glare. He was invited by Wally Whyton to join the Vipers, the one-time skiffle kings who were, by mid-1958, struggling to hold their own against rock 'n' roll. Jet moved into a shared basement flat in Eccleston Square in Victoria, which he also shared with his menagerie of small animals, including a fox and a skunk. Mostie felt at home, too; Vipers washboard player John Pilgrim and guitarist Johnny Booker each had pet monkeys called, respectively, Iggins and Elvis. Iggins used to sit on Pilgrim's shoulder while he played the washboard and, according to local legend, once crapped on Lonnie Donegan's shoulder.

It was the Vipers who came up with the idea of bleaching Jet's hair. 'I was quite bohemian, myself. I didn't mean to be, but I couldn't afford a pair of shoes so I used to go around barefoot. I used to walk from Eccleston Square to Soho.

'We were bored one day, all living in this basement, and someone said "What can we do next? I know, let's dye Jet's hair blonde!" Being so young and stupid, I didn't know that it was bleach and you couldn't get it out, you couldn't wash it out. Anyway, we did the first gigs and the birds were all over me, so I decided to keep the blonde hair. It was fabulous in Soho at the end of the '50s.'

*

In the summer of 1958, Bruce and Hank had renamed themselves. Bruce took his mother's name, Welch, which definitely had a more media-friendly ring than Cripps. He toyed with the idea of Buddy Welch, after Buddy Holly, though it would have caused a fair bit of confusion if the guitarist in the glasses was Hank and the one without glasses was Buddy. So Bruce it stayed. Number one at the time was the galumphing rocker 'Whole Lotta Woman' by Marvin Rainwater, who had been Marvin Percy until he took his mother's Cherokee birth name. Hank and Bruce practised the song for days until they had it down pat. When it came to ditching 'Rankin' for a more American-sounding surname, Marvin Rainwater provided further inspiration. Not wanting to lose his entire birthname, he became Hank B. Marvin with the 'B' short for Brian.

During the summer of 1958, Hank and Bruce would rehearse with the Chesternuts in Hampstead Garden Suburb by day and play at the 2i's several nights a week. As the coffee bar became something of a rock 'n' roll job centre for them, the Five Chesternuts broke up: Gerry Furst qualified as a chemist and Neil Johnson saw that as his excuse to get himself a proper job too. Pete Chester decided to work at his songwriting and put together a new line-up of the Chesternuts who would have a minor hit with 'Ten Swingin' Bottles' in 1960. Both he and Gerry

Furst would become the earliest members of the Shadows' extended family, reappearing like long-lost cousins at unlikely moments.

With no more opportunity for a free slap-up eggs and chips lunch, Hank and Bruce spent more and more time hanging out at the 2i's. 'We used to get eighteen shillings for four hours' work,' remembered Bruce. They played as the Geordie Boys, Hank on his Antoria and Bruce playing his American Vega, an acoustic guitar with a large, horseshoe pick-up.

Then Wally Whyton came down and heard Hank play. 'He was trying to update the Vipers,' said Hank, 'pushing them into the realms of rhythm and blues, as an extension of folk blues.' To reinvigorate the act, Whyton had already brought in Jet on bass. 'We did a week in Birmingham,' said Hank. 'Johnny Pilgrim, the guy who played the washboard, had been persuaded to buy a drum kit and he was awful! Johnny Booker did lead vocals and I played guitar.' They had moved on from Leadbelly's 'Pick a Bale of Cotton' to Chuck Willis's 'What Am I Living For' and Bobby Helms' 'No Other Baby' in a matter of weeks. The unfortunate Pilgrim, who couldn't keep up with the pace of change, would be replaced by a fifteen-year-old drummer called Tony Meehan.

*

Tony Meehan had never been outside of London when he joined the Vipers. 'I remember we stopped at a place called Barrow-in-Furness and Johnny Booker asked someone "Where's the ballroom?" and this bloke said "Go down there... turn right at t'robots." Robots were the traffic lights! It was the first time I'd ever heard a northern accent.' Just fifteen – in a group with real men, some of whom weren't even teenagers anymore – he was taunted mercilessly. In Derbyshire, the rest of the group told Tony it was a local tradition to cook your own Sunday lunch, then sent him into a field to try to catch them a sheep.

Tony Meehan had been born in Hampstead in 1943 to a large Irish working-class family. Music was his obsession from an early age, with no time for football or train sets. By the age of ten, he had already started saving up for his first drum kit and he ended up receiving one for Christmas, a 'Bitsa', which his parents had bought from nearby Blanks of Kilburn. When he was a little kid, he had lost half a finger when he stuck it in the axle of a soap box cart, but with his nine and a half fingers, he practised and practised. By the time he was thirteen, he was playing Irish dancehalls at weekends in Kilburn, Cricklewood and Willesden, playing waltzes, Irish jigs, foxtrots, anything.

He was kicking his heels in Kilburn one afternoon in 1958 when his friend Dave Rees suggested a trip to Soho. It was just three miles south but Soho, to young Tony, was another country. He'd first been with Dave a year earlier, when they'd gone to see the Vipers Skiffle Group at the Skiffle Cellar in Greek Street. 'We spent our last sixpence on a Coke which we shared. We had to walk home.'

Tony Meehan saw '50s Soho as an endless bohemian carnival. It was the most ethnically diverse, the most sexually permissive, the most physically loud and colourful place in Britain. Just a few streets, a square mile, but it added up to total liberty for the underclass; rock 'n' roll was just another subculture that slotted in effortlessly.

Tony Meehan fell in love with it. 'Some day,' he wrote in 1962, 'I'd like to write a book about the Golden Age of Soho. I remember it because I was there. We were all sort of semi-beatnik characters then, chasing after an ideal. It was the atmosphere ... it was sordid all right, but everyone there was human.'

On their second trip in 1958, making their way past Chas McDevitt's Freight Train coffee bar, Tony heard a beautiful noise underneath the Old Compton Street pavement. 'I was walking past the 2i's and this sound came out, like "*Whoa*. What is *that*?" We went in – I don't know how, because it was six shillings to get in. We could just about scrape together the twelve bob between us.'

Before him would have been the first full flower of British rock 'n' roll: sun-tanned Vince Taylor slumped by the jukebox; Cliff Richard in a black shirt and white tie, tousle-haired and grinning; chiselled Terry Nelhams, in a fine French crewneck, hitting on a girl with implausible stilettos.

On the tiny stage – eighteen inches high and about a yard wide – were two Geordies he didn't know: spotty, just seventeen and crying out in true, close Everly Brothers harmony. Their bassist looked and sounded incredible. Bright blond hair and dark hooded lids, no smile. Wasn't that... ? Yes, it was! Meehan remembered Jet Harris from a gig with Dickie Bishop at the Metropolitan Theatre on Edgware Road a year before.

'My father had taken me to the Metropolitan as a kid and I saw Charlie Chester, the pit orchestra, my first variety show. It was magic, absolute magic. It was for the working classes, it was their kind of club if you like – music hall was for people who couldn't afford night clubs.

Fantastic. It's not there now – it's Paddington Green high-security police station, which says a lot about our times.

'Anyway, Jet was playing stand-up bass at the Metropolitan and I thought it was absolutely astonishing. He was a jazz man. We went round to the stage door and Jet came out and I got his autograph. It's really weird. Uncanny. A couple of years later, I was in a band with him.'

By this point in 1958, playing at the 2i's, Jet now had his bass guitar and it was unbelievably loud. Tony had walked in wearing a cap just like one of Gene Vincent's Bluecaps. He felt pretty cool. So what if he'd been in shorts the previous summer? He had made his own drumsticks in woodwork lessons and here he was, a teenager in the 2i's in Soho in 1958.

'We went down the winding stairs to the cellar, which was crowded with people, and on the stage – this is uncanny too, really weird – was Hank, Bruce, Jet and a drummer. I can't remember who the drummer was. We sat down on these benches and my mate said "Why don't you sit in with the band?" Because that's what you used to do in those days. You'd ask, "Can I sit in for a number?" I was fifteen. They were all like men to me. They were seventeen! Hank and Bruce used to do this Everly Brothers thing. I thought they were wonderful. Anyway, at the break, I said "Do you mind if I play a couple of numbers?" They said "Can you play?" I said "Yeah, sure." I got up and we played "Be-Bop-a-Lula", and they were like "Hey, this kid can play!"

'And after that, lots of people were coming up to me asking if I'd like to do this or that. Suddenly I was in the music business.'

Almost immediately, Tony would leave school and replace the 2i's house drummer, Brian Bennett, who was away on a summer season in the Scottish seaside resort of Largs with a group called the Red Peppers. It wasn't exactly rollicking or rolling, thought Bennett, but it was steady money. And so, while he was away, Tony took the hot seat. He played a white marine pearl Ajax drum set (the kit had 'Tony' painted on the front of the bass drum by Eddie Stokes, who several years later would be responsible for the Beatles bass drum logo with the raised 'B' and the dropped 'T').

As well as his gig at the 2i's, Tony would play for singer Vince Eager at Churchill's club from midnight until three in the morning. When *that* dried up, he met Vince Taylor, the Hounslow-born American singer, and got work as the drummer in Taylor's Playboys along with guitarist Tony Sheridan and bassist Brian Locking.

One night, Johnny Booker of the Vipers saw Meehan at the 2i's and asked if he'd like to join them; they'd decided to lose Johnny Pilgrim, and his washboard, and Iggins the monkey. Pilgrim would go on to haunt Soho for years to come, in the slightly more sedate world of books, with a counter-culture bookstall on Charing Cross Road.

Bass-playing hero Jet had already become part of the Vipers by then, which blew Tony's fifteen-year-old mind. The cool cat that Tony and his mates used to call 'the Suede Kid', on account of his dapper clothes, did not project the precarious life of a Soho musician. When he got to know Jet in the Vipers, Tony was shocked. 'He struck me as a very quiet person, moody and often depressed. He was literally starving.'

They were living on crumbs, hoping for a break.

'In Soho in the early days, it was a hell of a struggle,' admitted Jet. 'I lived on the apple strudels at the 2i's. Me and Adam Faith, we sat in the gutter one day. His real name was Terry, which is what my name is. He was Terry Nelhams. We sat in the gutter outside the 2i's and I said "Oh, I'm starving, Terry." He said "So am I, Terry, but what are we going to do?" Anyway, someone just came along at that moment and gave us half a crown each. Half a crown in them days was a mountain of spaghetti bolognese, so we had one of them each. Of course, the months went on and I became Jet Harris and he became Adam Faith. Things worked out.'

During the summer of 1958, the new-look rock 'n' roll Vipers – with Jet and Tony – went to Abbey Road to cut half a dozen tracks with George Martin. Their version of 'Summertime Blues' was released as a single in October but flopped. By then, skiffle was yesterday's news and the Vipers name seemed antique; Jet had already jumped ship and got a job backing his mates the Most Brothers on an October tour. It would be headlined by the Kalin Twins, an American pair who had been number one for five weeks in August and September with 'When', a catchy if generic single that sat midway between the Everly Brothers and Paul Anka.

*

'The really great players in the 2i's,' Bruce Welch explained, 'were Hank Marvin and Tony Sheridan. They were both great. One afternoon, this guy came down and said he'd been looking for this guitar player he'd heard about, Tony Sheridan. He wasn't there on this day, but Hank was. And this guy said "I'm Cliff Richard's manager" and, of course, nobody knew who Cliff Richard was then. He said "I'm looking for a lead guitarist for this tour."'

'This guy' was John Foster, just eighteen, barely older than Hank or Bruce. Naturally, he was playing up this gig with his star attraction, Cliff Richard, as if it was a chance to play a three-week residency in Vegas with Elvis. 'Have you heard his single, "Move It"? Okay. Yeah, it's incredible, the most.' The first show would be in Hanley in Staffordshire.

Hank, fortuitously, had just returned from a week in Birmingham, playing with the Vipers. They were chopping and changing members, disintegrating fast, but Wally Whyton was still a comforting and influential presence.* He told Hank Marvin, as an aside, something that would fundamentally change his life. 'I was doing a lot of rock 'n' roll-style solos, which is a lot of double stopping, and Wally said "Why don't you play more single notes and get away from the basic rock 'n' roll stuff?" I'd already heard a bit of Django Reinhardt and Barney Kessel, and, over the weeks and months and years, I opened up.'

Hank's Vipers gig was already over. Now he only had the Geordie Boys to pay for his supper. John Foster asked him to play something, as Bruce recalled.

'So Hank played him a few licks, the intro to "That'll Be the Day"... If you could do the Buddy Holly intro, you were it, that was big news. So he offered him the job and Hank basically said "I'll do

---

* Whyton would go on to become a kindly children's TV presence in the '70s, and then the presenter of BBC Radio 2's *Country Club* for twenty years. No one has a bad word to say about him.

it if my mate can come along."' This act of generosity and comradeship from his old schoolmate would be the biggest break of Bruce Welch's life.

It was a done deal. As long as the singer got on with his new guitarists, then for the next three weeks Hank and Bruce would be members of Cliff Richard and the Drifters. The tour would be starting in October 1958. The Most Brothers would also be on the bill and the headliners were the 'When hitmakers' the Kalin Twins. Cliff Richard's first single 'Move It' – which had been recorded with session players – was in the shops but not yet in the chart.

'We went and met Cliff around the corner,' explained Bruce. 'He was being fitted for what became his famous pink jacket. He had a pink rock 'n' roll jacket, you know. He looked at us and we looked at him... We were all pimples and young, really young. And then we went out to Cliff's council house. He lived in a place called Cheshunt in Hertfordshire. We got the old Green Line bus just outside the BBC at Portland Place, went out to Cheshunt with our guitars, and met his mum, dad and three sisters in this council house. So we played in the front room and did "Whole Lot of Shakin' Goin' On", "My Babe", "That'll Be the Day"... like an audition, really. And Cliff said "Great, that's it." And next thing, we were on a three-week tour.'

This was not only the biggest break of Cliff's career, but the package that had been put together would leave the Shadows jigsaw one step closer to completion.

The Cliff tour, as far as Hank and Bruce were concerned, would be nothing more than three weeks' pay that they might be able to eke out until Christmas.

*

By the time the tour started in October, the Kalin Twins' 'When' had dropped down from its number-one position, replaced by Connie Francis' 'Stupid Cupid'. Cliff Richard and the Drifters' 'Move It', a far more thrilling teenage proposition, entered the top twenty, sneaking in at number nineteen, and began snaking past the Poni-Tails' 'Born Too Late', Johnny Mathis's 'A Certain Smile', the Olympics' 'Western Movies' and the Elegants' 'Little Star'. But when the tour started, its hit status was no certainty; 'Move It' was just a cool record, very American-sounding. 'It really changed English rock 'n' roll,' said Jet. 'First time I heard it, I thought it had to be American.'

Hanley was one of the six towns that made up Stoke-on-Trent, clay city, the home of British pottery. The Victoria Hall – where the Kalin Twins tour began on 5 October – had a queue around the block by seven o'clock. The crowd had looked quite different a few weeks earlier when *The Mikado* had come to Hanley, with Donald Adams in the leading role and Neville Griffiths playing Nanki-Poo, his son, disguised as a wandering minstrel and in love with Yum-Yum. *The Mikado* had premiered seventy-three years earlier. Time moved slowly in Hanley.

First on stage at Victoria Hall were the Most Brothers, purveyors of second-hand monkeys. Alex Walton and Michael Hayes had both been working at the 2i's, Alex selling coffee upstairs while Mickie sold Coke in the basement. Mickie, two years older than his stage brother, had been nineteen when they had made their debut single 'Whistle Bait' in 1957. His nickname was Mickie the Most because that was his favourite catchphrase: any film he saw, any record he heard, any new girl he met, he said they were 'the most'. Unfortunately for the Most Brothers, nobody thought their act was the most. 'Whistle Bait' – sadly not a cover of the Collins Kids' unhinged rockabilly single – was one of the weakest records of the entire British rock 'n' roll boom, which really took some doing. The 'brothers' could barely sing in unison, let alone harmony, and would go their own ways by the end of 1958. Mickie Most slowly realised that the real action was in the manager's office and most of the kids on stage were marks. He would become a millionaire by the end of the '60s.

One of the major British stars of the 1950s was Eddie Calvert, the Man with the Golden Trumpet, a moustachioed chap from Preston who looked sternly at the camera in every single picture (unless he happened to be holding his golden trumpet). In 1958, Calvert had his own fan club publication, *Calvert Cavalcade*, and two number ones to his name – 1953's 'Oh My Papa' and the zippy 'Cherry Pink (and Apple Blossom White)' from two years later. 'My playing may be corny, but the public like it that way,' he told reporters.

Eddie Calvert closed the first half of the Kalin Twins show. Quite likely, he got out of the building as quickly as he could before the teenage madness he suspected would follow. Eddie's producer, Norrie Paramor, was responsible for this Cliff Richard and his raucous 'Move It' and it was vastly outselling Eddie's latest, 'Little Pixie', despite its wall of impressive Latin percussion. Maybe those kazoos were a mistake, thought Eddie. Actually, he knew they were. No matter, Norrie had found him something called 'Americano' for his next single which might put him in good stead with the coffee-bar kids. Eddie really had no idea. The world was shifting under his feet. A few weeks earlier, his home town of Preston had been by-passed by the very first stretch of motorway in Britain, becoming a self-defined backwater. Looking out at the rough, spotty kids in the crowd, Eddie saw his career was about to be similarly by-passed.

Compere Tony Marsh would introduce Britain's latest teenage star Cliff Richard, with his group the Drifters, after the break. As the tour progressed, and as 'Move It' climbed the chart week by week, the reception they received grew louder and louder. This unsettled the sedate Kalin Twins. *Would Cliff and the Drifters mind swapping spots with Eddie Calvert?* they asked. *Then you could close the first set? And we'd be kind of both headlining?*

Thanks for asking, said Cliff, *but no*. And each night on the tour became a little more chaotic.

'Manchester Free Trade Hall, ohhh,' sighed Jet. 'Well, we couldn't believe what was happening! You know, the women screaming and the adulation was something else. This is why I personally get so angry when I see some of these TV programmes, the history of English rock. You know, they make out the Beatles started it, and it was Cliff. I mean, that record, "Move It"... that really changed English rock 'n' roll. I mean, it sounds really proper authentic. It was a bloody good record, and still is.'

'We used to wiggle our legs and I'd lay on my back with the guitar,' recalled Bruce. 'I used to say to Hank "Can you play rhythm while I get up?" because I couldn't get up and play rhythm at the same time. At the time, we were like the Sex Pistols of 1958, fairly raucous. I'd say to Cliff, "Do you fancy a riot tonight?" and he'd wiggle his legs a bit more and there'd be uproar, absolute uproar, screaming ... They couldn't hear him for screams you know, but we loved it, of course. Cliff was seventeen on that tour and we were sixteen. It was just mind-boggling.

'The greatest thing was we went back in October to Newcastle. We played Newcastle City Hall – we'd only been away six months. That time, and every time after that when we went back, all our schoolmates were in the audience. And the other guys in the band, the other Railroaders would turn up ... It was brilliant.'

3

HE'S GOT THE WHOLE WORLD IN HIS HANDS

Cliff Richard first came to England in 1948, just before his eighth birthday. Back then, he was called Harry Webb. He had been born in Lucknow in India and had travelled from Howrah, over the river from Calcutta, where his family were part of the significant Anglo-Indian community, a class that was a fiction of empire, mostly made up of people of mixed Indian and British heritage. It was a culture that would soon disperse after Harry and his family arrived in England, and then quickly dissolve.

Harry's father, Rodger, worked at the Howrah station restaurant, the railway company providing the Webb family with a flat, on a hill, with views down to the river. Handsome Harry studied Bengali and Hindi at school; the classroom wall had a map of the world with parts shaded in pink to highlight the extent of the British Empire. At lunchtime, he sat in the shade, eating sandwiches made by Habib, one of the family's servants, and at weekends he went to the cinema with Aunt Olive to watch cowboy movies and cartoons. As long as you didn't notice the train station's separate waiting rooms – 'first class', 'second class', 'Hindu' and 'Mohammedan' – then it felt like some kind of childhood paradise.

One day, Harry's mother Dorothy looked out of the window of their flat, down to the Hooghly River, and saw dead bodies floating in the water. Outside her front door, there were bodies in the street. Soon, there was a stench of burning flesh from funeral pyres. If Harry noticed any of this, he couldn't ever remember. But Dorothy and Rodger did. They were given shelter in a cinema by Muslim friends and fled for England – the place Anglo-Indians called home, even though most had never been – as soon as they could, leaving everything behind. The British Empire in India was in crisis and this was the beginning of Partition, with Pakistan breaking away from India and Crown rule ending abruptly and violently; the Webb family were just five of 14 million refugees.

With help from distant relatives, the Webbs found a room in a semi-detached house in Carshalton in Surrey, on the edge of London's southern suburbs. 'The five of us lived in that one room for a year,' Cliff would later tell the *Independent*. 'We didn't have our own toilet, so we were using chamber pots. It was our bedroom, and our kitchen, too – we had a paraffin stove, on which Mum cooked porridge in the morning … I can remember my mother crying a lot, and my Dad would say: "Don't worry, it will get better, we'll get ourselves out of this mess." But pretty soon there were six of us living in the room, when my sister Joan was born.'

They were placed on a waiting list and thrilled when they were given a modern red-brick house of their own in Cheshunt, on the polar opposite side of London to Carshalton. Eight-year-old Harry shared a bedroom with big sisters Jacqueline and Donella. At school, his dark skin and black hair marked him out as different. He was teased for being 'Indian' and one teacher asked him where he kept his tomahawk. 'I was teased and bullied the whole time, so I learned how to fight. I fought day in and day out then – I used to come home black and blue.'

He got older. Girls liked him. Harry Webb sang in the school concert and dreamed of making a record of his own, like those Geraldo and Jack Payne 78s they'd had to leave behind in Howrah. He sang with a skiffle group, but it wasn't for Harry. It was only when he heard 'Heartbreak Hotel' coming out of a car window in Waltham Cross that he knew exactly what he wanted to do. He wanted to be Elvis Presley – not be *like* Elvis, but actually *be* him. A kid called John Foster, who worked in the local sewage farm, saw Harry singing with some schoolmates in the Five Horseshoes pub in nearby Hoddesdon and told him he could make him a star.

Harry and his schoolmates called themselves the Drifters and Foster asked them if they wanted to play at the 2i's coffee bar, already well-known for its part in the Tommy Steele and Terry Dene stories. Did they ever! Foster got them an afternoon audition, which they passed and they played the same night. They had no lead guitarist, but Ian 'Sammy' Samwell was in the crowd that night and volunteered his services.

'Cliff had a small record collection,' said Samwell, 'mostly the songs we were performing on stage. The Drifters acquired a number of discards from a jukebox on an American airbase and this led to us performing some very R&B material like "Get a Job" by the Silhouettes and "Rock 'n' Roll Shoes" by Chuck Willis. We didn't know they were race records. We just thought they were rock 'n' roll.'

The Drifters were then offered a show in Ripley in Derbyshire, but the formidable promoter Harry Greatorex insisted on a named singer – 'Something Something and the Drifters'. So, on 3 May 1958, Harry Webb became Cliff Richard. Then, after recording Jerry Lee Lewis's 'Breathless' and Lloyd Price's 'Lawdy Miss Clawdy' in a booth at the HMV shop on Oxford Street, he got himself a deal with Columbia Records. It all happened in a matter of weeks.

Ian Samwell wrote 'Move It' while he was on the Green Line bus from Cheshunt, en route to Columbia Records. 'They say it's going to die but honey please, let's face it / Well they just don't know what's a-goin' to replace it / Yeah, ballads and calypsos have got nothing on / Real country music that just drives along.' The US had the Showmen's 'It Will Stand', Britain had 'Move It'. It was a manifesto.

TV producer Jack Good had jumped from the BBC's rather staid *Six-Five Special,* which had given the Five Chesternuts two minutes of TV fame, to a new ITV series called *Oh Boy!*. It was entirely designed by Good and when he heard 'Move It', he flipped. In Royston Ellis's 1961 book *The Big Beat Scene*, Good said, 'Cliff Richard in *Oh Boy!* was a figment of my imagination which this shy youngster from Cheshunt brought to life before millions of viewers. Using the raw talent that was there, Cliff was moulded into someone totally different from his real self. I wanted an air of mystery about Cliff. That's why I refused to let him talk at the beginning of the series. In fact, if he had opened his mouth, he would have been finished. On *Oh Boy!* Cliff was built into a sex bomb who was a cherubic-faced infant. That was how people saw him and wanted him. The image had to be kept for people to believe.'

The silent, cherubic sex bomb was about to ambush the Kalin Twins tour, with the most red-hot band in Britain right behind him.

*

Norrie Paramor had signed the unshaped Cliff Richard, but it was Jack Good who not only insisted on pushing 'Move It' rather than Paramor's preferred A-side 'Schoolboy Crush' on his *Oh Boy!* show, but taught Cliff the art of stagecraft. He told him to ditch his guitar, to shave off his Elvis sideburns and to perform not only with his body but also with his eyes. 'I always got him to look up at the camera, head tilted down and the eyes up and the angled shoulders forward. Then suddenly grabbing his arm as if he'd been poked by some hypodermic syringe.' The Drifters played in the shadows, menacingly, far behind him.

Oh Boy! was such a huge and instant hit show that a soundtrack album was recorded and readied for release by Columbia a week after Cliff's eighteenth birthday, on 21 October 1958. The album was a great, high-energy artefact of British rock 'n' roll. Cliff had a quarter of the running time, partly because its initial focus – Larry Parnes' boy Marty Wilde – wasn't involved.

Good would be in dispute with Parnes for a few crucial months. Parnes reckoned that Cliff was starting to get too much of the spotlight and withdrew Marty from the show in mid-October 1958 – big mistake. The show had started with Marty Wilde as the biggest rock 'n' roll star in Britain on the back of his moody top-five hit 'Endless Sleep', but once he was taken off the air, his career stagnated. The new kid benefitted. Watching *Oh Boy!* at home in Bradford, young art student David Hockney would sketch Cliff, over and over again. Soon after, he saw a newspaper article about a climbing accident with the headline 'Two Boys Cling to Cliff All Night', which then inspired a painting – codified and abstract – titled *We Two Boys Together Clinging*. He wasn't the only one thinking of clinging to Cliff. The *Daily Mirror* asked if Cliff was 'too sexy for television'. The answer, of course, was no. Everybody loved sexy Cliff Richard.

*

'Norrie Paramor didn't want The Drifters,' reckoned 'Sammy' Samwell. 'He only wanted Cliff.' Paramor had drawn up a recording contract, but didn't get Cliff to sign it until after the Drifters had recorded 'Move It', by which time it was clear that the singer worked best with his band. It had also become obvious to Sammy that Cliff was going to need a better guitarist than he was, so John Foster went to the 2i's, found Hank and Bruce, and Sammy switched to bass. Early on during the Kalin Twins tour, Jet Harris – playing bass with the Most Brothers – was approached by Cliff; it had become clear that the Drifters needed a better bass player than Sammy, who was struggling to play double bass. Jet's hard-driving, electric style was exactly what was required. Jet thought it over. He saw the reaction of the crowd to Cliff's performance and he nodded. 'I'm in,' he said.

'Jet Harris wanted to join, and Cliff wanted him, so I got fired,' Sammy later told Frank Broughton. 'The official story was that I had left to concentrate on songwriting. In fact, I had been given a five-year contract with a retainer. We were all friends and I stayed around writing songs for a couple of years.' Sammy also became their 'temporary acting unpaid sort of manager-cum-publicist' until they needed someone with more experience.

The first Cliff and the Drifters recordings that Jet played on were 'Livin' Lovin' Doll' and 'Mean Streak' in November 1958. Shortly after this session, drummer Terry Smart left and was replaced by the 2i's fifteen-year-old house drummer, Tony Meehan. He was the only choice.

'Unfortunately, the drummer, who was a really nice guy called Terry Smart, wasn't really up to it,' said Tony. 'And the others said to Cliff, "We've heard this young kid. He's pretty hot. You should get a new drummer." Terry was Cliff's best friend, it was one of those things. So they asked me if I'd like to join the Drifters. And I said, "Yes, I'd like to join the Drifters." And off we went.'

And now the Drifters were, no question, made up of the best rock 'n' roll players in the country. The classic line-up of Hank, Bruce, Tony and Jet would make their stage debut with Cliff at the Free Trade Hall in Manchester in January 1959.

'Cliff really did believe that we had something,' said Hank. 'He was very keen on promoting us, which I thought was great and, yeah, I think people should be aware that even in those days it wasn't like a singer and a backing band. It was more of a five-piece band that he happened to be the singer in. Like, say, the Rolling Stones with Mick at the front. We were a team, creating something.'

Cliff told his producer, Norrie Paramor, that there would be a practicality to his signing the Drifters and giving them their own recording career. If the Drifters became a big name in their own right, their shows would pull in more people. Cliff was full of teenage confidence and Paramor probably chuckled as soon as the kid sauntered out of the room. But he liked the band well enough that they were allowed to play on his third single, without the help of session players.

Very soon, the boy Richard was back in the top ten with his second hit, 'High Class Baby'. It was another Ian Samwell song, written about his fancy crush, a well-spoken, blonde actress called Julie Samuel who would go on to play Gerry Marsden's love interest in the 1965 movie *Ferry Cross the Mersey* and later become mum to singer Sarah Cracknell.

He may have lost *Oh Boy!* to Cliff, but Marty Wilde was a gentleman. Rather than grousing about his bad luck and worse management, he took the model of Cliff Richard and the Drifters to Philips, his label, who had previously insisted that he toured and recorded with older, session-playing jazzers. The Drifters would become the model for the Wildcats; if the best players at the 2i's were all in the Drifters, then the next tier down was pretty solid too – Big Jim Sullivan on guitar, Brian 'Licorice' Locking on bass and Brian Bennett on drums. The second-best guitarist, bassist and drummer in the 2i's, and therefore in Soho, and therefore in the whole country, were no slouches. He may not have had Tony Meehan's Parisian student air, but Brian Bennett was arguably the stronger rock 'n' roll drummer. The Drifters were happy in the knowledge that – within months of their formation – they were now a model, a beat group, a rock 'n' roll combo that everyone aspired to imitate.

*

Based in Hayes, Middlesex, EMI – Electric and Musical Industries – had become the biggest record company in the world after a 1931 merger of the British labels Columbia, His Master's Voice and the Gramophone Company, the original record label set up by the gramophone's inventor, Emil Berliner, way back in 1898. When World War Two was over, EMI was still comfortably the most successful British record company, with a bunch of subsidiaries, but its senior executive Len 'L.G.' Wood was well aware that it was reliant on its American repertoire – Frankie Laine, Johnnie Ray, Doris Day, Guy Mitchell – and that these licences could always be pulled from under their feet. Wood decided to rebuild EMI's pop business in Britain, rather than lazily relying on their American repertoire. This was smart business – the sales of records were about to boom. In 1952, L.G. Wood decided to appoint four new A&R men to EMI's pop labels.

The Guildhall-trained George Martin went to Parlophone to cover novelty and comedy records; Walter Ridley, a composer and arranger who had worked on Vera Lynn's BBC radio shows during the war, was given HMV; Norman Newell was handed Columbia's more straight-edged acts like Josef Locke; and dance band pianist Norrie Paramor was charged with finding Columbia new names for a younger audience. The year 1952 was a banner one for modern pop: the *New Musical*

Express was created, and with it the first 'hit parade', while the portable Dansette record player was launched, as was the equally party-friendly seven-inch single, playing at 45 revolutions per minute and 'unbreakable' according to the card sleeves they came in. EMI were the first company to produce the 45 in Britain, followed by Decca two years on, then Philips and Pye a full five years later. 'We had the finest team of artist and repertoire managers the industry's ever known,' bragged L.G. Wood.

Norrie Paramor wore his thinning hair slicked back, along with tinted glasses which detracted from his squareness and suggested there was something more going on.

Born in London in 1914, Paramor was very much a generation older than Cliff and the Drifters. Pete Townshend's father Cliff had been a musician, playing clarinet and alto sax with the Squadronaires, the biggest band during the war years. But Norrie Paramor was already something of a veteran by then, having been a pianist and arranger for Jack Harris and then Maurice Winnick's London-based dance bands, both big deals in the '30s. That's how much older Paramor was than his new charges.

During World War Two, he had scored music for Noel Coward, Mantovani and Jack Buchanan. In 1950, he recorded some sides for the Oriole label with Australian singer Marie Benson, which sold reasonably well and attracted the interest of EMI; he was appointed as recording director of the UK's Columbia label in 1952. Straight out of the box, he had a million seller in 1953 with 'O Mein Papa' by the trumpeter Eddie Calvert, which spent nine weeks at number one and, astonishingly, also blew its way into the US top ten.

He also cut albums like *Dreams and Desires*, *In London in Love* and *Jet Flight* under his own name, super-smooth string arrangements to ease people through the post-war trauma. He discovered Irish ballad singer Ruby Murray, who had a number one with 'Softly, Softly' in 1955, and created the Big Ben Banjo Band, who sold crazy amounts of albums over the following decade. He also put together the Big Ben Hawaiian Band and made a further six albums with them.

By 1958, Paramor was living at number 11, The Bishops Avenue in Hampstead, the most ostentatiously wealthy street in London. Behind the wrought-iron gates, there sat a cherry-red Jaguar XK 140 convertible; behind the front door were his wife Joan and three kids – Caroline, Jane and David – living under oak beams, walking on luxurious Persian carpets, drawing French drapes, the spoils of a successful music man. When skiffle had broken in 1956, it was too rough for Norrie and he left it to George Martin at Parlophone, who recorded the Vipers. But Norrie Paramor knew the secret of successful A&R was to give the people what they wanted; once Bill Haley had toured Britain, causing riots, and both Elvis and Buddy Holly had number ones in 1957, he knew he'd have to get with the new beat. Presented with the raw, unfinished Cliff Richard, he signed him and instinctively gave him Bobby Helms' 'Schoolboy Crush' to record, thankfully gifting Cliff and his Drifters the B-side, which was 'Move It'. Paramor's original intention had been to sign Cliff as a solo act and back him with jazzer Ken Jones' orchestra. But the Drifters' clean, tight sound – and their apparent professionalism to match their enthusiasm – convinced him to keep Cliff and the Drifters as a performing and recording entity. Norrie Paramor only needed to provide the polish.

*

Nineteen fifty-nine began with Cliff at the studio for his celluloid debut in a film called *Serious Charge* and with third single 'Livin' Lovin' Doll' in the top twenty. The song – written by Paramor – sounded like a rush job but, of all Cliff's early rockers, 'Livin' Lovin' Doll' had the most berserk energy. The pace was beyond galloping and the abrupt ending suggested they were trying to play it as fast as possible. Its vocal line was a staccato stutter, no words recognisable as the English language beyond the title, and it was wildly exciting. What it lacked, though, was any kind of hummable melody and 'Livin' Lovin' Doll' only made it to number twenty. It was quickly followed by the double A-side of 'Mean Streak', the last Drifters recording with Terry Smart on drums, and 'Never Mind', Tony Meehan's debut. Both sides were fierce rockers and gave the group a return to the top ten.

'It was so exciting,' said Jet Harris. 'I'd been in the studio before, but Hank and Bruce and Tony hadn't and it must have been wonderful for them to go in a studio, you know, Abbey Road of all places.'

The Drifters, their line-up still in flux, hadn't been seen as necessary for *Serious Charge*. But Cliff nagged Norrie Paramor to give them a shot at their own single. With Cliff's records selling so well, it wasn't really a wild risk as his more die-hard fans would buy it just to be completists. They were still essentially a vocal group, modelled on an American sound. Everybody wanted to be American. More precisely, everybody wanted to be the Everly Brothers and 'Feelin' Fine' clearly did. It was written by Ian Samwell and performed at an audition in Paramor's office by the latest line-up of Hank, Bruce, Jet and Tony. Hank later described it as 'a real up-tempo sort of punky-sounding thing', but it was one of Samwell's weaker songs; presumably either Cliff or Norrie Paramor had already turned it down. Production-wise, at least, it was a big step on from 'Teenage Love' and 'Jean Dorothy'. The group signed to Columbia as artists in their own right on 5 February 1959.

'Feelin' Fine' didn't really suggest what was coming next, unless you were looking into the distant future of the early '70s, to Hank and Bruce's most effective vocal harmony work. What it *did* sound like was a precursor of Merseybeat, with handclaps on the guitar break that pre-empted 'Hold Me Tight' or any number of early Beatles songs. 'Feelin' Fine' was frantic British rock 'n' roll, the kind that would ferment for two, three, four more years in the cellars and caverns of Liverpool. But that meant absolutely nothing in 1959. The single flopped.

Remarkably, 'Feelin' Fine' was also released in the US, on the Capitol label. Capitol Records! Just like Gene Vincent! Just like Frank Sinatra! That must have given them a huge thrill, though it came with legal consequences – American R&B stars the Drifters weren't quite so excited by 'Feelin' Fine''s stateside release, and the single was quickly withdrawn when they took out an injunction. Printing 'RECORDED IN LONDON' on the label wasn't going to sway Rudy Lewis and his gang, who at that point hadn't scored a Billboard top forty hit, let alone a UK hit – although within weeks they would cross over massively with the string-driven 'There Goes My Baby'. London's own Drifters would have to think up a new name on their future American releases; in the short term, they called themselves the Four Jets for US purposes only.

*

Serious Charge was set in Stevenage, notably in the old town that most outsiders are unaware exists. A Hertfordshire market town on the A1, it had expanded hugely when it became part of the post-war dream based around the 1946 New Towns Act. There were new shops and schools and wide-open spaces, plenty of fresh, clean air for the poor sods escaping bombed-out London tenements and terraces. The appeal of Stevenage's green vistas for newlyweds was obvious, the attraction for their offspring less so. What was there to do?

'Goodness, how fast this place is growing,' cried Hester, played by Sarah Churchill. Anthony Quayle's grumbling vicar had his hands full with the new town's youth. He looked permanently worried and snapped back at Hester: 'If we don't get hold of them, in twenty years' time you can shut all the churches and people like me will be out of a job.'

With the main 'juves' named Larry and Curly, screenplay writer Philip King was presumably a Three Stooges fan. Cliff's character – Curly – liked rock 'n' roll, and got to sing three songs, including the rough 'No Turning Back' and the gentler 'Living Doll'. But he didn't carry a flick knife like bad boy Larry. At a rock 'n' roll night in the church hall, Quayle had the squealing, knife-wielding Larry in an arm lock on the floor and asked the hoodlums to leave before he took 'great pleasure in throwing you through that window'.

Cliff's character Curly was the first to back track: 'Hey fellas, how about doing what he says?'

'Whose side are you on, anyway?' shouted Larry. The question was one that would be levelled at Cliff throughout his post rock 'n' roll career.

In a memorable coffee bar scene, Curly sang along to a record on the jukebox while girlfriends draped themselves over him, simultaneously doing the hand-jive. This was a genuine invention of British rock 'n' roll which meant you could dance when still sitting down; making the best of a constrained situation, making your own DIY fun, something the British working classes have always been good at. The song Cliff sang in the coffee bar was 'Living Doll', written – like the other songs in the movie – by Lionel Bart, who had risen to fame by co-writing all of Tommy Steele's breakthrough records. In the film, 'Living Doll' had a generic rock 'n' roll beat, like a faster-paced Ricky Nelson record, and Cliff sneered the line 'Got a rovin' eye and that is why she satisfies my soul' in the manner of low-level troublemaker Curly. On record, released several months later, it would sound very different.

Contractually, Cliff had to release a single to promote *Serious Charge*. Fan mail strongly suggested 'Living Doll', but Norrie Paramor was irked at having control of Cliff's releases wrested away from him. More to the point, the group hated the song.

*

While Cliff was filming *Serious Charge*, the touring schedule remained relentless. He moved out of his parents' house in Cheshunt and into a flat in Marylebone, which quickly – out of necessity – became a crash pad.

'We did everything together,' said Hank. 'We stayed in the same places, we went out to the movies together, we partied together, we on occasion shared girlfriends... we just did everything together, you know. It was a real fun, five-piece band, not a singer and a backing group – that was the feeling we had. And I think that's why the relationship got so strong, and I think that came across in the music as well. That chemistry worked in the music.'

Success and a hectic schedule caught Hank in a way he wasn't expecting, something that he kept to himself. The rest of the group probably thought he was being a bit moody and left it at that. His condition certainly wouldn't have rung any alarm bells. Pastoral care in the music industry in the late '50s was non-existent. According to their first biographer Royston Ellis, here are the places Cliff Richard and the Drifters played in 1959, on seven different tours of Britain. Buckle up. Walthamstow, Chiswick, Slough, Finsbury Park, Manston, Colchester, Worcester, Bristol, Reading, Dorking, Wimbledon, Hanley, Manchester, Bedford, Worksop, York, Dewsbury, Brighton, Cheam, Romford, Leeds, Pontefract, Scunthorpe, Newark, Burnley, Ipswich, Salisbury, Hull, Wigan, Newcastle-upon-Tyne, Sheffield, Edmonton, Birmingham, Cheltenham, Kettering, Grantham, Mansfield, East Ham, Dartford, Tooting, Doncaster, Southampton, Harrow, Bournemouth, Rugby, Guildford, Oldham, Bradford, Liverpool, Plymouth, Coventry, Rochester, Norwich, Lincoln, Lewisham, Preston, Derby, Kingston-upon-Thames, Wolverhampton, Shrewsbury, Huddersfield, Peterborough, Barking, Leicester,

Dover, Trowbridge, Cardiff, Dudley, Nottingham, Middlesbrough, Harrogate, Blackpool, Southport, Southend, Elephant and Castle, Stepney, Exeter, Luton, Canterbury, Chesterfield, Chester, Rhyl, Gloucester, Taunton, Weston-super-Mare, Northampton, Halifax, Sunderland and Carlisle.

They had to write while they were either backstage or in transit. Jet wrote the instrumental 'Jet Black', the Drifters' second single and their first self-written instrumental, in a coach in North Lincolnshire. 'Gee Whizz It's You', a stand-out on the 1960 *Me and My Shadows* album, was written by Hank and Ian Samwell on the plane home after a US tour, when an attractive air stewardess sashayed down the gangway towards them. Other songs like 'Please Don't Tease', 'She's Gone' and 'Thinking of Our Love' were presumably sketched out between Corby and Kettering, then worked up into an arrangement on the road from Worksop to Mansfield. There were no holidays. 'The most conflict we had was over the work we did,' remembered Tony Meehan. 'We worked very hard. We were backing Cliff, we were trying to do our own career, we were working seven days a week, not getting paid that well.'

Hank told the *Daily Mail*, many years later, how he might have spent any down time he had in 1959.

'When I was seventeen, in 1959, I would lie in bed for hours because I had no motivation. I thought *What's the point of getting up?* And now I know, looking back, I was probably a bit depressed at the time. I had everything going for me – but that's the thing with depression, you often don't know why it comes on. It then probably lasted for a few months then went and I was fine.'

To anyone outside the Shadows' circle, this would most likely have looked and sounded like a nervous breakdown. But there was no time for rest.

*

The February '59 tour included a week at the Lyceum, just off the Strand in London. It had a revolving stage and the boys had the idea to start off with their backs to the audience, who would see them once the stage had spun 180 degrees. Before Cliff even got to open his mouth, the Teddy Boys at the front pelted them with pennies – the huge, pre-decimal ones, the same that had gouged a chunk from Jet's bass at another rough show in Shepherd's Bush a few weeks earlier. This time, the onslaught of rotten vegetables and more destructive materials was so intense that the group downed tools and walked off. The entire week's booking was cancelled. The next day, the boys discovered that their hero, Buddy Holly, had died in a plane crash; they'd had better weeks.

Norrie Paramor had booked 9 and 10 February for the recording of Cliff's first album, backed by the Drifters, which would be recorded on a rare break, live, in front of an invited, entirely teenage audience at EMI's studio on Abbey Road.

The problem was that, by late January 1959, the group were frazzled – they were ill through lack of sleep and a seven-days-a-week schedule put together for them by a manager called Franklin Boyd, who had been recommended by Norrie Paramor. Cliff had developed laryngitis and his father Rodger Webb sacked Boyd for overworking and exploiting his son. Norrie Paramor can't have been too happy, either. They couldn't pull out of the Abbey Road dates.

The group's tiredness maybe gave the shows an even more frenetic edge than they might have had. They played Ritchie Valens' 'Donna' as a tribute to the recently deceased singer, killed in the same plane crash as Buddy Holly, but otherwise the *Cliff* album was almost entirely made up of rock 'n' roll covers – Jerry Lee's 'Down the Line', Elvis's 'Too Much', Little Richard's 'Ready Teddy' – though there were also a couple of instrumentals by the Drifters to give Cliff's voice a break. Jet's 'Jet Black' and Hank's 'Driftin'' would soon be re-recorded at Abbey Road and released as the Drifters' second stand-alone single. Cliff was raucous and, in spite of the slightly faked live situation, the album was a pretty good example of what a Cliff and the Drifters show would have felt and sounded like in 1959. All of the things that made *Cliff* exciting would be turned against by *Gramophone* magazine, whose reviewer was less than impressed:

'I find myself musing when listening to Cliff Richard that when the Beat Generation grows up it will be heartily ashamed of itself, and that records such as these will provide irrefutable evidence of the temper of our times; the unintelligible and unintelligent mouthing to a twangy guitar, the pile driver rhythm, the shrieks of rapture coming in smack on cue, and the lesson in mass hysteria that is given.'

*

The gay man's gaze steered so much of British popular culture in the '50s including the homegrown rock 'n' roll scene, much more so than it seemed to in the US. There was no quelling the demand for Lionel Bart's campy 'Living Doll' to be released on vinyl.

For the Drifters, the lyric was beyond the pale: 'Gonna lock her up in a trunk so no big hunk can steal her away from me'. It's easy to see why Cliff, Hank, Bruce and Jet would have winced. It was lightweight and silly, and would only be rescued from outright novelty by Bruce Welch. On tour in February '59, backstage at Sheffield City Hall, Bruce played around with the hated song – he slowed it down and gave it a country edge, which was then amplified by a beautiful Hank solo. They made 'Living Doll' bearable.

Cliff and the Drifters recorded just eight *Oh Boy!* shows in 1959 before the season came to an end in May. Disappointingly, it would never return. Like many semi-legendary TV series, its lifespan was surprisingly short, running on ITV from September 1958 to May 1959. There was talk of its return in September, but by then Jack Good had moved on, changed the format and launched *Boy Meets Girls*.

The Drifters had such a relentlessly busy package of live shows between January and May 1959 that, to their chagrin, they had to turn down *Oh Boy!* more often than not, along with the massive exposure it afforded them. Good would later grumble that 'there was Cliff going off into the sticks making a few hundred pounds for himself singing "Living Doll" or whatever, when he should have been on my show'. They did appear on 2 May, though, and would perform both sides of their proposed next single, 'Choppin' 'n' Changin'' and 'Dynamite', two blistering Ian Samwell rockers they had recorded back in March.

But the single would never come out.

After Bruce had come up with his arrangement for 'Living Doll', backstage in Sheffield, the group decided to try it in the studio on 28 April. At last, Norrie Paramor had this number down on tape, the track from *Serious Charge* that he was contractually obliged to release as a single. The hard-edged 'Choppin' 'n' Changin'' didn't have a chance.

Hank played a Dutch Egmond semi-acoustic guitar on 'Living Doll' (which looked and sounded like a Gretsch White Falcon) to give it what he called 'a country feeling', akin to James Burton's guitar playing for Ricky Nelson. His solo was closer to the warmly swaddled beat of Nelson's more recent singles – 'Lonesome Town', 'Never Be Anyone Else But You' – than anything Cliff and the Drifters had yet recorded. This was definitely the aim of all concerned, including Norrie Paramor. Yet, somehow, it was also the most distinctively English-sounding record they had made to date, as if the pegboard and white coats of the EMI Recording Studios on Abbey Road had somehow fused with their wannabe James Burton balladry.

Record Mail, EMI's own magazine for retail and designed to plug its own product, described Cliff's 'Living Doll' as 'a slow haunting ballad, with the essential beat ever predominant ... he will bring in an even wider public with "Living Doll", a factor always useful to a rising star'. The thin and derivative 'Living Doll' from *Serious Charge* had been transformed into a mellow, sundown swoon, all of its camp kinks smoothed over. The single went to number one within four weeks of release. It would quickly become Cliff's calling card, whether he liked it or not.

'As far as I was concerned, it was the beginning of the end of Cliff as a rock star,' said Jack Good, whose opinion of 'Move It' had done so much to give almost everyone involved in this story a bunk-up. 'There was a strong streak of Doris Day in him,' he added cattily. It certainly changed the public perception of the singer. Cliff signed an agency contract with Lew and Leslie Grade, who would immediately reshape his career. He would appear in his first pantomime at the end of 1959 and the Grades talked to ATV about him hosting a family-friendly TV series. The *NME* noted that he was a non-smoker, which was so rare in showbiz back then that it was almost an affectation. One more big win for the old guard over the youth came when *Record Mail* featured a photo of Cliff clearly wearing a crucifix.

*

The American influence on Cliff and the Drifters extended beyond guitars and cowboy movies and into literature. Royston Ellis, a British beat poet and 'a bearded, bisexual teenage speed freak' according to writer Andrew Hickey, had struck up a friendship with Cliff after he gatecrashed a Radio Luxemburg session. Another British poet, Christopher Logue, had been reading poetry to jazz accompaniment and calling it 'jazzetry'. Ellis was no big fan of Logue, but this planted a seed and he quickly had the idea of performing 'rocketry'.

'I met Royston in 1959 when he wandered into a studio in London where I was recording a programme for Radio Luxembourg,' wrote Cliff in 2014. 'He introduced himself as a poet and said that he wanted to dedicate his first book of poems to me. Of course, I was puzzled but agreed. After that, I used to see a lot of Royston as he became very friendly with Jet and Tony and he often came on tour with us.'

Ellis was smart, but also extraordinarily lucky. He was impatient and thought he should perform his rocketry with a pre-existing group rather than putting one together. Why not the biggest new noise in the country? That would give his poetry the biggest possible teenage audience.

He 'rather coyly' dedicated his first book 'to C – a drifter's boy, some rhythm and blues', thinking that was a good enough reason to catch Cliff's attention. He then wrote him a letter using a brown typewriter ribbon rather than the usual black, which was – unexpectedly for Ellis – read as gay code by Ray Mackender, a friend of Cliff's dad who had become one of his advisors when 'Move It' suddenly blew up. Mackender thought Ellis sounded like an intriguing proposition and invited him around to his house on Cheyne Walk, known as the Shrine. He liked Ellis's poetry and arranged an accidental-on-purpose meeting, telling Ellis the rest was up to him. And so, Cliff heard that a poet was going to drop by while they recorded a Radio Luxembourg session.

Jet was instantly taken with this bearded teenage boho who reminded him of Iris Orton and the wilder Soho characters of the '50s. Tony, likewise, saw a kindred intellectual spirit in Ellis and was all in favour of them working together. Hank and Bruce 'were baffled by my presence,' wrote Ellis in 2014, 'and when I broached the idea of the Drifters performing rocketry with me, they thought it was a joke.'

Cliff was 'polite and courteous by nature', said Ellis, and gave it some thought. He was clearly intrigued. He told Ellis that, when he was at school, he had also performed poetry to makeshift musical accompaniment – he even had a tape recording of it. Ellis was invited up to Cheshunt to hear the tape.

'It was a poem by Rudyard Kipling,' remembered Ellis, 'and the "music" was the sound of kids in his class banging on the tops of their wooden desks. Cliff's voice on the tape had a distinct Indian accent that suited the poem. He introduced me to Mrs Norris, his English teacher, who didn't pour scorn on my idea of rocketry, so perhaps that helped Cliff accept the idea that Jet, Tony and I had suggested, that the Drifters would perform with me.'

Ray Mackender booked them into Battersea Town Hall and the BBC recorded the event which, miraculously, survives on a newsreel. It came across like an early version of the Fall, or Half Man Half Biscuit, and it may have gone somewhere had the Drifters not then become the Shadows and grown too big for niche poetry performances. Tony Meehan may not have gone to art school, but he was the most literate Shadow, and took it seriously. Bruce smirked on stage as he stood behind Ellis reading lines like 'a long-haired, idle unbound boy and a glorious carefree maiden slump was in the front row of the stalls, content with the mumbling harmony of their own idea of love'. Ellis stayed tight with Jet, Tony and Cliff, who would occasionally go the pictures with him. The weekly music paper *Disc* thought it would be a good idea if Ellis wrote a book; *Driftin' With Cliff* emerged soon after in 1960, the first book on either Cliff or the Shadows.

By the time the book was published, the Drifters had changed their name. 'Perhaps *Shadowing Cliff* would have been a better title,' reckoned Ellis, 'as that is what I did for several months.'

Bumming around the country in 1960, he stumbled into the Jacaranda in Liverpool for a cup of coffee. A lad called George caught his eye and they got chatting. While the greasy rock scene was struggling in London, Ellis discovered it still thrived in Liverpool. George invited him back to his house on Gambier Terrace to meet two art students he was in a beat group with – John and Stu. 'They were introduced to me as the Rhythmettes,' wrote Ellis in *Myself For Fame*. 'Guitarists by night and art students by day – if they ever got off the pile of rags they were pleased to call their beds.' As requested, they backed an impromptu Royston Ellis poetry reading at the Jacaranda.

He introduced his fast friends to drugs – the strip from inside a Benzedrine inhaler that, if chewed, could keep you up all night. John and Stu were very taken with the idea of becoming Ellis's new backing musicians. The group was on the verge of splitting, so one day they hitch-hiked down to London to take Ellis up on his offer, knocking on the door of his mum and dad's house in Hatch End. 'Royston isn't home,' Mrs Ellis told the two lads, who looked sheepish and left no note. They returned to Liverpool, where John found he'd been kicked out of art college, so the band got back together for lack of anything better to do.

In the summer of 1960, a *Record Mirror* article reported that 'the bearded sage of the coffee bars' had been in Liverpool, and found a new five-piece to back him called 'the Beetles'. According to Ellis, they soon changed the spelling of the name to 'Beatles', with his encouragement.

When Tony Meehan read the story in *Record Mirror*, he was pissed off: what was wrong with using the Shadows as a backing group? Ellis pointed out that they were way too busy these days, but he'd be happy to perform with them again. Tony needn't have worried about being usurped by the Beatles, not just yet. And Ellis did stick around. A year later, he was piecing another book together, *The Shadows By Themselves,* during downtime as they filmed *The Young Ones.*[*]

*

Driftin' With Cliff was full of reportage-like vignettes of life on the road for a rock 'n' roll group in 1959. At one point, their coach was stuck at traffic lights in St Albans. Cliff was reading a sci-fi book when a girl guide strolled past and happened to look through the window. She was thrilled to see her dream boy Cliff looking back at her, winking. A crowd quickly gathered. One girl in the crowd particularly caught Hank's eye and this started a conversation on the sort of girl Cliff would eventually like to marry. 'If she knows how to cook Chinese food, all the better,' he said. Ellis wrote up both the mundanity and good nature of a teenage band on the road in the late '50s like the fellow traveller he was:

> 'Tea!' suddenly shouted Bruce, who craved for tea like a drug addict. They all took up the shout for tea, so Len [tour manager Len Sackson] instructed the driver to stop at the first café they came to. Not far down the road the coach pulled up outside a

---

* By 1961 Royston Ellis would be on TV talking to John Betjeman and reading his poems backed by a solo guitarist, seventeen-year-old Jimmy Page. If he'd been into management rather than poetry, he could have become a rich man. You couldn't fault his prescience. Instead, when Ellis turned twenty, he retired as the unofficial voice of the teenager, declaring he was now middle-aged. He began travelling, like a true beatnik, and writing books.

typical transport café on the A5. The boys went in and joined the many truck drivers. Here they each had egg, beans and tomatoes, and a pint mug of tea. Len said the tea would last everyone for the rest of the journey, but Bruce had already started on his second pint. They sorted out their sixpences and placed them in the jukebox. Cliff played Elvis Presley, his favourite singer. Jet put on Gene Vincent, his favourite.

Back on the bus, the boys had a cushion fight, all the way from Luton to Birmingham. They were still kids.

*

'Living Doll', backed by the hiccupping 'Apron Strings', had been number one for six weeks. It was followed by another ballad called 'Travellin' Light', with the previously discarded, self-descriptive 'Dynamite' on the flip. That spent seven weeks at number one on *Record Mirror*'s chart.

By the time 'Travellin' Light' came out, the Drifters no longer existed. An injunction from the American Drifters was looming and had to be confronted.

Jet: 'Hank and I went off on our scooters to the Six Bells in Ruislip to think of a permanent new name.'

Hank: 'We were prepared for a three-hour discussion.'

Jet: 'I'll never forget. We were drinking pints of Guinness, going through every name you can imagine – Zephyrs, Zodiacs, Tigers, Lions, you name it, for about an hour. And then we went quiet and

I just said Hank's Shadows? He looked at me... "Cliff Richard and the Shadows," he said. [Low, grumbly voice] "Yeah... that's it." So we fled back to where Cliff was living in Marylebone, back to the flat and said, "Cliff?"

'"Yes?"

'"Cliff Richard and the Shadows."

'"*YES!* That's it!"

'So it was my fault. But I can't imagine us as anything else.'

*

Cliff had sold well after it was released in April 1959, reaching number four and spending seven months in the top twenty. Cliff and the Shadows' next album, *Cliff Sings*, released in November, fell one place short of the top and was on the chart for eight months. This was quantifiable progress.

With 'The Snake and the Bookworm', the group showed they were digging deep for material on *Cliff Sings*. It was a Doc Pomus and Mort Shuman song, also cut by the Coasters, but the first recording by Pat Shannon had only just been released when Cliff and the gang recorded it. They made it their own – Hank interjected with his guitar, like a cheeky kid sassing storyteller Cliff. Likewise, Carl Perkins' 'Pointed Toe Shoes' wasn't in the arsenal of many provincial rock 'n' roll acts. Let loose to cut studio versions of items in their live set – such as a breakneck 'Blue Suede Shoes' – the Shadows were on fire. Their version of the Eddie Cochran single 'Twenty Flight Rock' remains a superb piece of British rockabilly.

There's one major problem with *Cliff Sings*. It was engineer Malcolm Addey's idea to split the album in half – eight songs with the Shadows and eight songs with Cliff backed by the Norrie Paramor Strings. All of these recordings were standards, designed to prove that Cliff wasn't the flick-knife-carrying tabloid monster of *Serious Charge*. Was he a snake or a bookworm? Here was the evidence. Any rock 'n' roll fans who thought that Cliff had abandoned them with 'Living Doll' had their suspicions confirmed. Worse yet, Cliff – used to bouncing off a band – was as unsteady as a kid riding a bike for the first time on 'As Time Goes By' and 'I'll String Along With You'. He had grown up with Peggy Lee and Nat King Cole playing in the Webbs' Cheshunt cul-de-sac and, given the same material, he sounded scared stiff. Fortunately, Columbia issued all sixteen tracks from *Cliff Sings* across four EPs: the kids could buy volumes one and two to get the goods; mums and their blanketed teenage offspring could stick with volumes three and four.

But the album reached number two in the album chart. Nobody could argue with the statistics.

*

Cliff's backing group's third single, 'Saturday Dance', was written by Hank and Pete Chester and recorded in August '59. Musically, it was barely an advance, still sounding like Everly Brothers karaoke in a Finsbury Park boozer. It had none of the charm and mystique of 'Travellin' Light', nor the restless power of 'Dynamite'. It was okay. This time around, on their first single credited to 'The Shadows', they did squeak into the bottom end of a couple of the UK charts (although not *Record Mirror*'s, so you won't find it in the *Guinness Book of British Hit Singles*). On the flip was a rare treat, kind of – Jet Harris handled the lead vocal on 'Lonesome Fella', a cowboy number that was too milky by far.

The success or otherwise of the Shadows singles without Cliff barely seemed to matter as they were invited to play *Sunday Night at the London Palladium*, a televised performance that brought in twenty million viewers. The boys donned tuxedos and, at the end of their performance, Cliff was presented with a gold disc for selling a million copies of 'Living Doll'. It was getting harder to say that Norrie Paramor hadn't steered them in the right direction.

After the London Palladium, where would they go next? Stockton-on-Tees. Cliff Richard and the Shadows would end the decade in panto, doing *Babes in the Wood* for four weeks on Teesside. That was the summit for British popular music in the '50s, whether you were Alma Cogan, Dickie Valentine, Marty Wilde or Cliff Richard – the Palladium and panto. Things would change in the 1960s, but by then Cliff Richard and the Shadows would be the establishment.

4

THE BREAKING POINT

It was a beautiful cover. The four Crickets towered over the photographer, grinning American-sized grins in sharp suits against a luminous blue-sky backdrop. In March 1958, "*The 'Chirping' Crickets*" LP was released in the UK. The Geordie Boys had their breath taken away by the contents, Buddy Holly's insane gift for songwriting and – impressing Hank in particular – for his boldness in proudly sporting spectacles on the cover.

But what on earth was that in Buddy's hands?

What primarily caught their eye was that guitar – a guitar like nothing they'd ever seen on Charing Cross Road. Britain was still starved of colour in 1958 because of post-war ink shortages; bottle green and battleship grey were predominant. And now here was Buddy, with his bright-blue sky and his bright-red futuristic machine. Hank and Bruce ogled the space-aged Fender Stratocaster. They knew they couldn't ever have one of their own.

The UK government had imposed restrictions on the import of US-made musical instruments in November 1951 – along with many other American products – in an effort to get the post-war British economy back on its feet. This had a big impact on the UK music scene and was as significant as 'Rock Island Line''s raw pig-iron energy in the development of skiffle. Quality instruments were in short supply. Budding UK guitarists had to rely on cheap European imports; wash-boards and tea-chest basses, out of necessity as much as expedience, were used for accompaniment.

By the start of 1959, Hank was playing a two-pick-up Antoria-branded LG-50 electric guitar, made by Guyatone in Japan. These were the first Japanese imports and helped fill the void left by the American import ban. This was also Hank's first solid body guitar and the first with an identifiably rock 'n' roll look to it. But still… that Fender.

'No one seemed to know about guitar maintenance,' remembered Hank. 'None of the guys we knew – it was just a mystery! I had this dreadful old Antoria, which I'd had for a few months. I bought it because it looked like a rock 'n' roll guitar. It had a small body, like a Les Paul body, and it had a headstock copied from a Fender, but it was big and clumsy. It was an unusual sound, a clacky, twangy sound, but the neck was awful. A thick neck, slightly concave, so by the time you got to the fifth fret, the action got quite alarmingly high. And then by the time you got to the twelfth fret, it started to come down again, because of the curve on the neck. The neck felt like it had been made by Fred Flintstone, it was just so bad.'

Cliff and the Drifters were all massive fans of Ricky Nelson – and especially of his guitarist, James Burton. They read somewhere that, like Buddy Holly, Burton played a Fender. That sound! That was the sound they aspired to and no amount of Norrie Paramor's studio expertise was going to make the Antoria sing like Burton's playing on Ricky's 'Believe What You Say'.

'So,' Hank revealed, 'Cliff said "I'd like to buy a really nice guitar for you – what do you reckon?"'

With several hits under their belt, they thought they might be able to try their luck. Hank and Bruce got hold of the address for Fender from Reg Clark, the helpful manager of the Jennings musical instrument shop at 100 Charing Cross Road. What did they have to lose? Customs officials weren't going to be kicking their door down just because they'd written to Fullerton, California, requesting a catalogue.

When the 1958/59 Fender catalogue finally arrived in London – the first Fender catalogue to have a full-colour cover – the Geordie Boys were enthralled by the cover star, a sharp red Stratocaster with eye-popping gold hardware. Assuming that Burton must play Fender's 'top of the line' instrument, the pair concluded that a Stratocaster – like Buddy and Burton played – was the guitar for them. It would be years before they discovered that Burton actually played a Telecaster.

Cliff kept up his end and agreed to finance the purchase. Then, with the help of Reg Clark, they placed an order with Fender. Reg also arranged the international payment through Jennings. Although one or two Fender instruments may have made it onto UK shores – with a handful of musicians bringing them back as hand luggage – Reg's request was the very first order from Britain that Fender had ever received.

Jennings had asked for a guitar just like the one on the cover of the catalogue. It is highly likely that Don Randall at Fender Sales read the letter and shipped them that actual guitar. It was a Roman Red Fender Stratocaster, with a bird's eye maple neck and gold-plated hardware (serial number 34346). It was the most expensive Fender anyone could buy at the time and so rare that another one like it has yet to surface.*

In March 1959, the Stratocaster arrived at 100 Charing Cross Road. Reg phoned Hank and Bruce, and they shot down to the shop so they could all unpack it together. What a moment. Reg would later vividly recall the overwhelming smell of the paint and polish as the tweed case was opened, and how gob-smacked they all were at the outstanding beauty and quality of the instrument. It was quite unlike anything they had seen. Even the Phillips screws – *the screws!* – were something they had never seen before. Every detail. Entirely futuristic. And it was theirs.

'Three pick-ups, and a tremolo arm, and a bird's eye maple neck,' Hank recalled. 'We didn't know what maple was, but the brochure had either rosewood or maple, and Buddy's had a maple neck. So that was it. It came over, and it was stunning. It was just wonderful to look at. It was like something from space, really, it was so futuristic in its design. It just looked sensational.'

---

* 1950s custom-colour Stratocasters are impossibly rare; almost all were sunburst finish. Fender biographer Martin Kelly believes that Hank must have been sent the one from the catalogue. Some Shadows fans claim Hank's first Strat was finished in fiesta red, but Fender had not introduced that shade at the time the catalogue was produced. There were several UK slang names for the colour – 'flamingo pink' and 'salmon pink' being two – but the guitar sent to Jennings was 'Roman red'.

Hank started using the guitar immediately. 'It just made us sound so much deeper and richer,' said Cliff. 'Hank was always a great player, but now he went up to another level.'

It's no exaggeration to say that this was the most important guitar purchase of all time. It would break open the UK music scene; every budding guitarist from the skiffle and rock 'n' roll scenes now wanted a guitar like Hank's. George Harrison drew pictures of Stratocasters in his school exercise books. And, in June 1959, the dream became a possibility for everybody else as import restrictions were lifted. Jennings weren't daft and quickly secured sole rights to import Fender guitars and amps to the UK. They were also the parent company for Vox amplifiers. By 1960, they were taking out ads for the dream team of a Fender guitar with a Vox amp. And they could have had no better advert for this than Hank Marvin, who was beginning to create magic with this exact combination.

*

'Travellin' Light' was a song by Sid Tepper and Roy C. Bennett. It may have had the dust of a dirt track in its mood, an Anglicised take on *On the Road*, with Cliff as Kerouac and Hank as Neal Cassady, no comb and no toothbrush between them (not a pretty thought). But Tepper and Bennett were Brooklyn born and bred, and had lived across the street from each other during the Great Depression. They weren't kids; they were Brill Building pros. In the pre-rock, nuclear family-obsessed '50s, they scored a brace of insanely catchy novelty hits about babies with Dean Martin's 'The Naughty Lady of Shady

Lane' ('And she's only nine days old!') and the Stargazers' 'Twenty Tiny Fingers' ('And the other one's got a big bald spot, exactly like his pop!'). They broached rock-lite in 1958 with Perry Como's 'Kewpie Doll', before aiming for the top with Elvis. For old-timers, they did all right, placing the forgettable 'Lonesome Cowboy' on the score of 1957's *Loving You* and the far better 'New Orleans' in the *King Creole* movie a year later. Leiber and Stoller were still Elvis's favoured writing team, though. If they couldn't get a song to the king, Tepper and Bennett reasoned, then they'd settle for a prince, somebody bequiffed and suitably attired, waiting outside the castle gates.*

According to Cliff, 'Travellin' Light' was a cast-off from the *King Creole* soundtrack, though its mood and lyric would hardly have suited the brassy urban melodrama. Its pace made it a logical successor to 'Living Doll', but it was superior in every way; it kicked up the sand, it had the mood, and the lyric. With none of the molestation of 'Living Doll', here was a carefree beatnik, hitching his way to who-knows-where, guitar over one shoulder. It was the first record to be credited to Cliff Richard and the Shadows. It was also the first single on which Cliff was accompanied by Hank's brand-new Fender Strat. Engineer Malcolm Addey smothered both Hank and Cliff in reverb, giving a wistful, slightly unreal feel that was perfect for the wandering minstrel, 'a hoot and a holler away from paradise'.

*

* Cliff wouldn't meet Sid Tepper, author of some of his biggest hits, until Tepper's ninetieth birthday in 2008, where they sang 'Travellin' Light' together.

Cliff's second movie, *Expresso Bongo*, was showing at cinemas across Britain in the first week of the 1960s. It was also the Shadows' first movie. There they were in the fictional Expresso coffee bar, playing 'Bongo Blues' as Johnny Jackson (Laurence Harvey) walks in wearing a trilby and a bow-tie, his stripper girlfriend Maisie (Sylvia Syms) on his arm. We see and hear the Shadows, playing Norrie Paramor's rocking composition 'Love', before we even get a whiff of Cliff: Bruce wears a tight white T-shirt, Chester-le-Street's own James Dean, with a pendant round his neck; Hank sports his Fender Strat, a collapsing quiff and a similarly American-styled dark hooped shirt; blond Jet has a varsity jacket, while Tony is stage-front, with a rather shocking convict cut and a long-sleeved pin-stripe shirt. They smile and maybe snigger a little. They look and sound the bee's knees. 'If things weren't bad enough,' Harvey moans to Syms as they walk into the caff, 'we have to pick on amateur talent night.'

Cliff played the gormless but handsome teen idol Bongo Herbert. Though there was a solid amount of Cliff biography in the script – early management being squeezed out, the switch from razor-edged rock 'n' roll to more wholesome entertainment – it was hardly complimentary: he is described as a 'snotty-nosed little Teddy Boy' and predicts his own future recordings will be 'this and that, a bit of variety… as long as it brings in the loot.' When confronted with the fanbase who made his name, Bongo sneers, 'What do I care about those grimy yobs?' And he frequently, urgently, asks his manager Johnny Jackson (played with a perfect Soho piquancy by Harvey), 'What am I gonna do when I hit twenty?' This all seemed like a remarkable, if unflattering, prediction of what lay ahead.

Two songs in the movie were parodies, designed to show the public that the slow-witted Bongo still held his mother and the holy ghost close to his heart. One was 'The Shrine on the Second Floor', from the original play, and the second was the Norrie Paramor-penned 'A Voice in the Wilderness', which turned a bible story into a remorseful love song: 'We had a quarrel, I was unkind / How could you leave me? Love made me blind.'

A few months earlier, Cliff and the Drifters had been jumping around the stage, falling on their knees, rolling on the floor. 'It was a very anarchic, rock 'n' roll presentation,' said Hank. They dressed in black shoes, black trousers and black shirts with a white tie, all of them living in the same dream. 'A Voice in the Wilderness' was where fact and fiction became truly compounded. There was a scene in *Expresso Bongo* where Johnny Jackson scammed his way onto Gilbert Harding's (real-life) TV panel show and grinningly told viewers that '"A Voice in the Wilderness" will introduce a new era in the hit parade.' Greedy hustler Johnny was spot on. Like 'Living Doll', no one in the group including Cliff thought much of 'A Voice in the Wilderness' and they plugged its flip side 'Don't Be Mad At Me' at shows and on radio sessions. Paramor frowned on this rebellion and was convinced that this was to the single's detriment. He thought it was the reason why it didn't give the group a hat-trick of number ones, stalling at number two behind Anthony Newley's 'Why' (which sounded like an *Expresso Bongo* parody of an icky teen ballad, but wasn't). After 'A Voice in the Wilderness', Cliff and the Shadows would continue to record rockers – but, almost always, they would now be B-sides or album tracks.

And so, with *Expresso Bongo* out of the way, 1960 got on with being the worst year in pop music since the dawn of rock 'n' roll.

*

Sometimes, they still had to pinch themselves. Cliff and the Shadows were booked to travel to the US in January to appear on a Biggest Show of Stars 1960 Winter Edition tour along with the great – Clyde McPhatter, the Clovers, Sammy Turner, the Isley Brothers, Freddy Cannon, the Crests, Johnny and the Hurricanes – as well as the not so good (milksop headliners Frankie Avalon and Bobby Rydell). Cliff's dad Rodger, his new manager Tito Burns and Shadows tour manager Ian Samwell flew out with them. They got to appear on network TV shows with Perry Como and Pat Boone, but more excitingly they were packed like sardines onto Greyhound buses with people they had previously only bought records by; unlike the Bedford van, their coach now had reclining seats, even toilets.

The place names seemed so exotic and exciting. Buffalo. Fort Worth. Kansas City. Philadelphia. They played Norfolk, Virginia, Gene Vincent's hometown, which gave them a real kick. But when they played in Lubbock, Texas, Buddy Holly's birthplace, Bruce remembered they were 'very apprehensive … we idolised him that much'. Southern shows, where their black compere was called 'boy' – or worse – by the locals, made them feel physically sick.

In the States, they played 'Forty Days', 'Whole Lotta Shakin' Goin' On', 'My Babe', new single 'Voice in the Wilderness' and 'Living Doll' – the bona fide top-thirty Billboard hit that had got them over there (it would go as high as number five in Canada). On a rare day off, like true western mythologists, they visited the site of the Alamo. With a few days off in New York, they made a pilgrimage to jazz club Birdland, met drummer Cozy Cole at the Metropole and bought pork pie hats that weren't yet in the London shops. They also heard Johnny Otis's 'Willie and the Hand Jive' for the first time and decided to include it in their set once they got home.

Tito Burns had ordered Cliff to return to London midway through the US tour to play at the *NME* Poll-Winners' Party – without the Shadows. He would be backed instead by the strangely named Parker Royal Four, who would later change their name to the Hunters and put out a few Shad-alike singles.

Burns clearly thought of the Shadows as nothing more than a backing group, rather than intrinsic to Cliff's work; back in Britain, they weren't even invited to a champagne party in Leeds to honour their singer's nineteenth birthday. It's hard to imagine Cliff was happy with this situation. Burns was overplaying his hand, Rodger Webb took against him and he was sacked shortly after the American tour was completed. Cliff's career didn't benefit from the tour; no one from his US label, ABC Paramount, had even showed up to say hello and his follow-up to 'Living Doll' went nowhere. The Shadows wouldn't ever play in the States again.

*

The calendar read 1960, but the '60s had not begun, not yet. Britain was still buttoned up, unable to express itself out of some misplaced loyalty to queen and country and Victorian values, whatever they were. Celebrity was no insularity. The panel show host Gilbert Harding, a few months after he had made his cameo appearance in *Expresso Bongo*, was interviewed on the *Face to Face* show, presented by John Freeman. Harding did not talk about *Expresso Bongo*. Instead, he revealed that he was 'profoundly lonely' and told a shocked nation that he 'would very much like to be dead'. Weeks later, on 16 November, he would suffer an asthma attack and die on the street outside Broadcasting House.

Arthur Seaton wasn't lonely, nor especially likeable either, but at least he didn't bow and scrape to his elders. He knew there had to be something more. 'I'm just out for a good time, all the rest is propaganda.' He was the main protagonist in Karel Reisz's film adaptation of Alan Sillitoe's *Saturday Night and Sunday Morning*, a juicy, violent, sexy slice of 1960 Nottingham life. Arthur wasn't much, a worker on a lathe in a cycle factory with little on his mind other than womanising and drinking ten pints on a Saturday night. Still, filmgoers rooted for him as he was trying get one over on the forces of mediocrity and it helped that he was played by a charismatic hard-ass, a Salford-raised actor called Albert Finney. He was a genuine Lancashire voice on the big screen who wasn't Gracie Fields. In 1960, this was a breakthrough. At the end of the film, Arthur decided to settle down and marry Shirley Anne Field, but his apparent surrender didn't matter so much. There were worse fates.

Finney had quite the year. He was also at the Cambridge Theatre in London, starring as Billy Fisher, or *Billy Liar*, playing a genuine teenage anti-hero. Like Arthur Seaton, Fisher was juggling three girlfriends at the same time: chaste Barbara, brassy Rita and free-spirited but plain-looking beatnik Liz. He lived in Stradhoughton, a fictional Yorkshire town where the highlight of the year came when comedian Danny Boon opened a new supermarket. Billy Fisher wanted to be a comedian.

Billy Fisher also wanted to be a novelist, a war hero, a dictator. Much of the play was made up of dream sequences, set in Ambrosia, a country located in Billy's own mind. In reality, he was a thief and a philanderer, and he virtually killed his grandmother by shouting at her. Not good. Plain-but-fun Liz gave him the chance to escape to London on the milk train, but he bailed at the last possible moment, preferring to stay in Stradhoughton with his own rich internal dialogue. When *Billy Liar* was adapted into a film in 1963, Liz would be played by Julie Christie, which made Billy Fisher look like a fucking idiot.

Pop music should have been a place where Britain's Billy Fishers could live out their dreams. And it would be. But the charts of 1960 were gummed up with goo. Rock 'n' roll had been neutered and spayed – almost all of its original protagonists were dead, disgraced, in the army or in the church. Smarmy Paul Anka and cocksure Bobby Darin now decided they'd wanted to be Frank Sinatra all along. Where exactly had the rock 'n' roll gone? In the States, it was in the hands of singers like Bobby Rydell with his painfully tame 'Wild One'. Sinatra had always known these goons wouldn't survive, that he'd be back, and he must have been laughing himself silly as he started to make regular incursions into the top twenty for the first time in years. He didn't even have to try; he could do it recording ancient jazz numbers like 'River, Stay 'Way from My Door' or even nursery tat like 'Ol' MacDonald'.

1960. 'Rue morgue,' wrote pop's biographer Nik Cohn, 'total wipe out.'

Rock 'n' roll's few survivors were clutched close, wrapped in cotton wool. The errant Gene Vincent – who had already been in enough scrapes to kill off most cats – was brought over to England by Jack Good, one of the few true believers, who had already made Cliff's career with his sage advice. He threw Vincent's sailor suits in the bin and dressed him in leathers, stuck him in the studio and stapled an old cowboy song, 'Pistol Packin' Mama', to the binding of Eddie Cochran's 'Something Else'. Bingo! Followed up by the better-yet 'Anna Annabelle' and 'She She Little Sheila', sweet Gene Vincent was reborn.

The Everly Brothers hadn't really gone away, scoring hits right through 1959 and into 1960. When their contract with titchy Cadence Records came up, they were signed up by film company Warner Brothers, who were looking to launch their new record label with a bang. It was a million-dollar deal in an age when that was such an unimaginable sum it may as well have been a billion-dollar deal. Their first single for the new label was given the catalogue number WB1, like the flashiest car on the studio forecourt, and pressed on gold vinyl. It was also their greatest record to date, 'Cathy's Clown', and went straight to number one in the States and the UK, where it looked down on the flotsam and jetsam for a full two months.

Norrie Paramor was busying himself with a new lad he'd discovered, a former miner from south Wales who'd quit the pits for the RAF and sang a bit on the side. He had been David Spencer, but now he was christened Ricky Valance – as if he was a Welsh reincarnation of Ritchie Valens – and Norrie gave him a song called 'Tell Laura I Love Her'. It had already been a top-ten hit in the US for Ray Peterson, but Decca, who held the rights in the UK, balked at releasing a song about a bloody car crash. It didn't bother Norrie, especially when young Ricky sang it like a cross between a choir boy and a sock puppet. Didn't he sound sincere? Weren't you moved by lines like 'as they pulled him from the twisted wreck, with his dying breath they heard him say "Tell Laura I love her"'? It got to number one.

Norrie also had an idea for the Shadows' next single – a make-or-break single, that much he knew.

The hated post-war national service – army conscription for teenage males – was finally being brought to an end in 1960. People coming out of national service would all be singing 'Quartermaster's Stores', Norrie reckoned. They would all be familiar with the army singalong and would surely dig a lightly rocked-up version? What Norrie didn't consider was that they'd probably have been over-familiar with it and glad to never hear the wretched tune again. The Shadows would record the thing, under duress, and have a little fun at the boss's expense by renaming it 'Quatermasster's Stores' after the current TV sci-fi sensation. It didn't really sound like a hit to Hank, Bruce, Jet or Tony, and – after three relative flops – it looked like their 'solo' days were numbered. They would once again just be Cliff Richard's backing band.

Something special was needed to save the day, to save the whole year.

*

Born in Paddington into a secure, middle-class upbringing, Jerry Lordan was a smart kid who had passed his eleven-plus and been packed off to Finchley Grammar school in September 1945. He was smart enough to teach himself how to play guitar, ukulele and piano.

He was also no coward, no Billy Fisher, and his parents' grammar school expectations for him – a doctor? A lawyer? – would be dashed as he toured Moss Empire theatres as a stand-up comedian and sang as half of a duo called Lee and Jay Elvin. They got to cut an Everlys-lite single for Fontana called 'So the Story Goes'; even by the standards of the Chesternuts' 'Teenage Love', it was a huge flop and copies are now like hen's teeth.

Restless and a little disillusioned, Lordan quit showbiz and got a job in a Piccadilly fleapit as a cinema projectionist, which at least had a smidgin of glamour. Bored as the projector ran *King Creole* for the twentieth time, he would listen to Radio Luxembourg and think about his aborted pop career. One day, another projectionist brought a guitar into the booth and started strumming. Jerry laughed. 'I can write a hit song on the spot,' he boasted. So he did. It was called 'A House a Car and a Wedding Ring'. Jerry made a demo, which reached arranger Johnny Franz and the song was recorded as a single on Decca by Mike Preston. Then, better yet, it became a hit when Dale Hawkins covered it in the States. Until now, Hawkins was best known for 'Susie Q', a single with a stinging James Burton solo that Hank and Bruce would have been very familiar with.

Not lacking confidence, Jerry Lordan left the film business to become a full-time songwriter in 1959 and quickly had a huge hit with actor Anthony Newley. The song was 'I've Waited So Long' and it featured in the movie *Idol on Parade*, a British take on the Elvis conscription story, something like a *Carry On GI Blues*. Lordan's own voice was sweet and melodious, easily a match for contemporaneous stars like Craig Douglas and Adam Faith, and he was soon convinced to sign to Parlophone and record his own material, working with arrangers including George Martin, Ron Goodwin and Bill Shepherd. Three middling hits emerged and he even cut an album called *All My Own Work*. Everything was smooth and ticking along. But that wasn't really enough for a smart lad like Jerry Lordan.

He realised he was often writing tunes that didn't particularly suit lyrics: John Barry had recorded Lordan's 'Starfire' for his 1960 *Stringbeat* album in 1960, and then there was something else he was working on called 'Apache'. The title had come from a Burt Lancaster movie, a favourite of Lordan's. 'I wanted something noble and dramatic, reflecting the courage and savagery of the Indian, two opposite qualities. The second theme was suggested to me by Dimitri Tiomkin's score for *The Alamo*. I was able to finish the whole thing in twenty to thirty minutes – it sometimes doesn't take long to write a classic. Not that I knew it was, initially. Certainly, I was very pleased with it. I wish that all my songs could've been written so quickly.'

'Apache' went from A minor to D minor and it was all-enveloping. Jerry Lordan had captured lightning in a bottle.

*

Bert Weedon was born avuncular. He was a kind-faced man from East Ham who, quite intentionally, put the guitar front and centre in British pop music. He was its greatest advocate, he was evangelistic about the guitar, in his humble Essex-borders way; this was in the 1940s, an age when big bands and brass instruments ruled, and the guitar was either seen as a novelty or used for percussion. The only time you heard a guitar take centre stage was on country, blues or folk records, and its only place in mainstream British pop culture was in cowboy films. If British rock 'n' roll was a structure with an initial blueprint, though, Bert Weedon's name would be stencilled bottom right.

Jazz and western swing were Weedon's main loves – not unlike Hank – but in the '40s he ended up on the only circuit that paid, with the dance bands; the Squadronaires, Ted Heath, Cyril Stapleton and Mantovani all benefited from Weedon's playing. He contracted TB after the war and doctors told him he had to avoid nightclubs, so he switched to session work instead, as well as cutting the occasional record. But his real contribution to the burgeoning rock scene was the 1957 book, *Play in a Day*.

Weedon had heard 'Rock Around the Clock' in 1954 and – instead of laughing it off as kids' music, like 99 per cent of his jazz and dance band contemporaries – recognised it as an exciting step on from western swing. He also saw it pushing the guitar to the forefront of popular music – at last! *Play in a Day* came out just as skiffle was booming, with rock 'n' roll still seeming like an impossible American landscape to most British teenagers. The book was a vital step, a key to the secret garden gate – after that, you were on your own. Even if you found it quite easy playing 'Jingle Bells' and 'There's a Tavern in the

Town' but got lost on the theory, you had still learned your C, F and G Majors from Bert Weedon. Hank and Bruce both bought a copy. So did Jimmy Page.

*

Jerry Lordan knew 'Apache' was strong, strong enough to completely alter the trajectory of his career, so he was initially thrilled when Bert Weedon agreed to record it. Weedon even started to perform the song in variety shows and on TV. But, to restless Jerry's frustration, the recording remained unreleased. Weedon had a plan to release the single in September, when kids were back from holidays, to optimise sales. He played his recording to Lordan.

'When I heard what he had done with "Apache", I almost cried, but I didn't think that I could protest too much. He claimed that he felt it needed toning down so that it was something nice for the kids, not too aggressive. I was heartbroken. It wasn't anything like I'd envisaged, to be honest. I was relieved when he decided not to release it.' Weedon's version was weak and pedestrian, with a meandering flute line that certainly didn't suggest any kind of noble savagery.

In early 1960, Lordan was on tour with Cliff Richard and the Shadows, promoting his latest single, the gooey 'Who Could Be Bluer?' 'It was really exciting. The reaction to Cliff was sensational [but] it made me realise I wasn't going to be a teenage idol. The Shadows had their Fenders by then. I genuinely thought at the time that they were something special, destined for greatness. I didn't realise that I was going to be instrumental, if you pardon the expression, in their success.

We travelled on the same coach and people were always whipping out the guitars, so I used to join in on my ukulele. As the tour was drawing to a close, I knew that they were looking for a new record to provide them with a hit.'

Jet Harris was the first Shadow to hear 'Apache'. 'I was travelling on the London Underground with Jet, on the way home to Paddington,' Lordan later told *Pipeline* magazine. 'I had the ukulele with me and, to this day I don't know why, but I hummed and strummed "Apache". Jet asked me to play it again. When I told him that I'd written it, he said straight away "You've got to play that to Hank and Bruce". I was delighted with Jet's reaction. I played it to Hank on the coach the next day. They agreed with Jet and wanted to record it as soon as possible. I had to tell them that we had recorded it already and they were utterly despondent until I told them that Bert had no immediate plans to release it. That increased the urgency to record "Apache", as soon as the tour was over. They had a sound, a style and, most of all, an image – youth, enthusiasm and energy. They were totally committed to it.'

At Abbey Road, Hank and Bruce would happily take prompts from Jerry about the arrangement so that their recording wouldn't suffer the way Weedon's had. Bruce put together a near-flamenco rhythm part. 'It was very much a joint effort,' he said, 'Jerry's initial ideas, Tony's pounding drums at the outset, the intro before the main theme was Hank's, my rhythm sound and so on. I wanted more power and clarity on the chords so I abandoned the electric guitar and borrowed Cliff's Gibson J-200 – he'd bought it after seeing Elvis in *Loving You*. I had it close-miked and really hammered the strings. We wanted more percussion so Cliff played bongos on the session.' It's worth noting that Cliff wasn't doing a session at Abbey Road that day. He was just there hanging out with his friends.

Another key ingredient to the song was Hank's new echo unit. In December 1959, Jack Good called the Shadows to tell them that Gene Vincent was appearing on his new *Boy Meets Girls* show. 'Jack knew Gene was one of our rock heroes,' Hank explained, 'so we drove up to Manchester and met him. Joe Brown was a regular on the show and he took me to one side and showed me this little device called a Meazzi.'

Luckily for everyone else, Brown couldn't get on with it. 'Joe gave me his Gibson and said, "Have some of that!" The echo he had on was the typical rock 'n' roll tape echo, the slapback kind of thing that you'd hear on Elvis and Gene Vincent records. Now, there was no way you could achieve that on stage and those guitar sounds were kind of wonderful. Suddenly with this [Meazzi echo unit] it sounded like a real rock 'n' roll guitar and I thought, *Wow, that's brilliant!* But Joe didn't like it. He liked that very dry sound, that sounded like he needed new strings – which he probably did. But I thought it was fantastic, so I contacted Vox, who were importing them, and got one. That was the beginning of it, really.

'I'd got the Fender Strat by then, so with the Vox amps and the echo, everything came together pretty much at the same time. But the great thing was the Meazzi had the multiple heads, which meant you had a variety of echo types: tripping echoes falling over themselves, depending on the position you put the echo control knob in – plus a knob that could alter the drum speed. And it really worked! Those great echoes on "Apache", "Man of Mystery" and "Wonderful

Land", for example, were truly wonderful effects that gave the guitar much bigger and glorious sounds. The Meazzi had a disc inside, like a turntable, and around the circumference you attached ¼-inch tape, overlapped it and stuck it on with Vaseline. In the early days, I'd do it. It was quite an easy job, just a bit greasy with the Vaseline.'

Hank acquired his own Vox-branded Meazzi 'Model J' Type 1B in spring 1960 and used it for the first time when the Shadows recorded 'Apache' in June 1960.

*

'I couldn't believe how great it sounded,' said Lordan. 'It was even better than I'd hoped. I sensed it would be a hit, and so did the Shadows.'

Just how great did it sound? It summoned up a world barely imaginable in a country still covered in bomb-sites and half-demolished houses. It was so dark and powerful.

Writer Luke Haines has called the Shadows 'the sound of god communicating via electric guitar' and 'Apache' 'the muezzin calling the demob masses of austerity Britain to prayer; the prayer that will lift the pea-souper and banish post-war drabness forever'. If Cliff's fire-starting 'Move It' and Vince Taylor's 1959 single 'Brand New Cadillac' would find later parallels in 'Anarchy in the UK' and 'White Riot', then 'Apache' was the dawn of post-punk – the rule-book had been torn up, and things could now become more adventurous. What exactly lurked in the shadows? Whatever you wanted to find.

Norrie Paramor wasn't sure about any of this. He was still rooting for his novelty army record.

'We'd booked in this session,' remembered Tony Meehan coolly, 'and told Norrie Paramor we were going to do a thing called "Apache". He had something else for us – "Quartermaster's Stores". Norrie's brother published it. It was a take-off of Johnny and the Hurricanes. That's what people did in those days.'

The Brian Matthew-presented radio show *Saturday Club* was the biggest show on the BBC for teenagers and its producer Jimmy Grant told Norrie, frankly, that he thought 'Apache' was clearly the better of the two songs. Fortunately, for the Shadows and for the future of British popular music, Grant held sway at a time when there was still very little teenage music played on the BBC. His opinion was enough to persuade Paramor; 'Apache' would become the A-side of the Shadows' fourth single in July 1960.

*

Most of Cliff Richard and the Shadows' contemporaries, even their heroes, had buckled in the face of relentless opposition to rock 'n' roll from the mainstream. Some were dead, the latest being Eddie Cochran, killed in a car crash in the decidedly unromantic locale of Chippenham in Wiltshire. Many others had simply wilted: exhibit one was Elvis recording a 1920s ballad called 'Are You Lonesome Tonight?', because it was his manager's favourite song; exhibit two was Lonnie Donegan's switch from the primal DIY roar of 'Rock Island Line' and 'Gamblin' Man' to the lame, extended gag 'My Old Man's a Dustman'. Who else was in the chart? What was the competition? The comedian Charlie Drake, a sponge pudding on legs, was there singing 'Mr Custer' and making 'Red Indian' noises. And then the Shadows rode into town with 'Apache', a record that stood up to this musical thuggery, clean and true and beautiful, giving the teenage listener room to breathe, a space of mystery and imagination. A new gold dream.

'People kept telling us it was going to be a hit, but we weren't sure,' Hank later told *The Big Issue*. 'It went into the chart at nineteen and started creeping upwards. Then I remember we were playing the London Palladium and we got a call from the record company telling us it was number one. We couldn't believe it. We all went potty.'

'Apache' single-handedly made kids in Britain realise they didn't have to work in a mill, or a mine, or an office; they could be a rock 'n' roll guitarist instead. Like Hank and Bruce, thousands of kids had first been inspired to pick up an acoustic guitar by Lonnie Donegan in 1956. Now *they* were the influencers and those same kids, plus ones who were several years younger – Pete Townshend, Brian May, David Gilmour, Peter Green – yearned to play an electric guitar just like Hank.

Others were drawn to Jet Harris's electric bass, which was scarcely less exotic. At this point, the Shadows had possibly the only Fender Stratocaster – and hence the only guitar with a whammy bar – and the only electric bass guitar in the country. Future drummers – Bobby Elliott, Clem Cattini, Ringo Starr, Mitch Mitchell, Cozy Powell, Dave Mattacks and John Bonham – were all watching Tony Meehan. He looked cool and relaxed behind his Ajax kit, the top British drum kit of the time, as played by jazzers like Jack Parnell. Kids noticed these details. Before the Shadows, before 'Apache', no one had really had the chance to study rock'n'roll players.

What this succeeded in doing was making the Shadows as exotic as any American group or singer. They bridged a gap in a way that even Cliff couldn't. They had the hardware, the means, just like James Burton and Jerry Allison. And now they were on TV, on British TV. They seemed within reach. Kids dyed their hair blond. Others sported their NHS specs with pride. The Shadows were heroes.

*

Back in the 1930s, Angus McBean lived in Acton and had a day job at Liberty's department store, where he restored antique furniture. He didn't want a day job. He sold his grandfather's gold watch to buy a camera and dark room equipment, grew a fine beard to indicate his independence and became a society photographer. No one from Acton became a society photographer – it was the privilege of the moneyed, the louche, a hobby for gentlemen of leisure. And so Angus McBean, son of a mining surveyor, had to work extremely hard to make his name.

The mechanics of printing fascinated him and he provided pictures for the theatre world. 'There must be huge splashes of colour,' he said. 'Wild music, beautiful people, magic, imagination, oceans of blood and wine, and always happy endings.'

His work appeared in Georges Bataille's surrealist *Documents* magazine. The French loved him, so, of course, the *British Journal of Photography* labelled McBean a charlatan. It was a peculiar insult for someone dead set on squeezing his subjects into a world entirely of his own making – candyfloss clouds, roman columns, floating heads, a McBean-built city of Anglo surrealism.

Now here he was in 1960 with the smooth-skinned Cliff Richard, the brown-eyed pin-up boy whom he had photographed and re-touched several times before. Usually though, by this point in his career, McBean was doing nothing more than straight portraits. This was because his own unique world had been entirely dismantled by the state.

During the London blitz in 1941, he had left London for Bath and set up a studio in a flat on Pierrepont Street, which soon became a safe house for gay men, and for servicemen stationed nearby. In November 1941, with the ongoing war not seeming to occupy their minds, Bath police raided the flat and arrested McBean and a sixteen-year-old. As Coventry, Liverpool and London burned, the police busied themselves by digging through diaries and love letters in McBean's flat. They arrested several other men and left two to commit suicide before they could be charged. McBean was sentenced to four years in prison for gross indecency.

Out of prison, with the war over, McBean had set about rebuilding his studio and his reputation. He did all right. He largely did what he was told and didn't often skew off into flights of fancy, or swim in oceans of blood and wine. He did nothing to get either Georges Bataille or the Metropolitan Police hot under the collar. This session, on this day in 1960, was for the first full studio album by Cliff Richard and the Shadows, and he liked Cliff Richard. McBean reached back into his pre-war mindset and came up with something quite perfect.

The Shads were off camera, a presence, with only Bruce visible. Cliff looked concerned, worried maybe about what the future might hold for him. He looked like he needed the support of that presence; the neck of Hank's guitar, on the left of the shot, was the only indication that they were musicians. Maybe that guitar was all Cliff needed to get him through.

McBean went on to photograph the Beatles for the cover shot of their first album, too, the rather less expressive *Please Please Me* sleeve (and, in turn, the matching sleeve for the unissued *Get Back*, which was used on the '*Blue Album*'). He was bold enough to work with LGBTQ+ figures like Quentin Crisp and Robert Helpmann. He went on to take definitive shots of Danny LaRue and Vivienne Westwood, and to appear in a David Sylvian video. But his legacy was largely gone, his place in history taken by usurpers who hadn't troubled the authorities. Harrow- and Cambridge-educated Cecil Beaton, who had taken his first portraits after borrowing his nanny's camera, and working-class David Bailey, who had the bootstraps back story, took away McBean's place in the pantheon.

What was to be learned from Angus McBean's story? To shut up shop. To keep prying eyes away from the window. After 'Living Doll', Cliff had quickly adopted an accent that was hard to place – somewhere in the south east, maybe, but possibly after an extended holiday in California. Not a trace of Lucknow. Wives? Girlfriends? Boyfriends? Don't mention them. Keep schtum and the media, the authorities, John Freeman, Russell Harty, Rupert Murdoch, none of them will interfere, none of them will touch you. Experimentation? Maybe, but don't be showy. The British hate the idea of anyone getting above their station.

Twenty-year-old Terry Nelhams was braver. Jet Harris's old mate Terry, the singer at the 2i's with the Worried Men and now known to the world as Adam Faith, had first hit number one with his fourth single, 'What Do You Want?', a year earlier. With his wobbly voice pinned down by John Barry's pizzicato strings, he had created a sound that was all his own and had been Cliff's only viable competitor all year. Faith took up John Freeman's offer to appear on the TV show *Face to Face* in December 1960. Other subjects had included Carl Gustav Jung, Augustus John, Lord Reith, Edith Sitwell and Bertrand Russell. Heavyweight company. It was a gutsy move.

Face to Face was filmed at the BBC's Lime Grove studios and came over like a therapy session. Freeman was rarely in shot, just the back of his head, while the subject tried to look calm under interrogation. Tony Hancock looked as though he might bolt from his chair at any moment. Gilbert Harding had been totally broken down by questioning. But Adam Faith wouldn't take Freeman's bait. They had expected this handsome working-class kid – from Acton, like Angus McBean – to mumble and sweat, to show that his musical knowledge didn't extend further back than 'Be-Bop-a-Lula' and to prove that he really didn't deserve to earn 'ten times as much as a cabinet minister'. Instead, he smiled to himself, took on board everything lobbed at him and gave it his best, in short, snappy answers. He treasured the 'personal and mental independence' afforded him by pop stardom. His favourite book was *The Catcher in the Rye*. He came across as cool, and very likeable.

Freeman: Would you like to marry?

Faith: Eventually, yeah.

Freeman: But not yet?

Faith: No.

Freeman: Is that because your manager won't let you?

Faith: Well, I don't have any of those sort of clauses in my contract.

Freeman: It is supposed to be very bad for a pop singer to be married, isn't it?

Faith: So I'm told, yeah.

Faith spoke in his own voice, with glottal stops and 'yeah' rather than 'yes', a gentle but recognisably working-class voice. At a stroke, his appearance on *Face to Face* changed people's minds about rock 'n' rollers, and in particular the public's perception of British rock 'n' rollers. In this, he even laid the ground for the Beatles to up-end British society three years later and for Penguin to publish John Lennon's classroom scribbles. All of this was possible. All of this was definitely possible for Cliff Richard and the Shadows, bigger names than Faith, with a wider reach and greater disruptive potential. They would have all watched this show. What could they do with this information?

*

In October 1960, *Me and My Shadows* was released in its distinctive McBean jacket. Ten of the sixteen songs were British compositions, all of which were either written by the Shadows or by a member of their expanding gang of compadres: Ian Samwell, Pete Chester, even Cliff chimed in to help Jet and Sammy with the spare, Spanish-guitar-driven 'I Love You So'. Here was early evidence of the Shadows' extended family, one that would remain tight-knit, but always open to true kindred spirits they met along the way.

1959's *Cliff Sings* had been carved asunder by standards and classics, so this was the group's first real studio album. There was no instant familiarity when you looked at the track listing. Excitement had built among Shads fans after EMI had bought time on Radio Luxemburg for a fifteen-minute weekly show, also called *Me and My Shadows*, which previewed Jet, Hank and Sammy's explosive 'I'm Gonna Get You'.

There were sixteen songs and they were consistently strong. Samwell's 'I Don't Know' and 'You and I' were Buddy-like, the latter reminiscent of 'Peggy Sue Got Married', a beat ballad more than a rocker that featured some lovely Hank guitar, getting the best from his Strat. Hank and Jet's 'She's Gone' was a stand-out – strong, moody, with stalking guitar and a plaintive Cliff vocal. Pete Chester's coffee-bar lament, 'Left Out Again', featured little more than Jet and Tony with a fast-plucked Hank guitar doubling up the bassline, while 'Choppin' and Changin'' – previously earmarked as a 1959 single – was another Sammy Samwell doozy, another tough-as-leather highlight and a true rocker with echoes of 'Move It'.

It wasn't all up-tempo: 'We Have It Made' and 'Tell Me' were soda-fountain ballads, leaning on the Ricky Nelson prototype; 'I Cannot Find a True Love' was a lovely bit of British outsider dreaming ('Is she here in London? Or in Memphis, Tennessee?')' while 'Evergreen Tree' was inspired by Saturday afternoons at the pictures, watching westerns, with a gentle clip-clop and a lonesome harmonica (played by Gerry Furst of the Chesternuts), as if Cliff was roaming the plains of the Bedford Levels on his old paint. It was quite haunting and even became a single in some far-apart territories: Italy, South Africa, India, Thailand.

If Norrie Paramor and Columbia were convinced that Cliff's market had shifted inexorably to ballads and weepies, they were in for a surprise. Written by Hank and Sammy on the plane home from the US tour, 'Gee Whizz It's You' was frenetic and fabulous, with Tony Meehan galloping home over the coda and Hank playing on the verge of total abandon. It was pressed in Britain as an export single, not meant for UK consumption but solely for Scandinavian countries and outposts of the empire. Once fans discovered they could order it, though, demand pushed it into the top ten, eating into the sales of Cliff's current moon-eyed single 'Theme For a Dream', which was still in the top five.

Me and My Shadows turned out to be Sammy's last hurrah. But what a way to go. Along with Billy Fury's *Sound of Fury*, released the same year, it remains the best British rock 'n' roll album.

*

Given the care and attention that the follow-up to Cliff's major breakthrough had received a year earlier, 'Apache''s sequel would seem rather thrown-together. The all-important follow-up was to be a double A-side of 'The Stranger', a confident twanging affair, combined with 'Man of Mystery', which had been written by veteran songwriter Michael Carr,* whose credits included several Gracie Fields songs and

* It was to be the first of several collaborations – Carr also had a hand in 'Kon-Tiki' (1961), 'The Bandit', 'South of the Border' (both 1962) and 'The Miracle' (1964). His

the early World War Two singalong 'We're Going to Hang Out the Washing on the Siegfried Line'.

Carr had been born Maurice Cohen in Leeds in 1905, but was raised in Dublin where his father ran a restaurant. Young Michael ran away to sea, ending up in the States where he worked as a pianist in Las Vegas, a cowboy in Montana and even spent time as a newspaper journalist, presumably with a card that read 'press' sticking out of his trilby. Moving to London, he teamed up with Jimmy 'Teddy Bears' Picnic' Kennedy to write a string of songs for Our Gracie, as well as jazz standard 'Dinner For One Please, James'. On the other side of the war, he wrote 'Lonely Ballerina' for Mantovani and seemed like a highly unlikely replacement for Jerry Lordan. No matter. The serpentine 'Man of Mystery' made it to number five on the *Record Mirror* chart and number six in the *NME*, where 'The Stranger', listed separately, peaked at number eleven. It was a decent showing.

'Man of Mystery' was already familiar to the public as the theme to a series of B-movies shown in ABC cinemas, *The Edgar Wallace Mysteries*, in a woodwind-led orchestral arrangement by the wonderfully named Francis Chagrin. The films were all introduced by a shadowy bust of the author, who had died in Hollywood in 1932 while working on the script for *King Kong*. The bust slowly revolved as the eerie 'Man of Mystery' played – Hank would later replicate this move on stage. The Shadows' version was played at twice the speed, with a heavily tremoloed Hank lead and an almost atonal solo.

---

last hit was Jackie Lee's much-loved TV theme 'White Horses' in 1968, the year he died. No one ever accused Michael Carr of being predictable.

The single was recorded at Abbey Road late at night, straight after a show at the Palladium. The session ran from midnight until 4 a.m. at the group's request. EMI was 'shocked and bemused at a request that would become commonplace over the next couple of decades,' Hank told Mike Read. 'You see, we were virtually making up our own rules as we were coming across new situations that neither we nor the record companies had experienced before. They weren't used to dealing with a self-contained unit like the Shadows, so at times they had to break down some of their old barriers and cope with four lads who were undoubtedly less conventional in their outlook and musical approach.'

They cut 'The Stranger' in an hour and a half and 'Man of Mystery' in twenty minutes. It showed. The last verse had a fluffed note which everyone present somehow missed; for years after, Hank would have to play the fluffed note exactly as it appeared on record to appease die-hard fans. 'Spot the wrong note, folks, and win a prize!' he'd quip.

Bill Crompton and Morgan 'Thunderclap' Jones were behind 'The Stranger' and, unlike the old-school Michael Carr, were another pair of Soho hopefuls who'd hung out at the 2i's. 'The Stranger' was a beautifully confident song and certainly a better recording than 'Man of Mystery'. Jones and Crompton had just been in the top ten with 'Heart of a Teenage Girl', as recorded by Craig Douglas, and would go on to write a slew of early '60s British 45s – Danny Rivers' 'I Got', the Vigilantes' 'Man in Space', the Fentones' 'The Mexican' and Don Lang's deathless tribute to the Shads' boss, 'They Call Him Cliff' – without achieving another major hit. Jones was later to be found entertaining the locals as a pianist at the Queens pub in Crouch End, north London, no doubt telling war stories about his brief brush with songwriting fame.

*

John Schroeder was Norrie Paramor's right-hand man at Columbia, a louche chap who would go on to discover Helen Shapiro and create the MOR jazz act Sounds Orchestral. Schroeder reckoned 'it was pretty obvious to both Norrie and I, right from the start, that the Shadows had the talent to be recording artists in their own right'. And so, as 'Apache' sat at number one, Norrie had suggested they find themselves a manager. Could he recommend anyone? Yes, he could.

Peter Gormley was a forty-year-old Australian who was also managing his mate and compatriot, an up-and-coming singer from suburban Sydney called Frank Ifield. Hank and Jet met the broad-brogued Gormley at his St John's Wood flat. He told them he wasn't after a fast buck and that they had to plan for the future. Show business was theirs for the taking, Gormley told them. Given they'd only just scored their first hit without being an adjunct to Cliff, this was quite the claim. Tony and Bruce then went up to meet him. 'You're not good-looking,' he told them. 'Well, none of you apart from Jet.' If they weren't going to cut it as matinee idols, explained Gormley, the Shadows needed to write their own material, diversify, look abroad, reach out, explore new markets. They liked his style immensely. He would remain their manager until he retired. 'Peter Gormley was like a father figure to me,' wrote Bruce, 'the dad I never had. We all loved the man.'

*

Albums were a major present that you might get for Christmas or your birthday, if you were lucky. With colour photos, much text, a Clarifoil cover and an inner sleeve with instructions on how to care for your record, they were a prize you would treasure like a hardback book. If singles were the equivalent of weekly comics, then EPs were more like annuals or summer specials, something to gleefully absorb in short bursts. They were more affordable than albums, a realistic present you could ask for without feeling guilty that you sounded greedy. You could even buy them with your pocket money if you quelled your desire for toffees and *The Eagle* and saved up for a few weeks. But they were still a quality item, with a glossy colour cover and sometimes even a sleevenote to memorise.

The Shadows' first self-titled EP was released in time for Christmas 1960 and they had clearly put some thought into it. Here was a mini-concept album, their take on the American West, and it became hugely influential in its sweep and atmosphere. It was led by Jerry Lordan's 'Mustang', approaching the viewer in a heat haze over the horizon. Moving on from the small-screen 'Man of Mystery', it included two movie themes: one was from the James Dean parable *Giant*, the other from *Shane*, and it wasn't hard to see the appeal of the latter movie, from 1953, to the Shads. *Shane* had seen tiny Alan Ladd up against towering, weasel-faced Jack Palance and his heartless cohorts, an underdog in sharp clothes taking on the iron-fisted conformists – the bully boys, the squares – and beating them. You didn't have to cave in. You didn't have to ape Sinatra or sing about chewing gum losing its flavour; you could stand your ground, make magical noises with your space-age guitar and be a hero.

But then once you'd broken through, once you were seen to be steering the ship, what then? 'There's no going back from it,' Alan Ladd had warned in *Shane*, though admittedly he wasn't talking about pop music but the altogether trickier notion of killing a man. 'Right or wrong, it's a brand, a brand that sticks.' For a short, precious while, the Shadows didn't have to overthink their position or their sound, or whether they were a brand or what their perceived brand was. 'Apache' had been such a colossal hit that they could have done whatever they wanted afterwards. 'Man of Mystery' b/w 'The Stranger' had cemented their position. The *NME*'s end-of-year polls placed them at number one in the 'small group' category – 'beat groups', or 'bands', were not yet part of pop's language. Now, this first EP was a celebration of their new-found status. They would end up releasing a stand-alone EP each year for the next four years, tracks that you couldn't find anywhere else, a thank-you to the devoted thousands. From being a mere backing group at the start of 1960, they were now out front, the most influential group in Britain by a distance. They had fame and status, and to their fans they seemed like friends, even spirit guides. But added responsibilities would be part of the baggage of fame and status. The future would be a little harder to navigate.

5

VIVA LOS SHADS!

In 1957, Richard Hoggart's study *The Uses of Literacy* had identified a new mass culture in Britain. He found working-class life was being shaped by outside influences; one hub of this change was the coffee bar, where 'most of the customers are boys aged between 15 and 20, with drape suits, picture ties and an American slouch. Most of them cannot afford a succession of milkshakes, and make cups of tea serve for an hour or two whilst – and this is the main reason for coming – they put copper after copper into the mechanical record player.' Hoggart may not have approved of a perceived Americanisation of British high streets, but this was the birth of teen culture, and a landscape still recognisable today. 'The Nickelodeon is allowed to blare out so that the noise would be sufficient to fill a good sized ballroom rather than a converted shop in the High Street. The young men waggle one shoulder or stare, as desperately as Humphrey Bogart, across the tubular chairs.'

By 1961, the Shadows were kings of the jukebox, or the Nickelodeon as Richard Hoggart would have it. Teenage boys and girls in any small town, county town or city across the country found sanctuary in their own particular café, or milk bar, or – in the bigger cities – coffee bar, spending the dead hours there after school or after Sunday lunch and before they headed off to the pictures. Some were for grammar-school kids, others for secondary moderns. Pubs barely came into this teenage world. Cafés for teenagers gave them a strong sense of identity and the jukebox gave them their own soundtrack. 'Apache', 'Man of Mystery' and 'FBI' sounded as if they were specifically designed for the jukebox.

There were no real teenage pop magazines in 1961, apart from the romantic ones aimed at girls with names like *Roxy* and *Marty*. There was *Hit Parade*, which had begun in 1954 and looked exactly the same in 1961, monochrome artwork and all, and felt like it was edited by starchy gents, definitely over thirty. The best place to find colour photos of your pop heroes was in the film magazines like *Photoplay*, or on record artwork. One reason that finding mint-condition pop records from the early '60s is so hard it's because they were fawned over, caressed, even pinned to the wall with drawing pins and kissed every night. The first Shadows album was finally released in 1961. The chunky knitwear on the sleeve might not have been what their female fans were hoping for or expecting, but the guitars looked great.

On that cover, so glossy it was almost reflective, Jet looked the business with his quiff, reddish-blond hair and Fender bass – and was that fan mail in his hand? Hank, in a ski jumper, was peering over his shoulder to take a look. Tony wore grey Farahs with white socks and white buckskin shoes, with a hooped jumper in several shades of brown, rather like a '70s sofa. He sat, contemplating, on a cushion, maybe wondering how much sleep he was likely to get that night before the inevitable six o'clock alarm. Only Bruce looked at the camera, the businessman, the leader. He'd made it from nothing, the rotten rows of terraces in Elswick, and he looked pleased with himself. He was buggered if he going to let anybody else loosen his grasp on wealth and fame.

The Shadows would be the peak of a year in which the group – with or without Cliff – absolutely bossed pop music in Britain, in Europe, almost everywhere. In the UK, it was a number-one album at the same time as 'Kon-Tiki' topped the singles chart and *Shadows to the Fore* headed the EP chart. Across the globe, groups emerged with the Shadows as their template. From France came Les Chaussettes Noires, in Spain there was Los Relámpagos. Tito's Yugoslavia, where they represented the dream of the free world, gave us Crveni Koralji – the Red Corals – and Bijele Strijele, the White Arrows. Shadows imitators were all over Scandinavia.* Further afield, Australia had the Strangers, Mexico had Los Sleepers and, in Brazil, with a truly giveaway name, there was the Jet Blacks. This was the tip of the iceberg. Across the world in the early '60s, the Shadows were unquestionably the most important rock 'n' roll band. They were worshipped.

*

* They were so big that the Shadows four-piece line-up and specific sound became a genre in itself, called 'piggtråd' in Norway and 'rautalanka' in Finland, which translated in both countries as 'iron wire' or 'barbed wire'. There were 'Shadowbands' by the dozen: in 1976, the Sonet label in Norway released a double album retrospective called Beat and Piggtråd; Finland followed suit in 1979 with the thirty-two-track Finnish Graffiti – Rautalankaa Ja Beat-musiikkia 1961–65.

How about the US? The place they had hymned with 'Mustang', and 'Apache' and the theme from *Shane*? The place they went to in their dreams every night? Bruce imagined taking the Shadows' thunder to the States, showing Duane Eddy a thing or two, putting Johnny and the Hurricanes' fairground organ in its place. He knew the Shadows were good enough. He had unshakeable faith.

And suddenly there was a group called the Ramrods, peeking into the Hot Hundred with a Shads-like 'Ghost Riders in the Sky'. Bruce knew that it wasn't just his imagination – there, on the fade, the Ramrods played Hank's intro to 'Apache', a hat tip, an acknowledgment from a genuine American instro group. They knew the Shadows, this group from Stamford, Connecticut with a girl drummer! It was *wild*! There it was, clear as a bell, the Ramrods' little tribute to the Shadows, as if 'Apache' was the ur-instrumental that their 'Ghost Riders in the Sky' could only dream of emulating.

So, Bruce wondered, why wasn't 'Apache' anywhere near the Hot Hundred? He didn't wonder for long, though; in January 1961, there it was – finally. Entering at number ninety-four, it then slowly circled the chart – eighty-three, sixty-seven, forty-eight – its progress humming ominously behind bigger names. It stalked its prey – twenty-six, twenty – overtaking the Everlys' 'Walk Right Back'. Then number fifteen – it overtook the Shirelles' 'Will You Love Me Tomorrow'. Then number eleven – it was breathing down the neck of Ben E. King's 'Spanish Harlem'. Number six, number four, number two… by 6 April 1961, only the Marcels' dang-ga-ga-dang-ga-ding-ga-dong-ding 'Blue Moon' was keeping 'Apache' from being the biggest-selling record in the US. The sound of the 2i's, from the west coast to the east, the ultimate coals to Newcastle from two Geordie boys with a penchant for fried-egg sandwiches... British rock 'n' roll had conquered the States. A homegrown song written by Jerry Lordan, the one he'd played to Jet between Marylebone and Edgware Road stations on the Bakerloo line, was now known by every gum-chewing, baseball-loving, Twinkie-munching teenager in New York, Chicago, Los Angeles and – naturally – Stamford, Connecticut.

There was only one problem. It wasn't the Shadows' recording at number two in the Billboard chart. It was a cover version by a thirty-five-year-old man from Denmark called Jørgen Ingmann. This fellow had a square head, and front teeth that bit down onto his fat lower lip when he smiled. He was no one's idea of a rock 'n' roll guitarist; he had been born before Bing Crosby had cut his first 78. He was almost – almost – as old as Bert Weedon. But somehow, probably just because his American label wanted it more than the Shadows' American label, Jørgen Ingmann had the American hit with 'Apache'. A huge hit. A number-two hit, with only the Marcels' deathless doo-wop holding it at bay. A million seller.

Did he have a 'Man of Mystery' to follow it up? A 'Mustang' up his sleeve? Could Jørgen Ingmann shock the US and become a Danish Duane Eddy? He could not. He followed 'Apache' with a piece-of-fluff theme from an Italian movie called *Anna*, a holiday trinket of a single, a plastic snow-globe with the Trevi fountain in the middle. 'Anna' didn't even appear to have drums on it, just a tambourine that Jørgen had bought from a toy shop in Aarhus. It did nothing and, by the summer of 1961, everyone in the US had forgotten Jørgen Ingmann's name.

Bruce Welch did not forget Jørgen Ingmann's name. The nerve of this bloke, with his plinky, piece-of-shit cover version! Bruce felt sick whenever he heard Jørgen Ingmann's name.

To compound his misery, a group called the Ventures had sneaked into the charts with 'Walk Don't Run', a tune written by cool jazz guitarist Johnny Smith, which they tore through like tigers and made their own. It became a transatlantic top-ten hit at the exact same time 'Apache' was number one in Britain.

The Ventures played Fender guitars – a Jazzmaster, a Stratocaster and a Precision bass. They sounded American. They may have been from hilly, heavily-wooded Washington state, the US equivalent of Yorkshire's West Riding, but the Ventures sounded tanned and surf-ready. They sounded no more like the Shadows than Duane Eddy or Johnny and the Hurricanes had done. They had every right to soundtrack their own lives, American lives, American teenage lives, but that's not how Bruce saw it. 'They cornered that whole section of the market,' he fumed. '*Our* market. We missed out completely.'

What's more, the Shadows had been offered 'Walk Don't Run' as a possible follow-up to 'Apache', but were given twenty-one days to record and release it before the Ventures' version came out in Britain. Not possible, said EMI. Bruce was fuming about this as well. He wanted to cover 'Walk Don't Run' and he didn't see this as double standards. He saw it as typical rotten bad luck.

Locked up in their new flat on Long Lane in Finchley, out in the suburbs with no fun for miles around, late in 1960 Hank, Jet and Bruce had written their own instrumental classic instead. 'FBI' would go on to become the first self-written Shadows hit early in '61 and one of their definitive moments.

*

'Sorry girls, they're not available!'

Jet had married Carol Costa in June 1959; Hank and Bruce had been at the wedding, but Cliff and Tony were away on holiday together in Spain. Outside the church in Hounslow were hundreds of kids, screaming and taking photos – Jet and Carol had to squeeze past them to escape to Grimsby, of all places, where they spent their honeymoon. Two months later, Bruce had married Ann Findley, with Cliff as his best man; again, hundreds were outside, scuffling in the street. Bruce's happiness had been somewhat ruined when he obtained his birth certificate for the wedding, only then discovering that he had been born out of wedlock. With Tony marrying Bridget de Mare in 1960, Hank completed the set at the very end of the year, while Cliff and the Shadows' 'I Love You' was sat at number one, marrying Billie, a girl he'd first met in Chas McDevitt's Freight Train coffee bar. Only their singer remained a bachelor boy. It didn't seem to affect their sales or popularity in any way.

Given their blue-ribbon year in 1960, new manager Peter Gormley helped the group to escape from an onerous publishing contract by setting up Shadows Music, which would give them a 75 per cent cut of their own songs. This was some years ahead of its time and another sign of Gormley's faith in their long-term potential. 'FBI' came out on 3 February 1961 while negotiations were still ongoing. To avoid losing chunks of income to their old deal, the Harris/Marvin/Welch number was credited to Peter Gormley on the label. Already, they trusted him not to run off with the proceeds.

The framework of 'FBI' was somewhere between a middle-European folk rhythm and the then-emergent Jamaican ska beat, with added evocations of organised crime and of agents intercepting actions from hostile states. The single was tight as a drum, with Hank's stinging, astringent line as sharp as an agent's shiny black shoes. For a two-minute instrumental, it packed in a lot of storyline: there was the menacing, unexpected change of octave; the violent smudging of the note twenty-six seconds in; and Hank's positively frenzied one-note break at one minute twenty-five that would make the Buzzcocks' 'Boredom' seem maximalist.

The British population may only have had a Hollywood version of what or who the FBI was, but the Shadows' reading chimed perfectly with that – even the law enforcers seemed cool in the US. As 'FBI' made its way up to number six in March 1961, Jennings supplied the group with new split-front AC30 amps, the style they would remain most associated with. These would initially go on sale to the public in a fawn-coloured covering but – given their now unique place in pop culture – the Shadows received their new Vox amps in a custom black covering. They looked terrific. Every '60s beat group would follow their lead and use Vox AC30s.

'Midnight', on the B-side of 'FBI', was another absolute beauty, with Hank's high, clean, echoing lead recalling Santo and Johnny's 1959 US number one 'Sleep Walk'. It was so dreamy, a cherished memory, a stroll by the dark blue waters, floating on a wash of Tony Meehan's echoed snare. What a record. The single was peak Shads.

*

To British ears, the Shadows' music felt like a tenuous connection to something not fully understandable. It might have been about some mythical America – the land of *Shane*, and *Giant*, and mustangs (either the Ford kind or the four-legged). It might also have been about a connection to an older world. 'The Frightened City' would be their next new record of 1961, released in late May, and the title alone was astonishing. The song managed to be taut and worrying yet entirely restrained, the menace this time was always just around the corner: Bruce's acoustic was to the fore; it contained some of Tony's busiest drumming; and Hank's deep, resonant, calmly authoritative lead gave the narrative of a city under lockdown.

You didn't need to know that it was another film theme, this time for a noir-ish British thriller about the London underworld starring Herbert Lom. Almost no one who bought 'The Frightened City' by the Shadows was old enough to see *The Frightened City* at the cinema. It could have been about some ancient, cursed civilisation, petrified by a vengeful spirit, its inhabitants cowering, running, and screaming. Or it could have been about London, its residents too scared to walk the monochrome post-war streets lest Herbert Lom's goons saw to you with a flick knife. You didn't need to see the film to get the picture. In my head, the city in question is a crumbling, beautiful place, Havana maybe, caught at dusk, with the streetlights on and low, thick grey cloud.

This disconnect, this allusion, was one thing that made the Shadows' music so powerful. 'The Frightened City'! It was an incredible title.

Whatever it conjured up in your head when you heard the opening rhythm on Jet's heartbeat bass and Bruce's acoustic – Latin-influenced but anxious, no siesta today – it was yours alone.

The lack of lyrics made the Shadows' singles more painterly than those of any other British '60s group. They gave you a title and the music; the rest of it, any story line, any visuals, were all in the mind of the individual listener. And if you had any kind of imagination, then 'Apache', 'Man of Mystery', 'FBI' and (especially) 'The Frightened City' were something to really lift you away from the drear of Dewsbury, Derby or Deptford, a three-minute soundtrack for your own, personal cinematic dreams.

On jukeboxes across Britain in the summer of 1961, 'The Frightened City' provided a pensive and abstracted coffee-bar soundtrack along with Del Shannon's 'Runaway', the Everly Brothers' 'Temptation' and John Leyton's 'Johnny Remember Me'. All four contained deep mystery, something of the eerie and unknown, and conjured up brushes with violence, even death. 'Back Home' on the flip was the pastoral coda to 'The Frightened City''s issues, all peace, with sparrows circling and gently brushing against Tony's cymbals as Bruce played the most basic blues riffs on a muted electric and Hank took us off to tropical climes; 'Back Home' doesn't make you think of Newcastle-upon-Tyne. The single reached number three, held off the top spot by Del Shannon and by Elvis's Neapolitan trip, 'Surrender', but stayed in the top twenty right through the summer.

Also out that summer, not that anyone outside of a couple of white African enclaves would have known about it, was *Live at the Colosseum*, an EP recorded live in Johannesburg. Here, 'FBI' sounds unbelievably powerful, a real evocation of how Hank's guitar would have pierced the air of provincial British cities, a siren call from the future. Tony Meehan in particular played faster and fiercer than the studio records suggest. 'Shazam', 'Guitar Boogie', 'Sleep Walk' and 'FBI' – there it is, bottled, an absolutely perfect time capsule.

The tour had taken place in March 1961. When they had landed with Cliff in Johannesburg, the reaction was rather different to the one in the US – the runway was engulfed with screaming fans. The South African golfer Gary Player was thoughtful enough to lend them his red sports car to get from the airport and into the city; we can only assume he was a fan as he never actually met the group. There were shows in Johannesburg and Durban, with the screaming almost as loud for the Shadows' set as it was for Cliff's. Apartheid wasn't exactly widely talked about in Britain at the time, so the all-white audiences came as something of a shock to the group. They managed to tack on a blacks-only show in Cape Town at the end of the tour, with profits going to charity, and while they didn't say anything out loud at the time, they wouldn't return to the country until apartheid was dismantled.

On arriving home from Africa, Cliff and the Shadows went straight into rehearsals for their second movie together, *The Young Ones* – shooting started at Elstree on 15 May. Cliff was the star, Carole Gray his love interest and Robert Morley his property-developer dad who was striving to demolish their ramshackle youth club. The film's set would remain standing at Elstree through the '60s and early '70s, and would be used for TV shows including *The Avengers*, *The Saint*, *The Baron*, *UFO* and *The Protectors*.

The boys would be picked up in a Bentley around 6 a.m., taken to the studio and plastered in makeup by 7 a.m. During the many hours when they were sat about doing nothing, they might go to a café to talk to Royston Ellis for his upcoming book. Jet and Hank often sneaked off to try to catch great crested newts, which they found in an enormous tank that had been used on the set of the movie *The Cruel Sea*.

Cliff's on-screen gang were a charismatic bunch: the dusty young lawyer Richard O'Sullivan, the pork pie hat-wearing Melvyn Hayes, the elastic dancer Teddy Green, the beatnik-looking Annette Robertson (who would later marry actor John Hurt) and the almond-eyed Carole Gray playing Cliff's girl. Hayes' role could have gone to Jet, which might have changed the dynamic and the future of the Shadows quite dramatically. 'I knew I could be an actor,' Jet said in 2005. 'Melvyn Hayes… there was talk I could have that part, but I had this mean and moody image – so they tell me, you know – and I don't think that would have suited me. I was offered a part in another thing called *Just For Fun*. Mark Wynter took it … a bit lovey-dovey, sort of tiptoeing through the tulips. Whispering sweet nothings to Carole Gray … my street cred would have gone.'

In the film, the gang's fundraising variety show took place at the old Finsbury Park Empire* which, having closed down in real life in

* The Empire had hosted names like Laurel and Hardy, Marie Lloyd, Max Miller, Tony Hancock, Harry Houdini, and W.C. Fields. Cliff Richard and the Drifters had played there on 1 December 1958. The last ever show at the Empire starred Emile Ford and the Checkmates, and the Lana Sisters who numbered Dusty Springfield in their line-up. The site is now an anonymous social housing block called Vaudeville Court.

1960, was cleaned up for one final performance and saw the Shadows play a manically fast number called 'The Savage' in matching silver-grey suits. Bruce's rhythm guitar playing defied belief, while Tony's fast fills almost got away from him. It's terrific, the highlight of the movie. They also got to play 'Peace Pipe' in the Simpkins Youth Club, in their casual clothes. In this scene, Jet was clearly the most photogenic, the star of the group.

The Young Ones, truthfully, was not *Expresso Bongo*, though it did also include another superannuated jazz singer, in a low-cut top and too much make-up, trying to seduce Cliff.

There were two problems with it. First, it was top-heavy with clunky showtunes and *High Society*-aping lines like 'Ever heard of Major Gagarin?', where it could have made far more use of proven hit writers Marvin, Welch, Harris, Chester and Samwell. Secondly, the story line involved a touch too much suspension of belief, although the friction between the New London, represented by avaricious property developer Hamilton Black (Robert Morley), and the Old London of wooden youth clubs and Victorian music halls (Cliff and his gang) was intriguing. Their can-do attitude ('Let's put on a show!') would have been more wearing if they hadn't also set up a pirate radio station on the BBC wavelength, broken into a derelict theatre, taken it over and eventually kidnapped the property developer (a step too far for Cliff's lukewarm character).

The central song wasn't 'The Young Ones' itself, but 'When the Girl in Your Arms is the Girl in Your Heart' – a Tepper/Bennett ballad which, in one unpleasant scene, seemed to appeal to old ladies playing bridge, kids in shades at a jazz club and pre-pubescent schoolgirls in their dorm. Hank and Bruce provided minimal backing for Cliff on screen for this sallow number and looked like they might fall asleep.

*

While filming *The Young Ones*, Cliff received the shocking news that his father, Rodger Webb, had died suddenly of heart disease. He was fifty-eight. Cliff was just twenty years old and was now effectively the head of the family with a mother and three sisters to support. He may have been one of the biggest pop stars in Europe, great fun and all that, but this was now a position he couldn't afford to relinquish. It was the first sign of major upheaval within Cliff Richard and the Shadows. The boy, not yet a man, began to look for succour in religion.

In 1961, he was dating Delia Wicks, an Australian dancer who was one of the 'Television Toppers' dance troupe on *The Black and White Minstrel Show*. They were serious enough for talk of marriage, but his dad's death changed all that; Cliff wrote to Delia to tell her they were breaking up. This made the papers. 'Being a pop singer I have to give up one priceless thing,' he told them. 'The right to any lasting relationship with any special girl.'

Cliff Richard was not only now supporting his family; he also knew he had become a figurehead for British pop music, a public-sector pop star. From this point on, he behaved more like a civil servant than a rock 'n' roller. He took his job seriously. This was a boy who had been laughed at for bowing to his schoolteacher when he first arrived in

England. The manners he had been brought up with in India now came into their own: he would put his private thoughts to one side and do what he thought was correct, what was expected of him. No matter how many times he was asked to sing the wretched 'Living Doll', he would never let his personal feelings show. Nor, years later, when he was singing 'Congratulations' or 'Goodbye Sam, Hello Samantha'. His own feelings about the songs were secondary. Neutrality and nobility came first. Cliff regarded this as his civic duty.*

*

On 22 June 1961, at the ungodly hour of 8 a.m., the Beatles were in a van heading to Harburg, fifteen miles south of Hamburg, where they had first signed up to play a set of shows in the same week 'Apache' had gone to number one.

They had just played at the Top Ten Club, coming off stage at 2 a.m. after seven or eight hours, and they were still hopped-up on Preludin. The Friedrich Ebert Halle in Harburg was a civic concert hall that doubled up as a recording studio and Bert Kaempfert was there, waiting for them. Kaempfert's name may have been regarded around the world as the last word in schlock, but in 1961 Germany, he was the number-one record producer, Spector and Meek and Leiber and Stoller rolled into one. Except, of course, he didn't like rock 'n' roll.

---

* In this, Cliff Richard is almost unique. His motive is often misread, but if people thought of him as a 'bread head', he would find that hurtful. That's not where the impulse to record songs he actively dislikes, like 'Congratulations', comes from.

The first thing he did was to dispose of Pete Best's bass drum and tom-tom, leaving him with just snare, hi hat and ride cymbal. The next thing Kaempfert did was suggest they record 'My Bonnie Lies Over the Ocean'. Kids would love it! Not 'the kids', just kids.

The session was led by Tony Sheridan, the guitarist from the 2i's whose tardiness back in 1958 had led to Hank and Bruce becoming Cliff's players instead. Sheridan sang 'My Bonnie' on what became the Beatles' first single, while John Lennon sang the hardly less uncool 'Ain't She Sweet'. Jerry Lee Lewis may have rocked up 'My Bonnie' before, and Gene Vincent may have cooed 'Ain't She Sweet', but the real meat from the Beatles' first go in a real studio was an instrumental, a Harrison/Lennon original called 'Cry For a Shadow'. The pair had written the song late in 1960 when they heard a rumour that the Shadows' 'Man of Mystery' was the last word in rocking instrumentals. Stuck in Hamburg, they were unable to hear the single, but they wanted to add it to their set. They asked Liverpool singer Rory Storm to sing it to them and worked out a rough approximation of the track from his humming. By the time they finally heard 'Man of Mystery', they realised their supposed cover was actually an invention of their own; they decided to call it 'Cry For a Shadow'.

It would be released in Germany in October 1961, by which time the Beatles had returned from Hamburg to Liverpool. George wrote to Stuart Sutcliffe, their bassist who had stayed in Germany, telling him 'everybody thinks it's great. I think a lot of people didn't really believe we had made anything, and no matter what anybody says it's Beatles on a "real" record.' George told the *NME* two years later that he 'didn't stop playing it for days'.

'My Bonnie' would eventually be released on Polydor in the UK on 5 January 1962, while 'The Young Ones' was at number one in the singles chart.

*

Ahead of *The Young Ones*, the Shadows' annus mirabilis had also found time for a second number-one single. Released in the first week of September, 'Kon-Tiki' was another slice of exotica rooted in Britain by its makers. Like 'Man of Mystery', 'Kon-Tiki' had been written by Michael Carr, who was smart enough to submit a demo with the more-than-capable Joe Brown playing lead guitar. It had been inspired by the Norwegian explorer Thor Heyerdahl, who had sailed across the Pacific Ocean from South America to the Polynesian islands in 1947 on a balsa-wood raft that he had named *Kon-Tiki* after an Incan sun god.

Hank's playing had the feel of Hawaii, with much use of the tremolo arm, while Tony played timpani that evocatively filled out the sound of his drum kit. The melody was a summer dream, which was needed both when it was recorded – back in January '61 – and when it was eventually released, in a cooling September. On the flip was '36-24-36', its less high-minded title apparently inspired by Jet Harris' girlfriend at the time, presumably the singer Patti Brook who he was seen stepping out with. Jet's clipped percussive bass set the tone and it bore a slight resemblance to Boots Brown's 'Cerveza', which they had played on their Radio Luxembourg show, *Me and My Shadows*. Either way, it had a groove that would remain a favourite of DJs some decades later.

September 1961 also saw the release of their first album. 'It's been worth the wait,' said *Disc*. 'The LP is a mixture of their familiar brand of modern instrumental showcasing plus solo spots from Messrs Meehan and Marvin, and vocalising from all four. There is contrast and variety and no risk of boredom or monotony. Especially impressive is Hank Marvin's Nashville piano playing, and thank goodness for one drummer who can play an extended solo which is logical and relevant without losing himself.' Tony's 'See You in My Drums' would turn out to be a swansong, though no one yet knew it. Other highlights included the jazzy Hank showcase 'Nivram'; 'Sleep Walk', the Santo and Johnny hit that they would frequently return to for inspiration; and the Norman Petty-written 'Find Me a Golden Street', which had started out as an organ instrumental. The title was taken from Revelations 21 by the deeply religious Petty. Its unresolved ending was a bonus cliffhanger.

Talking to *NME* about the album, Cliff said that 'as far as I'm concerned, this is the best LP ever recorded in Britain. I just love it and I play it at every available opportunity.' Its variety, clarity and effortlessness made it a treasured item, and is still the favourite album of many Shadows fans.

Jennings on Charing Cross Road had supplied Hank and Bruce with matching Fiesta Red Strats with rosewood finger boards, so must have been a little miffed not to see them on the album cover. Hank's fabled, original Strat was then returned to Cliff, who would have it repainted in white. Bruce would then 'borrow' the guitar from Cliff in the early '70s and, to Cliff's mild consternation, still has it today – repainted red. Hank had bought a Gretsch Country Gentleman in an attempt to get the Chet Atkins sound. He used it on 'Nivram' and Cliff's 1961 single 'A Girl Like You', but didn't get on with it and would sell it on in 1972. But 'Nivram' itself would remain a staple in Shadows sets, as if it had been a number-one single.

It wasn't just the futuristic guitars that kept the Shadows one step ahead of British competitors – and the most visually pleasing. At the end of the American tour, Tony brought a Gretsch 'progressive jazz' drum kit back with him. He was surprised to find that the snare drum was plastic rather than calf skin, which back in London caused much laughter. So Tony had it fitted with calf skin. Being a huge fan of modern jazz drummer Max Roach, and wanting to look the same, his four-piece kit was in champagne sparkle. You could see it in *The Young Ones* and understand how British drummers – making do with Chad Valley equivalents – would have been in awe of Meehan.*

*

'We all realised it might not last long if we didn't commit ourselves totally to the Shadows,' said Bruce. And when Bruce said 'we', he really meant 'I'. He 'believed so much in the group, I was looked upon as the regimental sergeant major, trying to motivate everyone, and often having a go if things were slacking. It wasn't personal ... I tried to keep up standards, and I was only adopting the right professional attitude in my opinion.'

---

* Unlike the iconic Fender Stratocaster, the Gretsch kit was sadly broken up and passed around Tony's kids. No one seems to know where it is today.

Though happy to admit this twenty-five years later, he may not have taken the military comparison so well at the time. These lads had just avoided national service.* And they were the biggest pop stars in the country. They should have been having the times of their lives. Wasn't it meant to be fun?

Talking to Royston Ellis, the more free-wheeling Tony Meehan was concerned for Cliff. 'To me he seems a highly sensitive young man, very conscientious to his public. In fact, so conscientious that he allows his life to be run by them. A young boy of twenty-one should be out enjoying himself, having fun with kids of his own age, going to parties, living it up a little. But Cliff is literally a prisoner. As a result of this, very few people ever get really close to him.'

Not all of the Shadows wanted to dedicate themselves totally to the cause; they had other avenues to explore. Playing the same show, in the same venue, with the same gags for weeks on end, hardly suited Hank, Jet or Tony's jazz sensibilities. Hank, so laid back, just got on

---

* Jet, being a little older, had managed to avoid it back in 1958. 'We were doing a rehearsal for *Oh Boy!* and the first to go up for national service had been Marty Wilde, and Marty had got out with flat feet. I said "Oh bugger me, Marty, I've got to go tomorrow over to Acton". The night before was the Albert Hall. We were doing a show and it was a miserable time for me, knowing that I had to go to Acton the next day you know, because national service would have meant two years away. I would never have got the job back after two years, no. You were stripped down naked, and there was a bloke walking round you and he's saying things to me like "You're very skinny Harris, aren't you?" I said "Yes, sir." You had to call him sir – he'd got medals on and everything! "What's that on your head? Is it a wig?" That was my blond hair. He said "Well what can you do, Harris? Can you cook?" I said "No sir." Anyway, he's walking around, he's scratching his head with a pencil. I was tiny, I must have been all of eight stone in them days. And a couple of days later I got the green card – B2 – meant I was unfit. But I reckon it was a wangle – we knew some influential people, you know, like masons and all that shit. I'd got my wages up to £250 a week, right? Who wants to go in the frigging army?'

with it and let nothing bother him. Jet had other, more existential things on his mind. Tony, though, didn't give a fuck. He drove Bruce round the twist.

'Tony Meehan was a teenager. Like most teenagers, he didn't like to get out of bed. He was also a prodigy, and was often told as much, which gave him an air of superiority.' Tony was also smart – his keen interest in psychology would lead to actual qualifications many years later – and he didn't want to be, or need to be, in a group with a sergeant major. 'He had no respect for anyone, least of all his elders,' fumed Bruce. His elders! Meehan was 'pompous', tutted Bruce. 'He wanted all the fame, the adulation and the money, but didn't want to do anything for it.' It should be noted that Bruce was still only nineteen in 1961, an age when you think you know wrong from right, when you have little real-life experience but everything is seen in black and white. Bruce had total conviction in his work ethic, his quest for what he considered perfection. Tony was a jazzer. Things happened when they happened. Anyone could have seen this combination wouldn't last forever. But, for now, Tony and Bruce suffered each other. Besides, a bit of tension wouldn't hurt the group's sound.

*

Tony Meehan's happy place was in the studio. He was dying to get into the control room, to have some influence over the sound of the Shadows.

'What I wanted to do was like the things I did with Jet afterwards

– bring horns in, bring strings in, voices, all sorts of things like that. There was a certain amount of conservatism, particularly from Bruce, who just wouldn't hear of any of that sort of thing. There wasn't really conflict, or friction, but there was a feeling of "we've done this, now let's move on". Seven days a week touring – it started to go a bit stale. And touring in those days was very tough. No air-conditioned buses and things like that, no toilets! You zoomed around in a Comma van and carried your own equipment. But it was great fun, enormous fun.

'The Shadows were the first guitar group. We were the innovators. There'd never been anything like it before. It was very revolutionary in its time – I don't know that anyone's ever given us credit for that. We really were quite an avant-garde sound in that time.

'And then suddenly everyone was doing that.'

'Apache' had only been the beginning. In 1961 and '62, there seemed to be an endless supply of new groups, teenagers with cheap guitars creating obscure instrumental singles. Many of them had previously backed singers – the Checkmates with Emile Ford, the Fentones with Shane Fenton. First out of the blocks were the Hunters, previously the Parker Royal Four and an adjunct to Cliff soundalike Dave Sampson. Their flash 'Teen Scene', in October 1960, had a satisfying air of dirty deeds. There was also the Moontrekkers' 'Night of the Vampire', banned by the BBC as 'unsuitable for people of a nervous disposition' – quite a feat for an instrumental. And then let's not forget the Cougars ('Saturday Night at the Duck Pond'), the Boys ('Polaris'), the Planets ('Jam Roll'), the Scorpions ('Riders in the Sky'), the Packabeats ('The Traitors'), the Flee-Rekkers ('Sunday Date'), the Nu Notes ('Hall of Mirrors'), and so on and so forth. Endless Shad-alikes.*

Hank and Bruce's former bandleader Pete Chester was still writing songs with them. He decided he could relaunch his own career with the all-instrumental Pete Chester Group; 'Forest Fire', a Chester/Marvin co-write, came out on Pye International in 1961. The group's name wasn't in keeping with the times, though, so they quickly became the Vigilantes, issuing 'Man in Space' as a tribute to Yuri Gagarin a few months later. Even Gentleman Bert Weedon's 'Ginchy' sounded a little less concerned with upsetting the children than his original 'Apache'. Among the best groups were old friends from the 2i's – Brian Bennett, Jim Sullivan and Licorice Locking – who had split away from Marty Wilde after he gave up touring in 1960 and changed their name from the Wildcats to the Krew Kats.

The Krew Kats were very much in the Shadows' shadows. They put up their own money to record 'Trambone' and 'Peak Hour' at IBC studios on Portland Place. For such premium-level rockers, opening their account with a version of Chet Atkins' 'Trambone' was an odd decision; it was certainly no match for the hectic flinty shuffle of Jim Sullivan's 'Peak Hour' on the flip. Glyn Johns was the tape op, but the group made all the production decisions, with Big Jim on his Gibson 345 played through a Vox amp. They took the finished recording to EMI where Norrie Paramor jumped on it. The high-handed Paramor unfortunately decided to stick the entire recording through EMI's own echo chamber – in a concrete dungeon far below

* All of these singles, incidentally, are worth your attention.

Abbey Road – to make it sound, to his ears, more pro. 'We had spent our own time and money getting it how we wanted it,' Big Jim later complained to *Pipeline* magazine, 'and by the time Norrie had finished with it, you couldn't even hear that I was playing the bloody thing finger style! I wanted "Peak Hour" as the A-side but Paramor wasn't having any of it. He insisted that his treatment had made "Trambone" sound more like the Shadows and therefore it was the more commercial side.' 'Trambone' sneaked up to number thirty-three in the spring of 1961.

Pick of the competition were the Outlaws, the house band at producer Joe Meek's Holloway Road studio, who had initially formed to back singer Mike Berry. They included Chas Hodges on bass, Bobbie Graham on drums and teenage guitar wizard Ritchie Blackmore – big-name session players. The entire oeuvre of the Outlaws was geared around 'Apache' and the Shadows' first EP. It was about deep Americana, Alan Ladd, Mercedes McCambridge, sunsets over the Nevada desert, all with that unmistakable, warm-dust smell of an Odeon cinema, and the promise of fish and chips for tea: 'Ambush', 'Valley of the Sioux', 'Last Stage West', 'Law and Order', 'Sioux Serenade', 'Ka-Pow!', 'That Set the Wild West Free' and 'Return of the Outlaws'. They cut a whole album called *Dream of the West* with a technicolour cowboys and Indians painting on the cover. It was one of the very few albums released in direct competition with the Shadows. And it was also magnificent, Meek daring to ratchet up the distortion and the sound effects in a way Norrie Paramor would never have conceived. But, like every other Shadows-inspired instrumental act from Britain, they found there was a sales ceiling. Instrumental nuts who couldn't get enough of the sound would push the Outlaws singles, or those of the Fentones, to the edge of the top forty, but more casual fans would simply stick with the original quartet and buy 'The Savage' or 'Wonderful Land' or 'Kon-Tiki' instead.*

*

As if there wasn't enough product in the shops, the end of 1961 also saw Cliff Richard's *Dream* EP released, which, on paper, looked like an ill-advised return to the standards that wrecked *Cliff Sings* two years earlier. The tracks all had 'dream' in the title and were written by Johnny Mercer, Nacio Herb Brown and Arthur Freed, Oscar Hammerstein – the legends of a bygone age. This time, the Shadows – rather than Norrie Paramor's strings – backed Cliff and it was a revelation. Here was his mainstream future writ large: he went deep, he paused in all the right, suggestive places, and genuinely came over as a crooner with aplomb. It was the Shadows who gave him the confidence to do this. Jet was back on stand-up bass, Tony pulled his dusty jazz brushes out from under his bed and the whole thing swung. It wasn't Gene Vincent and the Blue Caps, but it was hard to argue that it didn't work very well. 'They said I had gone mainstream,' said Cliff in his 2020 autobiography *The Dreamer*. 'Well, I had – and you know what? I was happy to. I might have loved Elvis, but what did I have

* The exception was a late-in-the-day instrumental hit, the Dakotas' 'The Cruel Sea'. Billy J. Kramer's backing group went as high as number 18 in the summer of 1963, just as the Shadows' old singles were being boxed up and put in the attic by Beatles converts.

to rebel against? I didn't hate my parents and family – I loved them! I wasn't horrified by the idea of becoming a clean, all-round family entertainer. I embraced it.'

6

STARS FELL ON STOCKTON

'One memorable day in the studio sticks in my mind,' wrote John Schroeder, assistant to Norrie Paramor at Columbia. 'Norrie had asked me to do a couple of tracks with the Shadows for their album. On two occasions they turned up late for the session and I had previously warned them about this. On the third occasion I am afraid to say I emphatically lost it. I gave them a fair old bollocking saying they were in breach of their contract. They were wasting valuable studio time, money and my time, and if they continued to act this way they would not only be jeopardizing their contract, we would have no choice but to charge them for the studio time and the loss of finance, deducting it from their forthcoming royalties. In other words they might very well not get paid anything for a very long time to come! That really put the shits up them and for some unknown reason it never happened again.'

The Shadows had just played a show at Cliff's old school in Cheshunt when Tony began to feel unwell. He asked the others if they could pack his kit away in the van (note – no roadies for the biggest group in the country). Bruce told him where he could stick it, assuming he was shirking again. Next thing they knew, Tony Meehan was lying on the floor. 'He looked like an extra-white washing powder,' said a remorseful Hank.

'I hit the bass drum,' remembered Tony, grimacing, 'and the fucking appendix burst.' He was rushed to hospital. 'I had to have an emergency operation. I nearly snuffed it.'

But his bandmates' reaction was understandable. Tony did have form. By 1961, he was married and had a baby boy; unlike Bruce, he wasn't wedded to the Shadows. During one argument backstage, he bit Hank's finger. Another time, he missed a train connection to get to a show in Leeds and turned up halfway through the set, still wearing his street clothes.

'When I joined the group I was a fifteen-year-old boy and not a man,' explained Tony. 'We toured constantly, doing shows twice nightly and three times on Saturdays. We never got a holiday and rarely a day off. My time-keeping problem was probably due to physiological reasons caused by constant tiredness, but I did what I had to do as far as the music was concerned.

'Initially we had a unique quality – we were all from different backgrounds, but the chemistry was there and very good. We could be very volatile, but we were creating something and trying to find ourselves. It doesn't often get recognised, but we changed the world's music. There wouldn't have been any Beatles, Rolling Stones or Gerry and the Pacemakers if it hadn't been for us.'

His morning lethargy was nothing unusual for a teenage boy. Add young children into the mix and it's hardly surprising he struggled to rouse himself to sit on a cold coach at 6 a.m.

'Bruce Welch had a difficult manner,' Tony told Jet Harris's biographer, Dave Nicolson, 'to do with his upbringing, I suppose. He took over and was domineering. Not long before he died, Peter Gormley told me that Bruce Welsh destroyed the Shadows. When I joined the Drifters, Jet was the best musician and the group leader. Bruce wanted to be leader, but being the worst musician of the group he couldn't get the respect.'

'In fairness,' said Cliff in *The Dreamer*, 'Tony had just had his first kid, he was never home and our schedule wasn't fair on his family. I can see that – we worked like dogs in those years.' He also understands how Bruce and Tony were never going to reconcile their approaches. 'Bruce is still the same today. If you dare to get to the studio even five minutes late, you will be greeted by a cold glare and one accusatory, barked word: "Waiting!" It became Bruce's catchphrase decades ago, and it still is.'

Talking to Royston Ellis back in 1961, latent psychologist Tony had this to say about Bruce: 'I always feel that he worries too much about unimportant things. Things like whether his shoes are clean, he revels in those sorts of worries. Maybe he is occupying his mind so that he doesn't have to worry about the important things, like whether we'll all be out of work tomorrow. Perhaps it's a sort of fear. He is definitely the least imaginative of the four of us, but also the most dependable.'

Royston Ellis's closeness to the Shadows' world had allowed him to expand his horizons beyond beat poetry: in 1961, *The Shadows By Themselves* was published. It wasn't the soft soap of Adam Faith's *Poor Me* or Cliff's *It's Great to Be Young*. The quotes rang true.

Tony may have described Bruce as 'the least imaginative' Shadow, but he didn't exactly go easy on Hank either. 'I find him very vague. Sometimes he is willing and sometimes unwilling to cooperate. I think he tries to approach everything from a neutral point of view but often gets his thinking coloured by his early, conventional upbringing. He's a very conventional person really, and inclined to be self-conscious. His tastes are very conventional and I'm sure he prefers to follow others with opinions, dress, in fact with his whole way of life. He is very simple in his ways, more uncomplicated. That's why people take to him easily.'

Jet was described by Tony as an extremely good bass player and a natural musician, but 'not an easy person to get on with. He's inclined to moods and he's very set in his ways. Also, he has had a lot of bad experiences with people and consequently he is inclined to be a bit wary of them. On the other hand he can be very charming, and he has the knack of making the most unusual friends.'

He kept his warmest words for his boss. 'I am very close to Cliff. Of all the Shadows I think I know Cliff the best. In fact, he is one of the few friends I have and really trust. I don't need friends like Jet does, and so only have a few. I think Cliff and myself got to know each other during our holiday in Italy two and a half years ago. I admire him very much … he is one of the few people I have met whom I would completely trust with anything.'

It's hard to believe that the publication of *The Shadows By Themselves* didn't cause ructions in the group, who presumably didn't get to look at it before it was in the shops. All this on top of Tony's punctuality issues! The nerve of the kid! 'No respect for his elders'!

'We were all stuck together, all the time, and little things did start to niggle,' said Tony in 2004. 'Bruce had this thing about tuning, and everywhere we went it was tuning, tuning, tuning. It became completely pathological. Every gig, you can imagine… Every show. Two shows a night, and then when we were working at the Palladium it was three shows on a Saturday. We'd leave the Palladium that night, get on a train and go to Blackpool or somewhere like that for a Sunday concert, and get five pounds from Cliff, come back on the sleeper and start again on Monday. We had a number-one record at the time. Not much of a life. We never got holidays. You weren't master in your own house and that was a big mistake.'

Tony Meehan was the baby of the group, but had ambitions that stretched beyond summer seasons in Blackpool. He wanted to produce records, arrange them, bring new ingredients to the Shadows' sound. With his interests in psychology and psychotherapy, the others must have idly wondered if he was ever looking into their minds. And now he was married, with a baby, and another soon on the way, he didn't think another trip to Manchester to promote their next single, with another ten hours spent in the Bedford van getting there and back, was a better place to be than at home with his new family. Possibly, he didn't say this out loud. Possibly, probably, he thought it was all bloody obvious, and if Bruce couldn't see that, then his priorities were out of order.

Tony quit the Shadows midway through a Blackpool season in October 1961.

In August 1961, the Shadows had begun playing their three-month season. One night, Tony was nowhere to be seen and they had to start the show without him. A couple of songs in, at the end of 'FBI', he slinked on stage to wild applause from a crowd who must have thought it was part of the show. But it wasn't. Backstage, Bruce tore into him. 'If that's your attitude,' snapped Tony, 'you better get yourself another drummer.'

'I left The Shadows because we had a row,' he said in Steve Turner's *Cliff Richard: The Bachelor Boy*. 'I was under a lot of stress and pressure, one way or another. I got tired of the whole showbiz thing. I wanted to do something with my music and they were getting into the whole *Summer Holiday* trip. I didn't like that direction.

'I went to work at Decca Records as a session musician, producer and arranger. There were no regrets. I did what I wanted to do.'

*

The fan reaction was one of total shock. To the outside world, the Shadows had seemed like inseparable friends. But, just as their first album hit the shops, Tony Meehan was no longer a member of the group.

In her Shadows fan memoir, Christine Colverson recalled that she was 'heartbroken! The blow was so shocking and so profound that even now I can't remember how news of this earth-shattering event reached my ears. Was it on the radio, in *New Musical Express* or from some beastly girl at school? I can only say that when I realised what had happened, I was very sad indeed. I appeared at the family tea table dressed all in black and got told off by Dad for being silly. Personally, I didn't think it silly at all.

'I clutched my copy of *The Shadows* LP to my bosom. It was the most recent picture of Tony that I had, and as far as I knew, it would be the last. The Shadows might go on (well, would they?) but things could never be the same again. And that meant the Golden Age of Rock 'n' Roll was over, too. The big question was "WHY?" It hung around unanswered for years.'

Christine and other Shadows fans got some answers, and heard Tony's side of the story, in the 13 October 1961 edition of the *NME*. It was in the form of a letter, allowing Tony to bow out with grace.

> I am a firm believer in following the policy which maintains that, since life is so short, it is most important that one should do exactly what one believes is right – and not follow the dictates of what other people think. It was this thinking which basically and primarily caused me to leave the Shadows.
>
> Quite frankly, I'd had enough touring. However well you may be doing in show business, I believe that it's equally important to have a personal life. Now, my private life is very happy indeed, and I want to enjoy it – but that is virtually impossible when you are forever on the road.
>
> I suppose I'm just not cut out to play forever in a group like the Shadows. Certainly it's not what I want to do. For months I've been straining at the leash trying to come to terms with myself – and now, at last, it's done!
>
> I want to emphasise, though, that I don't regret one single moment of the time I've spent with the Shadows. Quite apart from having shared three years with as great a bunch of fellows

as you could wish to meet, and having had some really wonderful times, it has been invaluable experience musically.

You see, anyone who wants to be a genuine musician must be able to play all kinds of music. In my opinion, some of the best young musicians in the country today have risen on the crest of the beat wave. I think that anyone who turns up his nose at rock 'n' roll is a fool. It is unquestionably the most powerful factor in modern music, and it's ridiculous to spurn it.

Ultimately I would like to form my own group (with a line-up something along the lines of tenor, baritone, trumpet, piano, bass, drums and guitar – but not, by the way, playing music of the style of the John Barry Seven). I appreciate that this aim would take months to be realised – if indeed it does ever come about – but it's something I would dearly love to do.

I'm also anxious to undertake as many sessions as possible here in London.

Many people scorn this attitude of what they term 'musical integrity', saying that they simply cannot understand how I could give up a lucrative position with the Shadows, in order to follow my own whims.

Well, it's just the way I'm made, I suppose. Besides, I'm hoping that it won't make too much difference financially. After all, session work in London – particularly in the recording studios – is extremely well paid. And if I can reach a high enough standard, whereby I am kept working pretty regularly, I reckon that I should do fairly well.

'He kept time on the drums all right,' said Hank in 2004. 'But Tony, unfortunately, was a very arrogant young guy ... he kept turning up late for everything. And really putting us in very difficult situations early on in our career. TV producers and agents, they don't look at one guy, they look at the band. You carry the can. Tony was young. For his age, he was very, very good. I liked what he contributed to those records, a slightly unusual style – he always reminded me of an embryonic Keith Moon.'

Tony knew he was leaving something special, something innovative, and something he would always be very proud of. 'The Shadows were the first guitar group. There'd never been anything like it before. I think the original group was the nucleus of that sound, from our various characters if you like. But I don't think it really progressed much after that.'

*

'The first thing you learn to do as a baby is clap your hands. It's natural. When I first picked up a pair of sticks, it felt like an extension of my arms.' The first time Brian Bennett picked up a makeshift pair of drumsticks was during the war, when a Glenn Miller show from the Aeolian Hall on London's Bond Street was broadcast over the radio by the BBC. Baby Brian Bennett was transfixed. Sticking his tongue out the corner of his mouth, and with a slightly furrowed brow, he emptied the kitchen cupboards of saucepans and wooden spoons and got himself a larder-ready drum kit. 'It chooses you,' he would say. 'It's a lot like falling in love. There's nothing you can do about it.'

Brian Bennett had a cheeky face from birth. His childhood was a happy one in Palmers Green, north London. His dad spent the war in Africa and, when he returned, he took the eight-year-old Brian on the bus down Green Lanes to Wood Green Empire. He saw his first orchestra there and he couldn't take his eyes off them. He wanted to be the drummer in a big band. That was it, that was all.

At Hazelwood Lane School in Palmers Green, there was an orchestra. One day, cheekster Brian sat in with them and blew their regular drummer off stage. The poor bloke was sacked. Brian not only stole this bloke's job, but also his girlfriend.

At weekends, he would disappear on a trolleybus south, into the West End. He would go into Doug Dobell's record shop on Charing Cross Road, the only game in town for budding jazz fans. Smiling Brian was only a kid but still confident enough to start conversations with Doug, and the other staff in Dobell's, and they effectively became his teachers. School was bollocks, he couldn't have cared less – Kenton, Basie, Ellington, that's what he wanted to learn about. The blokes in Dobell's would talk to Brian about nothing but music, the latest sounds and which 78s he should take into the listening booth. Brian absorbed it all.

Someone in the shop mentioned the broadcaster Voice of America and when he tuned in, Brian discovered 'Willis Conover's Jazz Hour'. Listening in from a Palmers Green bedroom, its exoticism was only amplified by the fact it was broadcast from Tangier and its signature theme was Duke Ellington's none-more-New York 'Take the "A" Train'; with Louie Bellson on drums, this was a sound that would make the hairs stand up on the back of Brian's neck. He learned from the American jazz greats – Shelly Manne, Buddy Rich, Max Roach, Sonny Payne – and quickly discovered he could play just about anything. He had a go at the violin, to please his parents, but no. Just drums. Drums, drums and more drums.

He left school at fourteen and, after dumping his satchel in the River Lea, he formed the Tony Brian Trio, working part-time with his dad at a printing works to help pay for a better drum kit. While other kids had paper rounds, Brian Bennett had bands – jazz bands, dance bands, wedding bands and, eventually, skiffle bands. He was paid properly, too, because he was good. He was the best – the Max Roach of Palmers Green. His only rival – though he didn't yet know it – was the baby-faced Buddy Rich of N8, Tony Meehan.

One afternoon in 1957, Brian went to the 2i's, like any other cocky London teenager with music buzzing around in his head, and became the house drummer in about ten seconds. Brian Bennett would have been on the coffee bar's tiny stage when a curious fourteen-year-old Tony Meehan first stuck his face around the door that year. And when Brian left to play a summer season in Largs before joining Vince Taylor's Playboys, it would be the even-younger Tony who got his old job.

By the spring of 1959, Brian was in a recording studio for the first time, with his mate from the 2i's, bassist Brian 'Licorice' Locking. They were playing on Marty Wilde's latest single, 'A Teenager in Love'. Wilde had, of course, been the initial star of Jack Good's *Oh Boy!,* but he had bad long-term judgement. His biggest hits would all be covers of American songs: Jody Reynolds' 'Endless Sleep', Ritchie Valens' 'Donna', Dion's 'A Teenager in Love'; Phil Phillips' 'Sea of Love'.

All were major American hits that British youth, radio-controlled by the BBC, were largely unaware of in the '50s. But once future generations discovered the originals, Marty Wilde's run of hits counted for nothing.*

Bennett and Locking were signed up to back Wilde on stage, with lead guitarist Big Jim Sullivan and rhythm guitarist Tony Belcher. Brian Bennett, literally, drove the bus and they played to just as many screaming girls as Cliff until Marty made the damn fool mistake of getting married – and to someone off the telly, at that: another *Oh Boy!* regular, the Vernons Girls' Joyce Baker. His fans revolted and he stopped having hits almost overnight. Cliff Richard looked on and took notes.

While Marty was away making a movie called *Jet Storm* – which was so bad that future Rolling Stones manager Andrew Loog Oldham apparently asked the Kilburn Essoldo for his money back – Brian Bennett got to play in the backing group for touring rock legends Eddie Cochran and Gene Vincent. Larry Parnes promoted it as 'a fast-moving Anglo-American beat show' and the bill was filled out by his charges Billy Fury, Joe Brown and Vince Eager, plus old 2i's mucker Tony Sheridan. Cochran and Vincent represented vitality, sex, danger. Neither was about to get pressured into recording a 'Living Doll'. They arrived in the UK in January 1960, with rock 'n' roll still standing. At rehearsals in Soho, Eddie taught Brian some tricks he'd picked up from legendary drummer Earl Palmer and they all got on

* This was a shame as Marty Wilde would prove himself to be a more than capable songwriter down the line with his own hit 'Bad Boy', Lulu's 'I'm a Tiger', the Casuals' 'Jesamine' and his daughter Kim's 'Kids in America'.

superbly. It was going to be quite the tour. Brian also saw the glint in Gene's eye and the glint of the knife he carried. 'I don't know what it is that makes you tick,' Gene told a heckler in Ipswich, 'but I sure hope it's a bomb.' In Leicester, Vince Eager's mum would bring nice guy Eddie Cochran her homemade apple tart that he'd been talking about ever since Vince had given him a slice in Ipswich. Outside Stockton, bad boy Eddie Cochran pulled the emergency cord on the train, just for laughs, and had to pay the five-pound fine.

After a show in Leeds, back in their digs, Gene Vincent banged on Eddie Cochran's door: 'Eddie!' he sobbed, standing there in his underwear. 'Eddie! They got my pants!' The ardent Leeds fans had literally torn Gene Vincent's leather trousers off of him. This was a proper rock 'n' roll tour and Brian Bennett loved it. It ran until April 1960 when the car that was driving Eddie Cochran and Gene Vincent to the airport, to catch the plane to take them home to California, left the road and Cochran was killed.

*

Stop the World, I Want to Get Off was the making of Anthony Newley, the star of screen and disc from Clapton Park. This was the darkest, furthest corner of the East End, sunk in the shallows of the Lea Valley, down river from Palmers Green where there were more trees and more light than the infant Anthony Newley had ever known. He lived about as far from the light and heat of the West End as you could do while still being thought of as a copper-bottomed Londoner. Clapton Park was an area that, after the war, would be razed to the ground and rebuilt as a vast, beige-brick estate. Few tears would be shed. All that would remain from his childhood was Newley's school, a Victorian edifice on Oswald Street, where he had broken hearts and driven teachers nuts with his bottomless reserves of brass and his unrivalled forwardness.

Out of school, he was a child actor. He won Petula Clark's lifelong affections when they acted together in the 1948 movie *Vice Versa* – him playing Dick Bultitude, her playing Dulcie Grimstone, doe-eyed with longing for the older boy. Nineteen-fifty-nine's *Idle on Parade* unintentionally made an actual pop star out of Anthony Newley; girls melted at both the sound of his outrageous vibrato and the sight of his brooding beetle brows. Petula Clark was apparently so overcome by Newley's hits like 'And the Heavens Cried' and 'Strawberry Fair' that she moved away to France.

Two years on from *Idle on Parade*, Newley was not only a pop idol but a star of the stage and a composer of modern-day standards, a self-taught polymath, the golden boy with a hit musical on his hands. With *Stop the World*, this no-mark from Oswald Street in the back-end of east London suddenly had Frank Sinatra and Sammy Davis on the phone, Matt Monro cutting his songs and Shirley Bassey slack-jawed in the front row. And, in the pit of the Queen's Theatre, Newley had just got himself a new drummer in Brian Bennett, the talented jazz nut who had agreed to play songs like 'Gonna Build a Mountain', 'Once in a Lifetime' and 'What Kind of Fool Am I' twice daily over the upcoming winter months, for twenty-five pounds a week.

Brian stood in the orchestra pit, nodding, as the show's previous drummer, Andy White, went through the fine details of the show.

Brian had a pen and a contract in his hands when the phone rang. It was Brian's wife, Margaret.

'Brian? Bruce Welch just called,' said Margaret, 'and he'd like you to join his group. It's the Shadows, you know?'

Brian knew. He'd heard the news and was half-expecting the call – him and Meehan had been circling each other for years.

'I knew Bruce, we'd bumped into each other on shows and things. There wasn't a sort of "Ooh, who are we gonna get?" It was like, "Well, we've got to get the best guy there is" and, without being presumptuous, you know, I was the choice.'

'It wasn't "Wow, I've made it!" It was "Shit, I've done all the one-night stands with Marty, I've worked with Eddie Cochran, Gene Vincent…", so I actually didn't really want to say yes. It didn't appeal to me. Bruce said, "It's the *Shadows* you know." I said, "Well, I've just married my girlfriend and we are just starting out."'

When he got home, Brian called Bruce to gently let him down – *Stop the World* was a big show, a rung up the ladder, a real money-spinner, far better paid than schlepping around in a Commer van with the Krew Kats. Besides, Brian explained, he had a summer season with Tommy Steele in Great Yarmouth to finish first.

This is the Shadows, said Bruce.

But Newley's promised me twenty-five pounds a week. Home by eleven every night. It's Tony Newley! Twenty-five pounds, Bruce! Can you believe it?

I'll double it, said Bruce. This is the Shadows.

When do I start, asked Brian.

Tomorrow, said Bruce.

Newley and Steele were fobbed off. The next morning, Peter Gormley drove Brian up to Birmingham to join Hank, Bruce and Jet for an appearance on *Thank Your Lucky Stars*. He mimed to Tony Meehan's drum part on their single 'Kon-Tiki', Britain's current number one.

Brian took Tony's place for the remainder of the Shadows' summer season at Blackpool. It wasn't a struggle.

In his open letter to the *NME* in October '61, Tony gave Brian his blessing, saying: 'I think the Shadows have secured a really fine drummer in Brian Bennett. I know him very well – he's extremely capable and in close touch with the idiom. What's more, he should have a good deal of fun with the boys.'

'I just used my ears,' Brian later said. 'Tony Meehan was one of the great drummers. He brought a lot to the band and was absolutely perfect for the Shadows. I liked his work and tried to be true to it, but over a period of time, without anyone noticing, I tactfully brought more of me to the table.' He impressed the other Shadows so much that they let him write the B-side of their next single, 'Stars Fell on Stockton'. He would still be called the 'new boy' decades later, but the Shadows had found the only drummer in the country who could not only replace Tony Meehan, but maybe improve their sound, keep a jazz edge but make them sound tougher, more focused.

The first new Shadows single with Brian as their drummer would be another Jerry Lordan song, his first A-side for them since 'Apache'. This new beginning for the Shadows was 'Wonderful Land'.

*

Nineteen sixty-two started with 'The Young Ones' at number one, which was dislodged by Elvis's daffy 'Rock-a-Hula Baby' from *Blue Hawaii*, then followed by 'Wonderful Land' for a full eight weeks. The Shadows' best single to date had probably been written by Jerry Lordan as a hymn to America, its glitz, its colour, its futuristic architecture and its endless horizons. The reality of the US in early 1962 was similarly starry-eyed, but not in the same way as the movie-loving Shadows might have imagined: during its stay at number one, the US president John F. Kennedy, leader of the free world, spent the night with the single representative of all Hollywood glamour, Marilyn Monroe. America had never been more American.

This may have been what Jerry Lordan had in mind, but 'Wonderful Land' also came out in a moment of great positivity for Britain. The Columbia single was released in its new company bag, with bold, bright colours in jazz stripes adorning the front. *The Times* had just issued its first colour supplement, with a feature on Mary Quant. The first James Bond movie, *Dr No*, was in production. For the first time since the war, Britain had a tangible dream of the future, a real optimism. People were moving to the new towns ringing London, the space and light in the bright, open spaces of Crawley and Stevenage. T. Dan Smith had a modernist vision of a new Tyneside, with a Paris-style metro sweeping from Jesmond to Eldon Square and towers of glass replacing Newcastle's soot-encrusted city centre. The future was sketched out in primary colours, with flyovers and underpasses, and 'Wonderful Land' was a new national anthem.

There was also a definite melancholy to the song, possibly in the melody and string arrangement's huge sense of promise, and its awareness that the promise is too huge to ever be truly fulfilled. Even in the twenty-first century, 'Wonderful Land' sounds vast, blue-skied, full of hope and still so sad.

Tony Meehan, session drumming on Holloway Road and arranging for Joe Meek, rolled his eyes when heard the single. Hadn't he been telling Norrie Paramor to add strings and brass to vary the Shads sound and hadn't they recorded 'Wonderful Land' months earlier with no orchestral embellishments? Norrie politely acknowledged the boy drummer and then seemed to ignore him. Almost a year later, in January 1962, Norrie had finally made sense of Jerry Lordan's complex composition – and all of its twists and turns, its mood ring of warm changes – by adding strings and brass. 'When we heard what Norrie had done, we thought, *That's magnificent. That's exactly what it needs*,' said Hank. 'The French horn sound, the beautiful strings ... It felt like an important interpretation of a great tune. Some people thought the tune was maybe too complicated, but we felt it should be a single. It sold like hotcakes.'

Hank also had no regrets about the change of personnel. 'Brian was a technically superior drummer and a great listener. He doesn't just *play*. He picks things up and cracks it. He has a very good musical brain.'

*

During a January '61 show at the Cavern Club in Liverpool, while the group had been playing 'Shazam', Jet had literally fallen off the stage. Fortunately for him, the Cavern had a rather low stage, but he still needed Hank to help him back up.

'We were told the Beatles were in the audience,' said Tony. 'We were told they were the big group in Liverpool, but it didn't mean anything to us. We went on, in this dingy little club. Jet locked himself in the loo with a bottle of brandy and wouldn't let us in. We had to break the door down. He was absolutely plastered. The first number was "Shazam" ... I could see him swaying in front of me and I was thinking, *He's never going to make it through this set*. Me and Hank and Bruce are looking at each other and everyone's shitting themselves, because there was a high degree of professionalism. It wasn't funny.

'You put your balls on the line every time you go on stage, because you haven't got a singer in front of you to take the rap. You want to put on the best show you can and there's this brandy-sodden drunk in front of me! Halfway through "Shazam" – bang! – he fell into the front row. It was just a tiny club like the 2i's, so he didn't fall into the pit. I wish he had! Broken his bloody neck! But we got him back on his feet and there was feedback, wires everywhere, it was chaos. "Oh shit! What do we do now?" So Bruce got on the microphone and said, "I'm awfully sorry ladies and gentlemen, but Jet has been unwell today." And someone at the back shouted, "Unwell? Fuck off, he's pissed!" You couldn't fool them ... Mind you, it was totally obvious.'

One of the first questions that Peter Gormley asked Brian Bennett on the drive up to Birmingham, hours after he'd agreed to become a Shadow, was whether he enjoyed a drink. 'Now and then,' Brian replied. 'Well,' murmured Gormley, 'don't get involved with Jet.'

Arriving in Blackpool for the resumption of their summer season, the first thing Jet did was to ask Brian if he fancied a drink.

Why not, said Brian, how about that pub over there on the seafront? Oh no, said Jet. Bruce might see them. So, instead, Jet led Brian into a nearby public convenience. They went into a cubicle. Brian wasn't sure what was coming next. Then Jet pulled out a couple of cans of beer. 'Bruce hates drink,' he laughed. 'He goes potty if he thinks I've had too much.'

Jet was more than familiar with the sergeant major routine by now. He'd have 'a few brown ales', get the treatment from Bruce and then go on stage in an understandably dark mood. As soon as Bruce looked away, Jet would turn to Brian on the drums and mouth 'the fucking bastard!', to which the new boy would shake his head and roll his eyes. There wasn't much more he could do.

'I couldn't afford to take sides, but it got pretty awkward sometimes, especially when rows would end with Jet in tears.'

Jet could pinpoint the start of his drinking problem. He blamed it on the breakdown of his marriage.

*

Back in April 1959, Cliff Richard had met a girl from Hounslow called Carol Costa, who in his eyes was Middlesex's answer to Brigitte Bardot. She had gone to see the Drifters when they played at the Chiswick Empire. The problem for Cliff was that Jet Harris had met Carol on the same night and the pair had quickly become an item. Before too long, Jet and Carol were living together in the spare room of Cliff's Marylebone flat. Cliff still had feelings for Carol, feelings that seemed to be mutual. They held hands and talked in a serious teenage manner whenever Jet wasn't there. They could, at least, have got a decent lyric out of this love triangle, but Jet seemed oblivious to what was going on behind his back.

Jet and Carol married just two months after they'd first met and that seemed to put an end to the matter. Cliff was happy for the couple, doubly so when Carol gave birth to baby Ricky in April 1960. But Jet and Carol would argue and, living in such close proximity, Cliff felt torn between social convention, stabbing his mate in the back and a genuine concern for Carol's welfare.

Cliff had also met Delia Wicks at the Palladium shows in the spring of 1960, but even then he couldn't break it off with Carol completely. The couple would meet secretly, but not secretly enough. Jet found out but said nothing – Cliff was effectively his boss. He knew they were meeting up in friends' houses, hoping nobody would discover what was going on. Eventually, Cliff's parents found out about the affair, which was humiliating and shaming for them as well as him. Being berated by his dad for sleeping with his bandmate's wife? It was a real low. This was the boy who had been brought up with such perfect manners. It was so ethically wrong.

Blackpool was the beginning of the end. Among the fish and chip parlours, the penny-shucking machines on the pier and the guest houses that smelt of overcooked cabbage, here were the seeds of the downfall of Britain's biggest rock 'n' roll band. Outside, the bracing, salty air would be gulped down by visitors escaping the mills and factories for a week or two each year, people with early onset deafness as a by-product of their trade, much like the musicians they queued to see in Blackpool's ballrooms.

The Shadows were playing a summer season there – and Elvis Presley was in the top ten with 'The Girl of My Best Friend' – when Cliff decided he had to end the affair. Still, he couldn't face telling Carol that it was over and asked Tony Meehan if he could do the job for him. Tony said he'd do it, but only with Cliff standing nearby. Carol asked to speak to Cliff. Tony handed him the phone. Everybody was crying.

What on earth did this do for the group's morale, let alone Jet's marriage and his mental state? It's remarkable they stayed together.

'I was stood behind Cliff every night and I didn't want to lose my job,' said Jet in 2005. 'It was never ever mentioned, the affair. You know what it's like, I was the last to find out. Everybody around me knew. I mean, Hank and Bruce said "She's not the one for you, you know", which looking back now was rather nice of them. Doom stuff. It was front page on the bloomin' *News of the World*, all that shit.

'I mean, life's funny ... When people have a go at Cliff to me, I shout them down, you know? We was only kids when all that happened, we really didn't know what day it was. We could play, we were a mean band, a good band, but life-wise we didn't know nothing at that time. We were just starting to learn.'

'Cliff was vulnerable,' reckoned Bruce, 'and I believe Jet's wife probably seduced him. Jet has said that Cliff and Carol made love on several other occasions in a friend's house in London. Jet couldn't handle the pressure and turned to drink for solace and comfort.'

Tony never liked Carol, saying she was 'a very hard character ... she had her eyes set on Cliff. I was probably the first to come across her affair and all of us told Cliff to pack it in and leave them alone.

Carol's affair with Cliff only lasted about six months. Jet always liked to drink, but the drinking accelerated over Carol. Whatever the reasons, Jet had major problems.'

Bruce remembered how Jet could hold court in a pub, the raconteur, surrounded by half a dozen blokes. He also remembered how these sessions often ended violently. In the early '60s, Jet's bottle-blonde hair was seen by some as an indicator that he was gay. 'Many times I had to drag him out of a brawl,' said Bruce, 'because his mouth had been working overtime. "Go on then, call me a poof again and I'll smash your face in" was one of Jet's favourite phrases. Here we were, one of the biggest attractions in the country, almost brawling in public. It had to stop and I became obsessive about telling him to lay off the booze. I guess I picked on him a lot, but it was necessary. It got worse when Carol filed for divorce, three years after they were married.'

The whole situation was impossible. With no opportunity to take time off to cool their heads, Jet followed Tony out of the door just six months later. 'My drinking was getting worse and Bruce's nerves were making me nervous. If there was a show at six-thirty, Bruce used to be suited up and made-up and ready to go on at four-thirty. He's a perfectionist, you know, which we all try to be, but you just can't do everything perfect, it's impossible.' After coming off-stage at the *NME* Poll-Winners' Party at the Empire Pool in Wembley in April '62, Bruce turned and said, 'We don't really need you, Jet.' He walked out on the spot.

'My playing was all right. I was never falling about pissed, but I was topped up nicely, you know? I came off that stage … I'd had a few and I said "Fuck it, that's it, that's me, I'm leaving." It was something that was coming in me, but I suppose with a drink it made me get it out. I went home and I thought, *I'm gonna do something myself.*'

Cliff still had residual guilt about the situation, hanging over from his affair with Carol Costa, but he knew as well as the others that the group couldn't have gone on the way it was. And Jet knew it, too. The following week, Hank told *Melody Maker*: 'It won't alter the group one bit.'

*

In March '62, Cliff and the Shadows played at the Eton Manor club in Hackney Wick, east London. Eton Manor had been set up by the famous public school to appease their guilt and help the less well off in London's East End, providing a hall and playing fields; there was even an Eton Manor football club. Princess Margaret and the Earl of Snowdon attended the show. The princess told Cliff that she was going to see *The Young Ones* at the weekend; according to Brian, she was giving him the eye throughout the show. The Shadows played 'Apache' and received shrieks and shouts from the Eton Manor boys, as well as polite handclaps (and the occasional wink) from the royal couple.

So now they were mixing with royalty. The Geordie Boys had a decision to make.

In the late '40s, when she was a child star, Petula Clark had appeared on a BBC TV show called *Cabaret Cartoons*, on which Mancunian cartoonist Harry Rutherford drew his guests as they sang and then revealed his cartoon of them at the end of the song. You never got to find out what Rutherford thought of his guests' performance because he wasn't allowed to speak. The BBC thought that his strong Manchester accent might offend its more sensitive viewers, presumably none of whom lived in Lancashire.

Things weren't so different in the early '60s. Liverpool rocker Billy Fury wasn't the most extrovert of stars off stage, but he played up his shyness and barely did interviews as he assumed nobody from London would understand a word he was saying. It wasn't purely about class; working-class London accents were entirely acceptable as Tommy Steele and Tony Newley had shown, which is why Jet Harris, Tony Meehan and Brian Bennett felt no need to moderate their voices in interviews. It was more that regional accents – from anywhere north of Watford – just weren't present on TV, or radio, or at the cinema. Films like the 1955 Diana Dors vehicle *Value For Money*, shot in Batley, West Yorkshire, had RADA-trained actors like John Gregson affecting 'northern' accents (as well as playing tight-fisted Yorkshire stereotypes) that would have been understandable to people in the south but sounded entirely phony to anyone from Leeds, Bradford or Sheffield.

Now they were major names in their own right, Hank Marvin and Bruce Welch made a decision to tone down their Geordie accents. Publicly, they would mimic Cliff's neither-hither-nor-thither, slightly mid-Atlantic voice, a classless thing that got him past BBC censorship. At least it wasn't the dreaded, BBC-approved 'received pronunciation' – or RP – that made everyone sound like a minor royal. This was a modern variant on RP, though, and it would be used by TV personalities of the '60s like David Frost and Cathy McGowan. The Shadows were becoming part of the new establishment.

*

The former Drifter Ian Samwell had been kicking his heels ever since 'Gee Whizz It's You' had dropped off the chart in 1960, drifting away from the Shadows. Then, in 1962, he landed an interesting gig at the Lyceum, off the Strand. 'They were looking for someone to spin records for a lunch-hour crowd. The house electrician had been playing the records until then. I had never played records as a DJ before. I was broke, so I agreed to do it.' It became a regular gig: every Tuesday lunchtime, and then every Sunday too.

And so, Ian Samwell had become the first club DJ in Britain, although no one would acknowledge this as a fact until decades later.

As a songwriter with the then-Drifters, Samwell had been to New York in 1959 'because I was under contract to a subsidiary of an American company, Hill and Range Music'. Incredibly, he managed to convince the Isley Brothers – fresh off their success with 'Shout' – to record his 'Say You Love Me Too', claiming it was 'possibly the first R&B song by an English writer to be recorded in America'. While he was there, Samwell bought, or was given, a ton of records, which he brought back to London. 'Times were changing, rock 'n' roll was over and pop was the big thing. Most of it didn't appeal much to me and I turned to rhythm and blues – Jackie Wilson, the Coasters, the Isley Brothers.'

He started DJ'ing at the Lyceum in 1962. Mecca, the venue's owner, made a life-size cut-out photo of Samwell and billed him as 'London's number one DJ'. 'The Lyceum's record collection was pretty pathetic, so I'd started to bring my own records. I played a lot of stuff you couldn't hear on the BBC, mostly rhythm and blues because it was hip and great to dance to.' He then set up a 'disco' night at Greenwich Town Hall, which was primitive but hugely popular. There were two record players with built-in speakers placed next to each other on a table on stage, with a house microphone in front of each one, and the music was played over the Tannoy. Such was the lot of the pioneer. After a while, Samwell started to invite acts down that he was friendly with to pull the crowds and give away promo copies of their latest singles: Kenny Lynch, Carol Deene, Jet Harris...

By 1964, Samwell was heading to New York twice a year to pick up new singles like Jackie Ross's 'Selfish One' and early Stax and Motown, before any of it was issued in Britain. 'There was a tiny basement on, I think, Lisle Street not far from the Flamingo. It sold illegal imports and was only open for about two hours at lunchtime, one or two days a week. You really had to be in the know to find your way to it. Everything they had was American rhythm and blues. It was all very secretive and exciting.'

His favourite slot remained the Flamingo on Wardour Street, also one of Jet Harris's preferred haunts, where 'the audience were either very hip or West Indian and I played bluebeat, which became ska. I produced Georgie Fame's first record there, an album called *Rhythm and Blues at the Flamingo*.' This would be Samwell's entry to another world: he also produced Fame's second album, then co-wrote the Small Faces' debut single 'Whatcha Gonna Do About It' and 'He's Got Something' for Dusty Springfield, before going on to produce albums for Linda Lewis, America and Prelude. By the late '70s, he was living in California. In a post-Shadows world, Ian Samwell did all right.

*

Jack Good was the white-cloaked philosopher, the original benefactor of British rock 'n' roll, the inventor of pop TV. Jet Harris had always been his favourite Shadow. One day in 1962, while the two of them were walking down Charing Cross Road, they saw a new future for Jet right there in a shop window – a six-string bass.

'Jack was with me. He said, "This is going to be something else!". I'd sat on my arse after leaving the Shadows, and Jack says "Come on, it's about time you did something", and I said "Ohhh… all right." And that's when I did "Bésame Mucho".'

Jet's first solo single would be produced by Good, who had a production deal with Decca which had already given him a number one with Lord Rockingham's XI's 'Hoots Mon'. Good was always image-minded; he had made Cliff what he was and he now intended to make Jet into a solo star. On the B-side was a cover of Ronnie Love's 'Chills and Fever', which years later would turn up on the soundtrack to Netflix drama *The End of the Fucking World*. Good told Jet he sang like a male Ann-Margret; Jet didn't have a clue what he meant.

'He was always quoting things about me, what was it? "Mean, moody and magnificent," he'd say. "The man who looked like Adam Faith before Adam Faith". That was another quote.'

'Bésame Mucho' did okay, but couldn't climb into the top twenty. 'Main Title Theme' from *The Man With the Golden Arm*, a mid-'50s Frank Sinatra movie about heroin addiction, was another matter. With Jet backed up by the full force of Charles Blackwell's brassy arrangement, it was vulpine, a prowling urban melodrama, Soho writ large and one of the coolest British records of the era. Decca issued the single, wisely, as 'Main Title Theme' so that the BBC wouldn't get upset about the allusion to drugs. It went to number twelve in September '62. The same month, Jet released an EP which included a beautifully deadpan cover of Johnny O'Keefe's Australian rocker 'Real Wild Child'. The EP's giddy Tony Barrow sleevenote described 'Bésame Mucho' as 'a compelling, thick-throated instrumental showcase for this man's unusually imaginative talents'. Barrow conveyed Jet's magnetism well. Jack Good, he wrote, had put together an EP of 'two instrumental tracks backed by two tracks designed to expose at greater length the curiously haunting singing and speaking voices of Jet Harris. There is much more here than string-twanging and lyric delivery. There is emotional strength and plaintive depth. Jet digs deeper than the cold, black print of his sheet music when he attends a recording session. And he comes up with searing sounds which seemed to be activated in the very soul of him.'

Jet's sound was 'unique and thrilling', said Barrow; both 'Real Wild Child' and 'Rave' were hard-headed, anticipating the R&B boom that was still two years away.

For live shows, after mulling over Jet Harris and the Nitesounds, he settled on the Jet Blacks for the name of his new band – Barry Lovegrove (guitar), Terry Webster (bass), Dave Quincy (tenor sax), Glenn Hughes (baritone sax) and sixteen-year-old Mick Underwood (drums). They spent October '62 touring Britain with Little Richard and Sam Cooke, with the Beatles added to their Liverpool Empire show. By now separated from Carole, Jet was back at his parents in

Willesden, with Wakefield-raised bassist Webster – fresh-faced and new to London – to keep him company.

The Jet Blacks would be filmed for a pop-exploitation movie called *Just For Fun,* playing the Dick Rowe-produced 'Man From Nowhere', shot in a deep-noir style, the star of the show looking icy and poised in almost complete darkness. Meanwhile, over in Italy, the enigmatic title and the subsonic sound of Jet's six-string bass were likely an influence on Sergio Leone and Ennio Morricone's earliest spaghetti western work.

*

In the *NME*, Bert Weedon had an interesting angle. 'At the risk of extensive criticism, I stick my neck out and say the Shadows should split up if they have a keen eye on their future. The worst thing in show business is to get a tag. You become known by one section of the public only. Soon I am sure Jet Harris will become a big star in his own right, and people who watch television and go to the pictures will have his name on their tongues – but they wouldn't have if he had stayed a Shadow.'

'Main Title Theme' came out in Britain while the Shadows were away in Greece making their next movie, *Summer Holiday*. By the time it reached the cinemas, the ominous clouds seemed to have passed.

7

EDGE OF REALITY

Their just-appointed manager Brian Epstein thought his new charges might learn a little in stagecraft from Britain's biggest band, so he took the Beatles to see the Shadows at the Liverpool Empire in 1962.

'Wonderful Land' was still at number one as the Shadows began their week in variety at the Empire. They shared the stage with Chinese acrobats the Pan Yue Jen Troupe, former skiffle hero Chas McDevitt, yodeller Frank Ifield – on the verge of a remarkable, if short-lived, run of hits – and Stoke belter Jackie Trent. The set started with 'Midnight' and they played 'FBI', but – intriguingly – not 'Apache'. Bruce was ill, so Peter Carter from Emile Ford and the Checkmates replaced him. The first night would only be new boy Licorice Locking's second gig as the Shadows' bassist, meaning that only Hank remained from the line-up of just six months earlier.

Being Liverpool royalty – even if the London record companies still weren't interested – the Beatles looked down from a theatre box. They must have been wondering if this was the last chance they might get to see the Shadows. They might have been wondering if Hank and three new faces even constituted the Shadows.

*

If the Shadows had been looking for the anti-Jet, they had found him in Brian 'Licorice' Locking. Out walked glowering Jet, in strode beaming boy Brian. One had the hooded eyes, the other had the milk-white skin. Their names both suggested darkness, but only one of them ever looked like they ventured out at night. Licorice gave the general impression that he was in bed with the *Beano* by eight. He was the Milky Bar Kid of British rock 'n' roll. Naturally, he would go on to become one of the most disruptive presences of the Shadows' entire career.

The boy Locking had grown up in Grantham in Lincolnshire, a railway town where the most exciting thing to do was get on a train heading north or south. You made your own fun and Locking was a joker. 'How are you today, Brian?' asked his teacher on his first day at school. 'I'm fine today,' he chirruped, 'but do you know what I did yesterday? I broke my neck.'

In the early '50s, he joined the Grantham Town Band, first playing euphonium, then flugelhorn. Aged fifteen, he had started playing his kid sister's harmonica and would put on shows for his friends in his mum's washhouse with a curtain drawn across the door. He graduated to playing in a harmonica duo with his mate Roy Clarke at the Granada cinema in Grantham every Sunday night. They specialised in Scottish reels. 'We were, without a doubt, the ambassadors of music for our Lincolnshire town,' Locking was keen to say. He left school in 1953 to work on the railways, never thinking he'd ever have another source of employment in Grantham.

Another local boy, Roy Taylor, was tall, square-jawed and strikingly handsome – he got his own mouth organ, joined in and the trio became the Harmonica Vagabonds, with 'HV' sewed in sequins onto their shirts. Just as the last sequin was stitched on, 'Rock Island Line' came on the wireless and suddenly all bets were off. Locking switched to tea-chest bass, a real one with a big stamp on it that read 'East India Company 2/6'. With Roy Taylor on vocals, the Vagabond Skiffle Group quickly became as popular as tulips in Lincolnshire market towns. The boy Locking earned his nickname when he drove his bandmates nuts by playing a plastic clarinet all the way to a date in Skegness. 'Put that licorice stick *away*!' yelled Taylor.

They became popular because they were good. Every town, even Grantham, had dozens of skiffle operatives in 1956, but the Harmonica Vagabonds were quality enough to enter the World Skiffle Championship. Having got through to the final at Streatham Locarno in south London, they had to settle for second place, but had earned themselves £150. They slept the night in the van, with Locking playing lullabies on his plastic clarinet. They woke at dawn and made the most of their first trip to the capital; the second-best skiffle band in the whole country recorded four songs in a booth at HMV on Oxford Street, including 'Be-Bop-a-Lula' and 'Money Honey', a decent indication of where skiffle – even in the provinces – was heading.

The next weekend, wearing bootlace ties and Ted threads, the Vagabonds ventured into Soho, to Old Compton Street and the 2i's.

Full of vim and teenage vigour, they climbed onto the stage and were quickly offered a residency. The Harmonica Vagabonds gave up their day jobs. The next time they played there, Larry Parnes spotted tall, handsome Roy Taylor – and the group fell apart. He was rechristened Vince Eager and a lifetime of being a footnote in the stories of Billy Fury and Marty Wilde opened up ahead of him.

*

Licorice stayed in London, his milk-white complexion never in danger as he spent most of 1958 hiding in the 2i's cellar. There would always be the odd job for a bassist as good as he was. First up, he joined Terry Dene for an eight-week tour of Scotland, with headliner Billy Fury. Every last inch of the central belt was covered. In Largs, he met drummer Brian Bennett who was with another support act called the Red Peppers, billed as 'Britain's brightest novelty group'. Brian and Brian decided to meet up again in London at the 2i's. They became firm friends, and a strong rhythm section. Neither looked like a star – no one was ever going to re-christen them Vince Eager or Johnny Gentle or Horace Hydrogen – but they lurked behind singers who most definitely did. First up, the two Brians joined the one-time Terry Nelhams, now Adam Faith, and his Worried Men. Then they joined up with Brian number three: Brian Holden from the aviation fuel depot out west called Hounslow. He had just spent a few years in the States – first in New Jersey, then in California – and when he returned to London, dressed head to toe in leather, he wasn't called Brian anymore.

Brian from Hounslow had become Vince Taylor from Hollywood. He may have struggled to hold a note but, oh, that tan! Post-war, bottle-green Britain hadn't seen skin that glowed quite like Vince Taylor's.

Guitarist Rick Hardy had also been in the Worried Men and met Vince Taylor soon after he had been pointed towards the 2i's by a friendly barman. 'Vince said they'd been living in Santa Monica, he somehow heard a Tommy Steele record and thought if this is rock 'n' roll in England, we'll take them by storm.'

He wasn't wrong. 'It was a bit magical,' said Brian Bennett. 'They were Americans, they dressed like Americans. It meant more if you were American. You were special. I remember this real suave-looking guy called Joe, the manager. Joe always looked extremely wealthy. He had the blue button-down shirt and a red tie and looked immaculate. Vince was very sharp, he had thick black hair, and straight white teeth and dressed expensively. They said that because Presley was so big in America there wasn't room for both of them.

'He had all the confidence, but I couldn't imagine him making it with that voice. I was the resident drummer down there, backing Licorice Locking and Tony Sheridan. We backed more or less anyone who turned up. That's how I met Vince. He came and got up on stage, had all the movements and all the girls loved it. But he couldn't sing in tune. He had no timing at all, so we had to nurse him into the beginning of a chorus.'

By October 1958, Taylor had finally settled on his backing group, essentially the best musicians left on the 2i's scene after the departure of the nascent Shadows, with whom he would start manoeuvres: Tony Sheridan on lead guitar, Tony Harvey on rhythm guitar, Licorice

Locking on bass and Brian Bennett on drums. That week they booked an audition for EMI and got a contract with Parlophone. Just a month later, their debut single was released – the raw 'Right Behind You Baby', originally recorded by Ray Smith on Sun Records. The following April, 'Pledging My Love', the old Johnny Ace weepie, became their second single, backed by Taylor's self-written 'Brand New Cadillac'. This time, Joe Moretti played the guitar, backed by Locking and Bennett with pianist Perry Ford. 'Brand New Cadillac' was supercharged rock 'n' roll, Gene Vincent's 'Race With the Devil' by way of a burn-up on the North Circular.

'Brand New Cadillac' was credited to Vince Taylor and the Playboys and, along with Cliff Richard's 'Move It', became one of the foundation stones of British rock 'n' roll. If Parlophone, or Jack Good, or anyone with the connections had flipped the single, Taylor's dreams of superstardom could have been realised in weeks. But the records weren't hits and Taylor was becoming increasingly unstable. 'It was a good band, but the chemistry wasn't right,' Brian Bennett told Kieron Tyler in the notes for Taylor's *Jet Black Leather Machine* compilation. 'Tony Sheridan and Vince Taylor were hard work because they both had egos and there were lots of rows. We had better offers somewhere else' – which is how Bennett and Locking hooked up with Marty Wilde.*

---

* Vince Taylor did become a major star in France, supporting the Shadows at the Paris Olympia in December '61 and causing riots the following year with his chain-swinging, leather-clad presence. Always game for anything that was being passed around, his fragile equilibrium was finally upended by LSD. David Bowie said he met Vince Taylor outside Charing Cross station in the mid-'60s; Taylor pulled out a magnifying glass, opened up a map, placed it on the pavement and calmly pointed out

They were all into jazz – Licorice, Brian and guitarists Big Jim Sullivan and Tony Belcher. Licorice wasn't really a rocker; he was into contemplative jazz. He bought all of the Poll Winners series of albums by the likes of Barney Kessel, Oscar Peterson and the Modern Jazz Quartet. When he toured with Eddie Cochran and Gene Vincent in 1960, alongside Brian Bennett and Joe Brown, Cochran said that he liked the rhythm section's sound but 'You guys swing it too much, there's not enough drive!' Then he gave them each a masterclass in how to play full-bore rock 'n' roll. Locking took notes: 'We were in absolute awe.'

Bennett and Locking then got a gig with Tommy Steele, as the rhythm section for Steele's Sunday night concerts. 'This involved us flying all over the country in a small eight-seater aircraft in rain, fog and storms, and having the time of our lives for an eight-week season.' While they were playing Great Yarmouth, Bennett suddenly joined the Shadows, leaving Locking as half, maybe less than half, of a great rhythm section. With panto season over, he spent a few weeks touring with Adam Faith, who was just back from Scotland after hunting for the Loch Ness monster in a truly rotten movie called *What a Whopper*. And then nothing.

Licorice wrote to his parents to say he was coming back to Grantham; the call of the rail, the lure of the signal box was strong. The 2i's contingent, that tight-knit clan, had either moved on to the

---

the sights where UFOs would land in Britain. Bowie later based Ziggy Stardust on Vince Taylor's rise and fall. In 1996, Bowie told the BBC's Alan Yentob that Taylor was 'out of his gourd. Totally flipped. He came out on stage in white robes and said he was Jesus Christ. It was the end of Vince, his career and everything else.'

Palladium and Eamonn Andrews, or they'd gone back to their trade. Johnny Gentle became a joiner. Vince Eager worked on cruise ships as a 'cruise director'. Terry Dene found religion, Dickie Pride found heroin. There were worse fates than working on the trains.

And then the phone rang in the hallway of the Lockings' Grantham terrace. It was Brian Bennett to say Jet had left the Shadows. There was an audition the next day at Bennett's house in Winchmore Hill. Could he make it? Licorice would have joined without any incentive at all – hell, he was unemployed. He'd probably have joined a reformed Vipers Skiffle Group if they'd asked.

In April 1962, with 'Wonderful Land' still at number one, the unassuming Licorice Locking became a full-time Shadow.

*

Jet Harris had looked like a Shadow. He had named the Shadows. To many people, he was the Shadows. Jazz-cool Tony Meehan being replaced by everybody's mate, cheeky Brian Bennett, was one thing; Licorice Locking taking over from Jet Harris was something else.

The entire dynamic of the group shifted. Hank was now the single focus, backed by three players who were all 2i's-trained, the best in the country – I mean, two of them had played on 'Brand New Cadillac'! – but they had no image whatsoever. The new-look Shadows smiled in every photo, every last one. They looked like they worked in the local bakers. They looked like they could make a mean split tin, but Brian and Brian were really quite different to Jet and Tony, who had known where the action was. Hank aside, the Shadows – groundbreakers and heroes to a generation – now looked like any other instrumental group in the country. And by 1962, there were dozens of Fentones and Outlaws, Saints and Dakotas. They were almost as ten-a-penny as skiffle groups had been in 1957.

*

The public weren't as okay with Jet and Tony's departures as Hank might have first thought. For the next Shadows single, Hank bought a flamenco guitar specially for the occasion. He needn't have bothered.

'Guitar Tango' was a curious choice after the majesty of 'Wonderful Land'. The melody was strong; it was sent to them in the post, according to Bruce, by a pair of French songwriters who seem to have done little else, on the off chance the Shadows might record it. And they did, initially with Jet in April '62, but no one thought it sounded that hot. Hank had bought a Spanish guitar for the occasion, one which he later said he lent to George Harrison for the solo on the Beatles' 'And I Love Her'. They re-cut 'Guitar Tango' with Licorice on bass and full *Tommy the Toreador* brass fanfares. Norrie's string arrangement was rich and redolent of a particularly scorching day in Extremadura. Primarily, it worked as a showcase for Hank's incredible playing – he left no doubt that if Julian Bream ever decided to vacate his chair, Hank B. Marvin could be Britain's premier classical guitarist. What it had to do with rock 'n' roll, however, was a moot point. The flip side, 'What a Lovely Tune', gave no succour, a slight gag of a society couple's fumblings on the balcony set to a palm-court backing.

Maybe the Shadows didn't want to seem too reliant on Jerry Lordan; he surely had something more suitable up his sleeve. It was Licorice Locking's first appearance on a Shadows record, but the bass part came in a distant fourth to Hank and Bruce's matador stylings and some superb cymbal work from Brian Bennett on the verse. It would have made a strong album track, but given that they had some fences to mend with fans who thought of Jet and Tony as equal partners in the Shadows' saga, 'Guitar Tango' felt like a misstep.

In a letter to the *NME*, a fan called Keith Conroy called it 'shameful'. David Jacobs' eyebrows went into sad arcs on *Jukebox Jury*: 'I simply don't know what it's all about,' he sighed. Bruce said the group 'were furious ... one paper called it the worst record they've ever made. In truth, they were worried that the record didn't sound like the "safe" Shadows, which was exactly what we were trying to break away from.' The loyal Norrie Paramor had a right to reply in the *NME* and said, in his most headmasterly voice, that he thought 'Guitar Tango' had 'tremendous individuality and freshness'; it showed his boys to be more versatile than many realised. Maybe so.

It may also have seemed like they couldn't win, but then up popped Jet like a bad penny with his single that tore 'Guitar Tango' to pieces.

'Main Title Theme', from their former bassist, loomed over the holiday souvenir sound of 'Guitar Tango' like a thunder cloud.

Licorice, poor soul, didn't need this pointed out to him. 'To be honest – and this is absolutely true – I was always aware that Jet was a hard act to follow. We couldn't have been more different, could we? Totally different. I was always conscious that it was a bit of a tough task because of his image. I wasn't the blond, moody type. And he was so popular it was ridiculous. He was the kingpin for looks. I was a completely different kettle of fish. I knew he was a jazzer, and there's a lot of hidden talent there that's never come out.'

'Guitar Tango' made it to number four, eight places higher than 'Main Title Theme', but Jet knew which was the better record. He contemplated his future. Maybe he should reunite with Tony Meehan? They'd been the most influential and popular rhythm section in the country, after all.

*

The Shadows steadied the ship when director Sidney J. Furie asked them to provide the music for his courtroom drama *The Boys*. Atmospherically, it was a close cousin of *Never Let Go* and *Beat Girl,* hard-nosed British films from 1960 which had both been scored by John Barry. The boys in question were Dudley Sutton, Ronald Lacey, Tony Garnett and Jess Conrad, who had planned to rob a garage. Three Bennett/Marvin/Welch tunes for the movie were given impressively utilitarian titles: 'The Boys', 'The Girls' and 'Theme From *The Boys*'. They were released on an EP. 'The Boys' saw Licorice picking out the familiar 'FBI' bassline, as if to say 'Don't worry folks, "Guitar Tango" will *never* happen again.' Released as a stand-alone single in Australia, it went to number one. Neither 'The Boys' nor 'The Girls' evoked Ronald Lacey's frightening, beady-eyed meanness, but the main theme was melancholic and more suited to the film's downbeat storyline of petty crime and murder. *The Boys* EP did good business and Licorice was seemingly accepted as part of the gang.

The Shadows' second album, *Out of the Shadows*, appeared in October '62. Little on it bore comparison with the drama and aggression of the first album. It was altogether sweeter, as if 'Guitar Tango' had been a dry run. Only 'The Rumble' (not the Link Wray song) and 'Tales of a Raggy Tramline' had the fire of the debut, and both of them had been recorded before Jet left. Of the less edgy numbers, 'Spring is Nearly Here' had been written by Brian in the theatre pit at Great Yarmouth, with Bruce adding the middle eight; it was gorgeous, softer, but a proper new cinematic direction. The wistful, exotic 'Some Are Lonely' dated from December '61 and was written by Cliff.* There was softness again and some nocturnal, dreamy echo from Hank. 'Cosy' was another gem in the 'Sleepwalk' mould, while Brian's 'Little B' was a showcase for his power and precision. But – 'Little B' aside – the group would rarely revisit *Out of the Shadows* on stage.

*

As if solo Jet clad in black wasn't enough of a threat, in September 1962 another group appeared to shake the Shadows' place at the summit. Joe Meek had been producing singles in the style of the Shadows for years from his hand-built studio above a leather goods shop on a

---

* Cliff has always told people that he isn't a songwriter. He's put this down to his extra press and promotional duties on tour, while the rest of the Shadows would be back at the hotel kicking their heels and jamming new ideas. Had he been the guitarist rather than the frontman, there's enough evidence dotted around his catalogue that Cliff was a decent songwriter whose talent might have blossomed with encouragement. He just chooses never to talk about it – an interesting point of comparison is George Harrison, who was much more vocal about his lack of songwriting opportunities in the Beatles.

windswept, polluted stretch of Holloway Road in north London. Only this time he had put together a group called the Tornados, who were powered not by lead guitar but by keyboards, with his sidekick Geoff Goddard playing the melody of Meek's own 'Telstar' on the Clavioline. With an other-worldly grasp that Jerry Lordan would have been proud of, mystifying sound effects and what sounded for all the world like harmonising cosmonauts, 'Telstar' reached number one in Britain in October '62.

If 'Wonderful Land' had embodied hope for the future in a rebuilt, post-war Britain, then 'Telstar' upped the ante by encapsulating the dreams of the space age, the white heat of technology, impossibly wide intergalactic vistas.* The single was like science fiction coming to life, in your front room, on your record player. 'Telstar' also did what the Shadows had always dreamed of doing: the Tornados' earth-shaking, futuristic anthem-for-the-world went to number one in the US.

*

As usual, there was no white Christmas in Britain in 1962, just a very foggy one. But the snow started to fall on Boxing Day and it did not relent. It was so heavy in the final week of 1962 that Big Ben rang in 1963 ten minutes late, with snow weighing down the hands of the clock.

* The Shadows would go on to record a rather plinky-plonky version of their own in 1981, with a pre-set drum pattern, which only served to emphasise the power of the Tornados' original.

January 1963 would be the coldest month of the entire century. People couldn't wait for February to roll around, but that then brought gale-force winds which created snow drifts twenty feet high. With football matches postponed for weeks on end, and their income shrunk to zero, Halifax Town made the most of it and converted their pitch into an ice rink. No football, no horse racing, no milk deliveries – the freshly frozen country had to get used to drinking black tea and making its own fun.

Anyone who did make it down the icy streets to the cinemas or the record shops were presented with posters of Cliff Richard, arms outstretched, eyes closed, with an expression that suggested he'd either just had a religious awakening or he was soaking up the sun rays and loving it. Behind him, we could see the Acropolis. 'THE "YOUNG ONES" HAVE GONE ABROAD!' read the poster and, in January 1963, everybody wanted a slice of that cake. Before the film was released, there was a taster single, a double A-side, one side jaunty and one a ballad, both by Cliff and the Shadows. It went to number one in the second week of release, dislodging 'Lovesick Blues' by Peter Gormley's other charge, Frank Ifield.

'The Next Time' was a country-flavoured ballad, structurally similar to Perry Como's '50s hit 'Idle Gossip' (which Cliff had already covered), but made comfortably 1962 by the Shadows' empathetic backing: brushes for Brian and a gentle strum from Bruce. Cliff's vocal performance was warm, regretful and perfectly pitched, and sat on top of Hank's upfront piano line – a demo version shows how Hank had initially tried the song with a 'Travellin' Light'-style mooning guitar, but by the time the single came out, 'The Next Time' had his fiercely compressed block piano chords, possibly Joe Meek-influenced – Nashville-via-Holloway Road.

Flip the single over and you got 'Bachelor Boy', a Richard/Welch co-write that would quickly become another enduring nickname for 'the Peter Pan of Pop', until at least the late '80s. 'Son, you'll be a be a bachelor boy, and that's the way to stay': did Cliff's dad really give him advice along those lines? Almost certainly not, but it was his passing in 1961 that had made Cliff reassess his role as a professional entertainer and his concern for his public image. The song would nag at Bruce for years, too; he knew he would have to face jibes for his line about '*a* wife and *a* child' until his dying day. The song would later become a possibly unwitting inspiration for the chorus of the Beatles' 'You've Got to Hide Your Love Away'.

Also at the cinemas during the frozen start to 1963 was *It's All Happening*, in which Tommy Steele – as Billy Bowles – played the hard-working, unrewarded assistant to A&R man Max Catlin (Michael Medwin) at KLO Records. All of the acts in the movie – second-stringers like Danny Williams, Marion Ryan and Carol Deene, plus a past-his-prime Russ Conway – were EMI acts. The studio in which we saw John Barry conducting a session bore a strong resemblance to one at Abbey Road and the modern offices had the sleek sheen of Norrie Paramor's workspace in Manchester Square. But if KLO was a barely disguised EMI (who released the soundtrack on Columbia), the film painted a rather grubby picture.

The surprisingly close-to-the-bone script was by Leigh Vance, who had written the screenplay for *The Frightened City* and would end up in Hollywood, writing for *Mission: Impossible*, *Cannon* and *Hart to Hart*.

Vance's A&R men at KLO were all married and having affairs with their secretaries, who were initially misled about their respective boss's marital status. 'They are always married,' deadpans Max Catlin's secretary Delia, played with cold resignation by Jean Harvey. 'Sometimes it lies low, out of sight, like an infection. But dig deep enough and you'll find some pudding-faced little number in Hatch End who got her hooks into him in kindergarten.'

To get a deal through with a nonagenarian financier called Lord Sweatstone, Catlin puts on a private show of 'London's sexiest singer, Sonia Delahey' singing 'Call Me Kitten You Big Cat You' (which, sadly, we don't get to hear). The sexism is intentionally dreadful and down-trodden working-class Billy Bowles only breaks free by putting on a big climactic charity show, thus earning himself both the hand of his girl – Angela Douglas – and a record contract away from KLO.

The roots of *It's All Happening*'s turbulence would have been clear to anyone working at EMI.

Parlophone's George Martin had never hidden his mild revulsion with Norrie Paramor's willingness to insert his own songs into his artists' repertoires. This was a common practice: Columbia's Norman Newell did the same, as did John Schroeder, writing Helen Shapiro's brace of number ones 'You Don't Know' and 'Walking Back to Happiness'. Schroeder, Paramor and Newell were all more than competent songwriters – nobody was really questioning the quality of 'The Frightened City' – but it was Paramor's use of pseudonyms to hide his prolific output from his bosses that Martin thought unethical. 'My Feet Hit the Ground', the flip side of Cliff's 'High Class Baby', was co-penned by Ian Samwell and 'Joseph Seener'; Craig Douglas's 'Riddle Of Love' by 'Phil Silversteed'; and Eddie Calvert's 'Montparnasse' by 'Sidney Norman'. All of them were Norrie. There was a back note of bitterness when George Martin snipped 'If you have an artist like Cliff, once you've got him up there, all you've got to do was find a reasonably good song and give it to him and you've got a second hit.'

Martin and Paramor were paid roughly the same by EMI, around £3,000 per annum, but the former was living in a small flat within walking distance of Manchester Square, having an affair with his secretary, separated from his wife and two kids. Happily married Norrie, on the other hand, was out in the fanciest part of town. And in an era when the car you drove said a lot about your status, Paramor had a brand-new Jaguar, while cash-strapped Martin drove a second-hand Mini.

At the start of 1962, George Martin's roster at Parlophone was made up of what Mark Lewisohn described as 'dissidents, madcaps, fools, wizards, fine singers and talented musicians'. He had former Goons Peter Sellers and Spike Milligan, comedian Charlie Drake, novelty revivalists the Temperance Seven, Flanders and Swann, Bernard Cribbins and even the BBC Radiophonic Workshop on a remarkable single Martin produced with them called 'Waltz in Orbit', released under the name Ray Cathode. Martin upset his bosses in 1962 by preciously insisting that a Bernard Cribbins album, rather than being recorded in time to cash in on the success of hit singles 'Hole in the Ground' and 'Right Said Fred', 'must be allowed to blossom of its own accord like a rare desert flower'.

In March 1962, George Martin was collared by David Frost, then a twenty-two-year-old TV researcher. Frost paid for lunch, asked some questions about the mechanisms of EMI and received Martin's unfiltered thoughts on Norrie Paramor. A few months later, when Frost was one of the stars of the new satirical TV show *That Was the Week That Was*, he declared to the nation that 'Norrie is an ordinary man writing ordinary tunes with ordinary words. During the last ten years, Norrie Paramor has used all his power and all his influence, and made everything ordinary.'

On the big screen, though, it seemed to be Paramor's Parlophone rival who was getting it in the neck. Luckily for George Martin, *It's All Happening* was a flop compared to the new Cliff Richard movie.

*

The storyline of *Summer Holiday* was more far-fetched but much more fun than *It's All Happening*. And it seemed even more far-fetched and idyllic in iced-up Britain than its creators might have intended. The title song felt like it had always existed, like 'Happy Birthday' or 'White Christmas', and came to Bruce and Brian in a matter of moments, with the two effectively finishing each other's lines. They must have been delighted. The new Shads line-up got to play three songs on their own in a mocked-up Paris club; Cliff fell in love with a cross-dressing stowaway;* there were controlling showbiz parents; and there were some interminable scenes with Ron Moody and his mime troupe. But, overall, it was genuinely uplifting and the snowbound country fell for it.

---

* This was elfin actress Lauri Peters, who had just married actor Jon Voight.

The opening scene was a masterstroke: a brass band played the title song on Bognor Regis beach in the monochrome rain. This was a post-war Britain that everyone was used to, still just eight years past the end of rationing. Then, everything turned to colour as Cliff drove a red Routemaster bus into Aldenham bus depot and shouted 'I'VE GOT IT!' He may as well have shouted 'WE'VE DONE IT!'. They'd melted the snow. They'd cancelled the rain. At least for the next two hours.

Although there were choreographed scenes and no one gets to actually kiss, the songs and routines in *Summer Holiday* were mostly hipper and more teenage than the Hollywood musical knock-offs of *The Young Ones* and, while it isn't 'high '60s' in the way 'Get Off of My Cloud' or *Alfie* is, *Summer Holiday* feels identifiably 'Britain in the '60s'. The sands may have been shifting under their feet, but during the big freeze, Cliff and the Shadows absolutely bossed British pop culture. For week after week, *Summer Holiday* and its accompanying hits – three number-one singles – were unavoidable.

The one souvenir you could take with you from seeing a movie was the soundtrack album. And, if you couldn't afford the whole album, a single. The album reached number one on February 1963 and stayed there for fourteen weeks. 'The Next Time', backed with 'Bachelor Boy', went to the top on 3 January, at the end of the first week of heavy snow, and the Shadows – or permutations of the Shadows – would remain at number one until 11 April. There was a three-week break for 'The Wayward Wind' by Frank Ifield, but then even he was their friend and management stablemate. Behind his desk, Peter Gormley must have felt like he was sitting on a solid-gold chair.

The film included one peculiar track. 'Really Waltzing' wasn't a great song, but it provided an intriguing, meta comment on Cliff and the Shadows, as if the forces just around the corner had somehow made them turn self-reflective. Sat around in Greece, waiting for Una Stubbs to come out of make-up, they could look back at 'Living Doll', or at pantomimes in Stockton, and somehow see them in context. 'I know this kind of music makes me sick and you sick … still, I'm aware,' sang Cliff to Laurie Peters, no longer dressed as an urchin boy. Cliff Richard was always going to be happier at number one with a song he didn't like than at number sixteen with a song he did. He was aware, all right. The Shadows, now rid of their art-school element, shadowed his thinking.

*

'Dance On!' was released as the Shadows' twelfth single in December '62, just as the public's anticipation for *Summer Holiday* hit a high. Could the fanbase take even more Shadows product? It could. The tune was written by the Avons, who had enjoyed their own hit single in 1960 with the grisly 'Seven Little Girls Sitting in the Back Seat'. They sent their vocal version of 'Dance On!' around as a demo, but Bruce thought it would make a better instrumental.

He was right. It worked like clockwork. But was that what they wanted? The criticism of 'Guitar Tango' had stung them and brought out Hank and Bruce's conservative side; 'Dance On!' sounded a little too much like the Shadows on autopilot. Hank's ear-catching riff on the intro sounded like the ignition turning in a Norton Dominator, then the bike revving up – but it promised a lot more adventure than 'Dance On!' went on to provide. Maybe it was hamstrung by its title, excised from the original lyric,* which made you realise how much power and invention those early Shadows titles had. There was no frightened city beyond the walls of this dancehall, no issue that Cliff and the Shads couldn't resolve by getting everyone to put on their dancing shoes. 'Dance On!' was fine. It was okay. It was just… there was no mystery to it.

The flip side was called 'All Day' and was written while the boys were hanging about, kicking their heels, during either the Yugoslavian or Greek scenes of *Summer Holiday*. The poor lambs had been sat around all day with nothing to do but soak up the sun, drink ice-cold continental beers, learn to play bouzoukis and write their next single. All day, for days on end. Pardon me while I take out my tiniest violin.

Their first single to appear on the new, black Columbia label with a large '45' on the right-hand side, 'Dance On!', gave them their fourth number one, dislodging Cliff's 'The Next Time'/'Bachelor Boy'. It was the second time the Shadows had knocked their guv'nor from the top spot and they would repeat the feat just a few weeks later. Hey, it was like 1960 all over again. They were on top of the world.

The only fly in the ointment for this Cliff/Shadows one-two seemed to be the record at number three, which would knock the docile 'Dance On!' from the top after a single week. It was called 'Diamonds'.

* Kathy Kirby would have a top-twenty hit with the vocal version a few months later.

*

After he had walked, or was sacked, Tony Meehan had turned to record production, hanging out occasionally with Joe Meek and learning from scratch under the auspices of Decca's Dick Rowe.

In November 1961, Decca had announced a 'root and branch' makeover of its pop singles A&R team: Rowe described it as 'a dynamic new policy' designed to catch trends as they broke and to 'increase Decca's success with singles by British artists'.

In the 3 February 1962 issue of *Disc*, Rowe was interviewed in a piece headlined 'Decca Get Ready For Big Pop Drive'. He sounded almost scientific in his prediction of where pop was heading. 'I think there are about five separate markets for discs. We talk about teenagers, but even that section is divided into three. Those between 12 and 14 are not romantically inclined, and like the thumping rock style best. Those between 14 and 18 are romantically minded and enjoyed the ballad style of people like Presley and Cliff Richard. Those between 18 and 22 go for artists like Sinatra, and people older than that have other tastes.'

Mike Smith, who had been Dick Rowe's assistant, was promoted to A&R man and was now able to make his own creative decisions. Given that Smith was just twenty-six years old and still lived at home, this was a genuine step out of the past for Decca. The second key member of the team, and the one who unsurprisingly took the headlines, was Tony Meehan. He was now both an A&R man *and* a record producer. He signed a singer called Louise Cordet, of exotic French heritage, who also happened to be the goddaughter of Prince Philip. Her debut single was 'I'm Just a Baby' – cute, catchy, ridiculously coy and written by Jerry Lordan – which reached the top twenty in the summer of '62.

One of Mike Smith's first discoveries was a Liverpool rock 'n' roll outfit, who he'd seen playing at the city's Cavern Club, called the Beatles.*

Decca Studios on Broadhurst Gardens in West Hampstead was an imposing red-brick building that had once served as the town hall. On New Year's Day 1962, the Beatles arrived there to record and audition, freezing cold but bang on time. A sleepy Mike Smith turned up late; New Year's Day hangovers didn't officially exist, unless you were Scottish. For the rest of Britain, New Year's Day would remain just a regular working day until 1975.

Mike Smith loved the energy he had seen at the Cavern and wanted to give the Beatles what Decca referred to as a 'commercial test'. He was young, relatively inexperienced and – when he finally made it to West Hampstead – he had a swimming head. Not only that but his face was cut and bruised, medals from a car crash he'd survived on the edge of Basingstoke just before Christmas. But, hangover or no, he was solely in charge of this session. It didn't go well.

---

* Their manager, Brian Epstein, had gone to EMI first, where he had a friend on the inside called Ron White. At the next EMI A&R meeting, in December 1961, White played the Beatles' German-only single 'My Bonnie' 'to each of our Artistes managers' which, almost certainly, would have meant the four heads of A&R: Norrie Paramor, George Martin, Wally Ridley and Norman Newell. Citing EMI's roster, which apparently had 'sufficient groups of this type at present', the Beatles were rejected. EMI's official line, from December '63 onwards, was that only the middle-of-the-road men Newell and Ridley had been there, most likely a smokescreen so that Norrie Paramor and George Martin weren't tarnished by having turned down the Beatles.

A few days later, Smith was told by Dick Rowe that he could only choose one of the two groups he had recently auditioned – the other was a group from Essex called Brian Poole and the Tremeloes. History has judged Rowe and Smith harshly, but the Tremeloes were a wise enough signing. They were an adaptable instrumental band and, living in Dagenham rather than 200 miles north of London, they would quickly be used in Decca's studios to provide backing on records by Tommy Steele, the Vernons Girls, Lynn Cornell and Jet Harris.

The Beatles audition, or commercial test recording, may not have worked out for whatever reason, but Dick Rowe was a reasonable man and broached a compromise with Brian Epstein. For a relatively small fee, say £100, his A&R man-cum-producer Tony Meehan could privately record the Beatles' first UK single and Decca would then release it for them. After all, Rowe himself had spotted the twelve- to fourteen-year-old market's appetite for their 'thumping rock style beat'. With all his experience, Meehan was still only eighteen and Rowe knew that he understood teenagers.

When Meehan was later interviewed by Beatles chronicler Mark Lewisohn, he recalled what Rowe had told him. '"There's a chap here I'd like you to meet. I know you're busy but can you fit him in? He's a very, very interesting man and he's got another one of these groups." That's exactly what he said – "another one of these groups". Dick seemed more interested in Brian Epstein than the Beatles, for some strange reason.

'I just said, as any professional person would do in the middle of their work, "Look, I'm busy, contact me later and I'll be available." That's all that happened. Dick never told me anything about them and

I never discussed them with Brian [Epstein]... It was just a complete mess, as things generally are – a dreadful corporate blunder.'

On 10 February, Epstein dictated his reply to Decca: 'Whilst I appreciate the offer of Mr. Meehan's services, I have now decided not to accept. The principal reason for this change of mind is that since I saw you last the group have received an offer of a recording contract from another company.' In truth, they hadn't. Lewisohn's research turned up an itemised invoice sent to Brian Epstein by his lawyer on 15 February. It read 'Perusing Decca Agreement', which suggested Epstein had given the notion of Tony Meehan producing the first Beatles single a fair bit of thought. It's a nourishing thought that Tony got so close to producing the Beatles' first UK single. Maybe he'd have chosen 'Bésame Mucho', which they'd played at their audition, and which Jet would coincidentally record as his Decca debut six months later.

'Tony Meehan was really cocky,' George Harrison would tell the *NME* in 1977. 'He was the star and he decided he could choose who would be on the label or not.' This would have been Tony Meehan's job at Decca to be fair, but in any case Meehan was fairly sure he'd never even met the Beatles at this time, and that George was confusing him with Mike Smith. No matter. Harrison would still be fuming about Meehan's apparently cool reaction to the Beatles' Decca audition when interviewed again in 1992: 'He was this... *kid*!'

*

In late '62, the inevitable happened. Tony Meehan teamed up with Jet Harris once again. He had already played drums on Jet's recordings;

now that he was in the producer's chair, here was a chance to show Hank and Bruce the brave new world he'd envisaged for the Shads. Straight away, he came up with the ultra-modern production on Jerry Lordan's 'Diamonds', a number one in February '63, which featured eerie wordless voices, mariachi brass, an avalanche of a drum solo and Jet's bottomless six-string bass sound.* The pretty acoustic counter-melody on acoustic guitar was played by a teenage Jimmy Page on his very first session. 'Diamonds' strode up the charts with a swagger. It was a wonderful single with complete authority. Jet and Tony liked their lamb chops, the same as Hank and Bruce, but you could tell from 'Diamonds' that Jet and Tony preferred the pan hotter and their meat a little bloodier.

'Dance On!' sounded like an underthought demo by comparison. Unlike 'Bésame Mucho' and 'Main Title Theme', 'Diamonds' was a definite extension of the Shadows' sound, with their original mystery intact. The duo couldn't have made their point any better.

*

Jet Harris and Tony Meehan would have two more fast top-five hits in 1963 – 'Scarlett O'Hara', another Jerry Lordan composition that was almost as good as 'Diamonds', went to number two, while 'Applejack' would peak at number four after it was released in August.

---

* Jet didn't play his Fender VI on 'Diamonds', but a regular Gretsch Country Gentleman guitar tuned down two semitones.

April saw Jet and Tony on tour, topping the bill over Helen Shapiro, John Leyton and Mike Sarne, fresh from his novelty number one 'Come Outside'. They played no Shadows material. Instead, their sets comprised 'Main Title Theme', 'The Magnificent Seven', 'No Other Baby' and 'Frankie and Johnny', plus their own 'Diamonds', 'Footstomp' and 'Hully Gully'. In June '63, they released the *Jet & Tony* EP, combining the A- and B-sides of their first two singles. It spent five months on the chart. If you already owned the singles, then the sleeve was worth the money by itself. Jet and Tony were caught in monochrome, cool and unsmiling, looking more like refugees from the Gerry Mulligan Quartet than anyone who'd had anything to do with 'Dance On!'.

*

Back in November '61, just after Brian Bennett joined, the Shadows had played the Olympia in Paris for the first time. 'That was an absolute highlight,' Brian remembered. 'It was pre-Beatles Paris in the early '60s, so we were the kings, walking through Montmartre and everybody would know who we were. I remember Oscar Peterson and Quincy Jones backstage, Ella Fitzgerald standing by the side of the stage going, *"Yeah!"* while I played [drum solo] 'Little B'. I couldn't believe it.'

Also backstage was comedian Jacques Tati, who asked them to write the title music for his next film. They did; he never called back. They hung on to it, titled it 'Foot Tapper' and it appeared – appropriately – in the Paris club scene in *Summer Holiday*. Extracted from the score and re-recorded with a proper ending, it became the Shadows' fifth number one in the spring of '63.

Not every moment was so golden. The group's wages were still a flat £50 a week, pretty good for your average Herbert but, if you included their singles with Cliff, 'Foot Tapper' had just given them – and EMI, and their management – their *twelfth* number one. It would also be their last.

Meanwhile, the group who Tony Meehan had been so close to recording a year earlier were fast becoming a phenomenon. *Summer Holiday* was replaced at the top of the album chart by the Beatles' debut *Please Please Me*. They had been signed by Parlophone and handed by EMI's L.G. Wood to George Martin as an act of punishment for taking his secretary to an official company event rather than his wife. The Beatles' first hit single, 'Love Me Do', had only been released six months earlier, but by May '63 they would be top of both the singles and album charts. The four band members balanced each other perfectly, in sound as well as personality, much as the Shadows had done in 1960.

*

With the Tornados, then Jet and Tony, and now the Beatles breathing down their necks, the Shadows turned once more to Jerry Lordan, who had kept possibly his most beautiful song for them tucked up his sleeve – 'Atlantis'. In some ways it was 'Wonderful Land' redux – a sparkling intro, a warm heart-tug of melancholy, with a similarly complex chord structure that wrong-footed you just as you thought you were coming to the chorus.

But it wasn't as clearly optimistic. It had nothing in common with 'Summer Holiday' and 'Foot Tapper''s sunny bonhomie. 'Atlantis' was about something mythical, something lost. As the mark of an era's end, it couldn't have been more perfect. Years later, Liverpool's Radio City listeners would vote it their favourite single of the '60s, bar none.

'Atlantis' peaked at number two, which would have given no one any immediate cause for concern. The Beatles were great – Cliff and the Shadows loved their records, and they were quite happy to pull up seats for them at the top table. But the record that kept 'Atlantis' from the top wasn't by the Beatles. 'I Like It' was Gerry and the Pacemakers' second number one of 1963. Like 'Please Please Me', it had been recorded at Abbey Road and, like 'Atlantis', it was released on the Columbia label. But it lacked the urgent thrill of 'Please Please Me' or the emotional depth of 'Atlantis'.

It was number one largely because Gerry and the Pacemakers were from Liverpool and 1963's kids had decided Liverpool beat groups were all they needed. Their older sisters could have Billy Fury and Cliff Richard; their older brothers could mourn Buddy Holly and mime guitar to the Shadows. These younger kids wanted the now sound of the Beatles, Pacemakers, Searchers, Swinging Blue Jeans, Fourmost and any other guitar/bass/drums outfit who were familiar with clubs like the Cavern, the Iron Door and the Blue Angel.

Number two in the chart – there were no alarm bells. But, following on from their last number one, 'Atlantis' would turn out to be the Shadows' final top-three single. More than even the departures of Jet and Tony, the deep aquatic sadness of 'Atlantis' signalled the end of the Shadows' golden age.

3

THEME FROM A FILLETED PLACE

The 1963 summer season on the Lancashire coast again caused issues for the group. Bruce was still having trouble tuning his guitar and it was becoming an obsession. The group were playing two shows every night, with an opening spot at 6.15 p.m. Bruce began arriving at three in the afternoon just to tune his guitar. The tension was getting too much for him – he began screaming at the rest of the group to be quiet while he was tuning up. His quest for perfection suggested obsessive compulsive issues. It wasn't just his guitar. Bruce worried that his suit wasn't pressed correctly, that his amplifier might pack up or that his microphone might not be switched on. He simply couldn't relax.

'It was an impossible situation,' said Brian. 'You couldn't clean your teeth or even clink a glass. His nerves were shattered by his mad fixation. I didn't know whether his obsession was due to the fact he wasn't a great solo player and felt a little inhibited by his own technique. Being a drummer, I wasn't too worried about it. Besides, once we'd been on stage for a couple of numbers, his guitar would have gone slightly out of tune anyway, but you could hardly detect it with everything else that was going on.'

To make matters worse, Licorice's punctuality was no better to Bruce than either Jet or Tony's. 'One evening he missed the start of the show completely and I told him in no uncertain terms to buck his ideas up and get to grips with himself. That was good coming from me, in my state.' It seemed that Licorice had been out walking the streets of Blackpool, knocking on doors, trying to interest people in the Jehovah's Witnesses. When they played in Preston, he again missed his call on the stage at the ABC theatre because he had been canvassing with copies of *Watchtower* in his back pocket. The group was already on stage by the time he got to the theatre.

That wasn't all that was driving agnostic Bruce spare; Licorice's proselytising had been going on within the group, when he was out of earshot. Coincidentally, Brian Bennett, though he never really mentioned it, had grown up with the Jehovah's Witnesses. His mother had become one during the war while her husband was away fighting and she had to bring up baby Brian on her own. He was an only child. His parents were only children. She met a Jehovah's Witness and found that it helped her. When Brian's dad came back, he wanted nothing to do with it. Young Brian went along with it, but as soon as he could duck out, he did.

Licorice found that a pliant Hank, though, was a ready convert to the cause.

Brian Bennett's son Warren explained how the Jehovah's Witnesses had some kind of sway over 'Licorice, Brian, Hank, Cliff's mum… Cliff tried it for a couple of weeks. Bruce can't stand anything to do with religion and would make a point of saying so. If Hank had to go to Kingdom Hall and couldn't work late, Bruce would say something like "Ah, God getting in the way of another fucking album!" That kind of thing. He hates anything to do with religion.' The friendship between Hank and Bruce would never be quite the same again.

*

Licorice Locking's style was functional. He was in the Shadows out of convenience, a friend of Brian Bennett's, and the amount of time he spent talking and thinking about religion was causing Bruce to contemplate his own future. Maybe he should have been more lenient with Jet. The thirsty bugger was now at number two in the chart with 'Scarlett O'Hara', another Tony Meehan collaboration and another Jerry Lordan song. Maybe the group had finally run its course? Maybe it was time he left? He was just twenty-one, but doctors convinced Bruce he would have a nervous breakdown if he stayed in the group.

Bruce decided to take a desk job, working in the Shadows' office. 'We're going to miss him very much as an integral part of the group,' a solemn Hank told the press, 'quite apart from our own personal feeling. However, we hope his departure will not affect the group's popularity. It'll be a big responsibility for me to be solely in charge of the team, but I can always phone the office for Bruce's advice.'

'It's going to be a terrible wrench for all of us after five years of close harmony,' said Cliff, 'but you can't argue with your health.' In the end, though, Bruce didn't have to visit the stationery cupboard, or have his name engraved in Stippolyte glass on the office door.

The call of Jehovah was strong. Licorice decided to stand down from the Shadows and Bruce – his mind seemingly cleansed of stress by Licorice's departure – changed his mind about leaving. It was late 1963.

*

Once again, the Shadows needed a new bassist. Initially they attempted to convince John Paul Jones, who was then playing with Jet Harris and Tony Meehan's backing group. He carried a cigarette holder, which Bruce wasn't sure fitted the image of the Shadows. Jones also understandably felt some degree of loyalty to current boss Meehan and would have felt like a cad leaving his current group for the drummer's old band. He did all right in the long term; in 1968, he joined Led Zeppelin.

Hank recalled how Bruce's trouble tuning his guitar didn't depart with Licorice Locking: 'He'd sit in front of the mirror – he reckoned you could tune up better in front of a mirror, don't ask me why. It got to the stage where he was throwing his guitar on the floor, he would walk out of the show and leave us to do it without him. It was just appalling, really. In hindsight, he should have gone the way of Tony Meehan. I should have had him shot! You'd just ended up making excuses for him all the time.'

The rest of the group came up with a radical idea to try to cure Bruce's issues. According to Hank, they 'had the guitars checked out by Vox, or by Jennings who made Vox, and they said, yes, there did seem to be a problem in the fretting. The frets were not quite in the right position. Now, I find it very hard to believe this was truly the case. But anyway, because of the problem, we approached Jim Burns, who had been making very, very good guitars for a number of years, and got him to make us a guitar that we could design with him, in terms of its appearance and in terms of the sound we wanted to achieve. And that's what led to us moving over to the Burns Marvins.' New guitars would fit the new line-up, and a new rhythm section to genuinely rival Tony and Jet – Brian Bennett and the virtually unknown John Rostill.

*

John Rostill had not played at the 2i's. He had not worked on the Coke machine there, nor kicked his heels waiting for Tony Sheridan to turn up, nor sported a bright-pink jacket. He had not thrown his aunt's boyfriend down the stairs, pissed on a monkey nor indeed had any kind of hit record. John Rostill's professional career had started at Tooting and Mitcham Football Club when he was paid fifteen shillings to play at the club's dance. Quiet John. Saturnine John. Handsome bastard John. If he'd been so inclined, he could have had Joe Meek or Gordon Mills shape him into a moody matinee idol, a younger Engelbert, a shyer Tom Jones.

But John was only interested in guitars. He'd grown up in Mitcham, the pylon-covered flatlands where Surrey melted into south London. It was a good place for birdwatching when he was a kid, but when he was fourteen, ornithology was shunted to one side because – like thousands of other kids – John Rostill heard 'Rock Island Line'. As late as 1967, when everybody was tripping over themselves to praise Jimi Hendrix and Peter Green, John Rostill stood firm and said he owed it all to Lonnie Donegan. His parents wouldn't buy him a guitar at first, so he decided to design and build his own – the body, the neck, the fingerboard, the frets. But he didn't string it. Maybe finishing the job would have taken some of the pleasure away; he hung it on the wall instead. Building it took a lot of hours alone in his room, a lot of dedication. It wasn't that he didn't like company, but John Rostill needed his space, a quiet place.

For Christmas in 1956, his parents bought him a Spanish guitar and 1957 was spent playing Donegan's 'Don't You Rock Me Daddy-O' and 'Lost John' at fetes and garden parties with his mates. He built them tea-chest basses. He made himself useful. He met Bruce Baxter, who was in the year above him at Rutlish Grammar School, and they would rehearse every day in John's parents' garden shed, eventually forming the Dynamos, a group with no bassist and different drummers on a weekly basis. The shed was also a workshop where John built his own amps. He rigged up an electricity supply from the house by using the wire washing line – his earthing wasn't perfect, though, and his mum got a real shock when she tried to hang out the washing after a night of heavy rain. It was just as well her clothes prop was wooden.

John Rostill finished school with no qualifications. He got a job with Triumph, the bra manufacturers, but despite being surrounded by lace and straps and cups and clasps, he turned to jelly every time a woman tried to talk to him. He didn't mind the job so much, as the Dynamos were getting to play random gigs around London, with John by now having bought a black and red Hopf electric bass with the money he'd saved from his bra work.

In 1959, John Rostill and Bruce Baxter saw an ad in *Melody Maker* for 'young rocking musicians'. They turned up for the audition at the National Union of Railwaymen's concert hall near Euston Square in matching outfits – blue corduroy drape jackets with gold backcloth, drainpipe trousers and black suede winklepickers. They were given the gig by a singer called Terry Loony who – this being 1959 and not 1977 – used the stage name Terry Young. Young had sung at the 2i's, which impressed his younger charges no end. But now he'd decided to form a band of his own: Terry Young and the Youngsters. If you thought he was protesting too much, you'd be right – Terry was considerably older than Rostill and Baxter. Still, with his brother Barry Loony (now Barry Daniel) on drums, he had himself a group. Young convinced Rostill and Baxter to take a flat in Fineview Villas in St John's Wood.

One day, John's parents returned from a weekend away and discovered he'd left home, just like that, moving from Mitcham to somewhere that his new flatmate Bruce Baxter described as a doss house. But Young and the Youngsters got regular work, so John upgraded to a Fender bass and bought a Vox AC30 amp, like the ones the Shadows used. Young got to pick the group's set and it was all American covers – Presley, Darin, Holly, Vincent, Cochran. Cliff and the Shadows were forbidden. That didn't stop Rostill and Baxter from playing 'FBI' when they rehearsed every night in St John's Wood, until they were too tired to play anymore.

If he wasn't playing his bass, John would be in his room building himself another guitar. 'He designed it and drew it to scale on paper,' remembered Bruce Baxter. 'It was semi-acoustic, but it had a very curious shape. He hung it on the wall. It was like a Salvador Dalí Fender. I'm sure it would never have played.'

Terry Young and the Youngsters edged towards professionalism. They played regularly in ballrooms managed by Peter Walsh, who also managed the Anglo Everlys act, the Brook Brothers, who briefly became stars with 1960 hits 'Warpaint' and 'Ain't Gonna Wash for a Week'. In the summer of '61, the Youngsters were at Butlins in Clacton; they had got the job by auditioning with an ace keyboard player from Leeds called Alan Hawkshaw,* who was in Joe Meek's act, the Checkmates. Young had slipped him a fiver and asked him to pretend he was a Youngster for twenty minutes. By the time they turned up for their season at Butlins, Young simply said Hawkshaw had quit the group. The contract still held and the Youngsters played a four-month residency. Hawkshaw, by a wild coincidence, would end up as a part-time Shadow a few years later.

Young was snide. He kept his musicians in the dark, made sure they lived close by and banned them from drinking or even talking to girls when they played. Keeping up with the burgeoning beat boom, they became the Terry Young Five, then the Terry Young Six – also on board by now were Bournemouth-born tenor sax player Kevin Drake and a talented pianist from the West Riding of Yorkshire called Barry Booth. They played with the Beatles. They played with Roy Orbison. They played with the Shadows. They backed Chris Montez, Tommy Roe, Louise Cordet, Jimmy Justice, Paul and Paula, Phil Everly, Frank Ifield, Shane Fenton, Patti Brook – the great and the good of the ABC circuit and many visiting American dignitaries. Terry Young kept sticking out rotten solo singles, produced by Tony Hatch for Pye,

---

* Among record collectors, Hawkshaw might be best remembered for recording the much-sampled single 'The Champ', under the name of the Mohawks, in 1968. The previous year, he had played organ on a Shadows session for the first time, and would remain a key, peripheral figure in their story. To the general public, he is best known for writing the theme to Channel 4's *Countdown*, recording it with Brian Bennett on percussion in 1982.

but his band remained nothing more than hired hands. Still, that was enough for an inventive bass player like John Rostill to get noticed.

When they backed Ketty Lester, touring on the back of her super-sultry 1962 hit 'Love Letters', her arranger Lincoln Mayorga asked them to play a song he'd written called 'Mad Goose'. Mayorga was something of a hero to instrumental fans as he had put together a rocking outfit called the Piltdown Men, who had a string of minor hits on Capitol, with titles cut to fit: 'McDonald's Cave', 'Goodnight Mrs Flintstone', 'Piltdown Rides Again'. Somehow the Terry Young Six – minus Young – ended up recording 'Mad Goose' rather than simply rehearsing it, and it appeared on Pye International under the name the Sons of the Piltdown Men. Pye International's remit wouldn't usually extend to guitarists from Mitcham, so we can assume there was some subterfuge here. No matter. 'Mad Goose' b/w 'Be a Party' (Pye International 7N 25206) would be John Rostill's first appearance on record.

Barry Booth was an accomplished keyboard player. He would go on to be Roy Orbison's musical director and cut an album of exquisite sketch songs called *Diversions*, in 1968, with lyrics from the pre-*Monty Python* Michael Palin and Terry Jones. In 1963, he was wise enough to be a member of the Musicians' Union and thought he was earning a minimum wage with the Terry Young Six. He was shocked when he discovered that his union rates were a damn sight more than Young was paying Rostill, Drake or Baxter. When he told them, Rostill and Drake realised old Terry Young was paying them peanuts and had been ripping them off for years. They didn't bother turning up to the next show.*

* Young would replace Rostill with Danny Thompson, later of Pentangle. The Terry Young Six broke up a year later.

Rostill and sax player Drake had become close friends. They freed themselves from Terry Young's mean, bony grip and moved down to Bournemouth together, where shy John stayed at Drake's parents as they got a new group together called the Interns. Out went the sky-blue suits and silver shoes, in came frighteningly realistic surgeons' outfits (with non-NHS silk shirts underneath). To complete the gag, John bought an old ambulance to get them from gig to gig. Bournemouth suited his speed. Drake and Barry Booth had encouraged the self-taught bassist that music lessons were nothing to be scared of, so in Bournemouth he decided to take bass lessons from a Mrs P.G. Curtis; he also learned to play cello and toyed with the idea of becoming a session player. Everyone told him he was good enough – one of the best. 'John was a natural musician and very talented,' Mrs Curtis told Shadows historian Rob Bradford years later. 'He was very assiduous. We did a lot of work on correct finger positions on the fretboard. He wanted to emulate the Shadows' style, you know, using chords and playing counter melodies on the bass guitar. He was a nice, clean, fine lad.'

Hanging around on Bournemouth's geriatric seafront, with his collar turned up against the sea breeze, the nice, clean, fine John Rostill operated the lift up the cliff in the summer months. He was also a deckchair attendant, folding and unfolding them, getting splinters in his bass-playing fingers, hurling the bloody things when he should have stacked them neatly. It had to be done – endless nights with the Interns at Bournemouth's Le Disque A Go! Go! playing the usual rock 'n' roll, Merseybeat, R&B and Shadows material weren't going to pay the rent on their own.

On a drizzly November night in 1963, after the Interns finished their set, an older fellow approached them. The club's owner Allan Azern remembered that 'they went into a huddle in the corner for about half an hour or so. They seemed very excited. Then John Rostill and Kevin Drake left. I asked the others what had been going on. When they told me that John had been invited to audition for the Shadows the following day, I just couldn't believe it.'

Brian 'Licorice' Locking had made his final appearance with the Shadows at the London Palladium. They needed a replacement urgently and the former bass player with Terry Young Six was on their wants list. The group's road manager David Bryce drove down to see John in Bournemouth at the Le Disque A Go! Go! and to invite him up to London for an audition the following morning. John Rostill was thrilled – these were his heroes, knocking on his front door – but he was also worried sick. 'I'll never pass the audition,' he kept on mumbling to Kevin Drake, pacing, sweating, his perfect quiff threatening to collapse over his furrowed brow. 'I've got to look smart. What about my shoes? These shoes are terrible. I need a new pair. The shops will all be closed. What the hell am I going to do, Kevin?'

Kevin lent him a nearly new pair of black shoes, even though they were a size too small and pinched his feet. The audition was a breeze.

The Shadows had shared a bill with the Terry Young Six several times during 1962 and '63, at summer seasons playing to ruddy-faced holiday makers in Blackpool. 'It was John, not the drummer, who pinned down the beat in that band,' reckoned Bruce Welch. 'Also, he was a very good-looking, smartly dressed guy. He reminded me of Don Everly. He looked the part. He was someone who had stuck in my memory.

'So when the time came to replace Brian Locking, John sprang to mind. We attempted to recruit John Paul Jones and failed. We offered John Rostill the job instead. He came up on a Sunday morning to the Palladium and we played through 'Dance On!' That was it. It was really as simple as that. He couldn't believe it, but we knew that he was a great bass player.' John played the one song and that was enough; the three remaining Shadows were convinced. He was a steady, loud, inventive bassist. He would play chords on the bass, slapping the strings hard. He was also a prolific songwriter. He could write either on his own or with any member of the Shadows, as it turned out.

Not quite sure if he was in a dream, John Rostill continued to see Mrs Curtis for music lessons. Learning the finger positions for 'FBI' and 'Apache' in her parlour now had a rather more practical application. He phoned her up just before his first TV appearance to let her know he would be on the telly. 'You just keep watching me,' he told her, 'and I'll try to wiggle my fingers.'

To Bruce's relief, John had no religious hang-ups, either. And, most importantly, he helped Bruce with his obsession over tuning. Offered a bonus of £10 a week, more than half the average wage in 1963, Rostill agreed to tune Bruce's guitars before every performance. Bruce was impressed with the way he used harmonics to tune instead of more conventional tuning. This was new to him and he trusted him completely. John joined the Shadows in Christmas 1963. Straight away, he was on location in the Canary Islands shooting another movie, *Wonderful Life*, with Cliff and the boys.

'The whole ten weeks was a mixture of fun and boredom, I think, to most of us,' said Bruce, 'but to John it was a never-to-be-forgotten experience, as he hadn't yet played a note for the Shadows but found himself in the Canary Islands making a film.'

*

Jet Harris and Tony Meehan were more than keeping their heads above water in 1963. 'Diamonds' had been a number one, its power and widescreen majesty showing the Shadows what they were missing. The new team couldn't really have wished for a better year.

Jet was now dating Billie Davis, a rising star with a striking look – wide-set eyes and a blunt, jet-black fringe. She had just secured her own first top-ten hit with a cover of the Exciters' 'Tell Him'. While the backing may have been Decca's attempt to mimic the New York-sized original, Billie's voice was more than distinctive, soulful, somehow strong and fragile at the same time. She had broken through just ahead of Cilla Black and Dusty Springfield, whose debut solo hits came a matter of weeks later. She was part of a new breed of British girl singer – and at the forefront.

On 28 September 1963, Billie Davis was doing a Saturday gig in Evesham in Worcestershire. Jet Harris had picked up an *NME* award earlier that day and hired a driver to take him and Billie over to the show. 'The gig was great,' she later told Jet's biographer Dave Nicolson. 'We were well up. He was number one and I was number ten in the charts. Coming home in the back of the car, we were very tired and sleepy. And a Midland Red bus suddenly pulled out into the road and our car went into it.'

'That really put the tin hat on it,' said Jet. 'I was asleep on Billie Davis's lap in the back of the car and a bus went into us. The bus was a write-off, that's how bad it was. I caught the ash tray full on my head, and from then I was in and out of hospitals. I couldn't look at a guitar. I wouldn't even touch one.'

The car had no seat belts. Jet fell forward and split his forehead. Billie had also been lying down; the impact broke her jaw, although she didn't realise this at the time. 'There was blood everywhere. I got out of the car, carried Jet out, put him on the side of the road. But the lovely thing was some fans had been following us from the gig on their scooters and motorbikes and they helped us. Jet's two *NME* awards plaques were in my hand when we were collided and both were badly scratched.

'I thought that I was fine and went over to get on the bus for a sit-down. A little old man was sitting on the bus and had his head bumped when the car crashed into it. I said "Are you all right?" The ambulance man saw me wandering about and said "Who are you? What are you doing? Were you on the bus?" I said "No, I was in the car" and I turned around and looked at the car – which was a Humber Supersnipe, a really heavy car – and I realised it was a write-off, and I'd been in that car. My knees then went a bit wobbly and he said "You better get in the ambulance."'

*

'Because Jet was a married man and he was having an affair with a young singer – which was me – it hit the tabloids.'

The press, if anything, were more heartless in 1963 than they are today. Billie Davis went home to her Marble Arch flat and tried to sleep. Suddenly she was woken up by a man, shaking her and asking where Jet was. The stranger was Mike Hellicar, who might have sounded like a character from *Journey Into Space*, but was a notorious, hard-boiled hack from the *Daily Sketch*, who had broken into her flat.

Meanwhile, Jet should have still been in hospital, but he wasn't – he was going on benders. The press wouldn't leave them alone. Jet and Billie decided to escape to Brighton and stay with friends, but the press followed them. 'My jaw was wired, so I couldn't sing,' said Billie. 'I couldn't do anything. I lived on baby food. I can remember getting on this train with Jet – we were so naïve, even at that stage. Getting off at Victoria station, I remember looking up the platform and seeing all these photographers. I looked at my friend Annie and her boyfriend who were looking after us, and who had the flat in Brighton, and I said "Somebody really important must be on this train". And, of course, it was us! A tabloid journalist wrote an article – "the couple who caught the 10.25" or something like that.'

Jet and Billie were in London on their way to Harley Street to see a Dr Meyer who had previously treated Judy Garland and Alma Cogan. The doctor was furious with the crowds gathering outside his surgery. 'Leave the kids alone,' he shouted. 'Let them rest. They're ill, they've had an accident.' Billie said Jet went to pieces after the accident. He had a scar on his head, with more than thirty stitches. The psychological damage wasn't as visible.

*

Jet and Tony had been booked to appear on *Ready Steady Go!* to play their third single together, 'Applejack'. It was the only live music show on TV at the time, and broadcast every Friday night. *Ready Steady Go!* was a big deal.

'I'd booked a spot on *Ready Steady Go!* for "Applejack",' said Tony. 'He was in a car crash and had his head smashed open, but he could walk. He could have been patched up, walking wounded... he could have mimed, but he wouldn't. He was drunk and he was obnoxious. I said, "Just do this one show, then you won't have to play for a month. Go away, get better, go to the south of France." It was important. But he was in a very belligerent mood. We had a fight – thwack! Unfortunately, it came to that. I knocked him over a desk and he walked out. I had to do an interview while they played the record.'

Billie Davis sat at home watching as Cathy McGowan interviewed Tony Meehan. She couldn't understand why Jet wasn't on screen. Suddenly there was a knock at her door and there he was. He'd run away, he said. He couldn't cope. He had turned up for the pre-show rehearsal, at which he said Meehan and the show's producers had managed to gently coach him through a couple of shots at 'Applejack', but he clearly wasn't fit to appear on TV. He especially didn't want people to see the scar on his head, which was prominent. He just couldn't face appearing on TV; he couldn't face anybody. He had run from the studio and made it over to Billie's just as the show went on the air. The stress of the crash and its aftermath would tell on Tony Meehan, too, and he would virtually retire as a drummer within months. He was just twenty years old.

Years later, it became apparent that – even before the crash – Jet had been in no condition to sustain the spotlight. His drinking had made him incredibly unreliable. When Meehan recorded both 'Scarlett O'Hara' and 'Applejack', he had had to bring in Joe Moretti – the star of Johnny Kidd's 'Shakin' All Over' – to play Jet's guitar lines.

'We'd made "Diamonds",' said Tony Meehan. 'We went out for serious money, with a band you'd kill for, a *fantastic* band. "Diamonds" was the first record Jimmy Page ever played on. Glyn Johns was the tape operator and he'd introduced me to Jimmy. "Will you give him a chance?" I said, "Tell him to come along." And he never looked back. These people were just starting, you know?

'Jet, he was in bad shape by then. But the band had Joe Moretti on lead guitar, tenor sax, flute, clarinet ... We auditioned John Paul Jones – he was John Baldwin then – and said "Yep, you're good." That was his first job ever, he was about eighteen. He was the bass player and I was on drums. We toured for about a year.'

This live band, with a brass section, was a dream for Meehan. 'We were about ten years before Chicago and sounded like Chicago. We were a very go-ahead band. It could have been massive. But I'm afraid the bottle put an end to it. You couldn't get much out of Jet in the studio either. Unfortunately, Jet's drinking got the better of him.'

Who knows what might have happened in 1964 if the Midland Red bus hadn't stopped Jet and Tony's career in its tracks. But it felt like the duo would have come apart sooner or later.

'Sometimes he was okay,' said Tony, 'sometimes he was half-pissed, other times he couldn't stand.

'Jet Harris was the one in a million who blew it. He was a very brilliant musician who went to pieces. He was so destructive in every way. Look at the lives of people he has affected. Jet and I could have had the most fantastic career together ... when our duo broke up, I was upset, as we both had a strong affection for what we were doing.'

A while later, Jet confessed to Tony that he knew the drink was to blame. There had been Cliff's affair, and there was also the car crash, but he was married to the bottle. 'He'd drink two bottles of vodka and ten pints of beer a day ... That was his life for years ... I always expected to pick up the paper to see Jet Harris had been found dead in a bedsit somewhere. It wasn't pleasant.

'It put an end to my career as well, because I couldn't face it after that. 1964. Suddenly there was a lot of money in the music business and all these villains started to get involved. The music business was bad enough, but these were real rogues, hard bastards. Because I was fronting the band, I had to do a lot more solo work, a lot more flashing around, which wasn't my bag at all. So there was a lot more stress. I was doing so much playing it started to affect my hands. I had so many splits and sores I used to carry a bottle of surgical spirit. I used to pour it on and then I could play. I had blisters on the blisters, I'm not joking. I was at a club in Manchester and said "Look at my hands, I can't play, I can't do this." And the manager said, "You're booked to play. You'll play." And I just thought, *That's it, fuck it, never again*. And I just packed it in. I thought I don't want to be anywhere near these people. My heart wasn't in it.'

9

THE RISE AND FALL OF FLINGEL BUNT

As the Shadows played Stockton for what felt like the 300th time, fifty miles up the road, Newcastle was becoming Brasilia-on-Tyne. The streets of Elswick, on which Bruce had grown up, the dirty brick terraces he had hated, were being torn down.

T. Dan Smith had a fierce determination to eviscerate Newcastle's slum housing, all those scrunched-up terraces that lined the north bank of the Tyne: Byker, Elswick and Scotswood. They would be replaced with modern public housing, including the Byker Wall, a housing estate that could really put Newcastle on the map.

There would be a motorway road system to relieve traffic in the city centre; unbelievably, at the beginning of the '60s, the main shopping street was still part of the main road between London and Edinburgh. The coal-filthy Tyne was to be cleaned and purified; Newcastle Airport would be redesigned for international flights; the university would become independent from haughty Durham; Tyne-Tees television was to have a brand new HQ; and the Northern Stage theatre would be built. Smith had an urgency to re-invent Newcastle as a cross between Brasilia and Manhattan, a northern powerhouse instead of an isolated outpost. Nobody would ever be ashamed of their Geordie accent again.

*

When they wanted to escape from Stockton, the first instincts of Newcastle's musical modernisers was not to head north, back home, but south, and then further south. At the suggestion of manager Peter Gormley, Hank and Bruce – as well as Cliff and Frank Ifield – had bought plots on the Portuguese Algarve in Albufeira where they built villas, all in a row. They had all amassed some serious money. Bruce described Albufeira as 'the perfect place to get away from it all and escape the pressures of the music business. It was unspoilt, undiscovered by tourists, and an ideal spot to relax.' Cliff would keep his villa until the 2020s, with his vineyard next door; you could even buy bottles of Cliff's homemade wine at Albufeira Airport.

By the beginning of 1964, Hank and his wife Billie had bought an impressive new house in Totteridge, north London, for £12,500 at a time when the average annual wage was £1,000 and the average home cost £3,360. Brian Bennett and his wife Margaret moved into Hank and Billie's old place in Winchmore Hill with their young lad, Warren. 'Suddenly we didn't have to worry about how much money we spent,' Hank told Mike Read. 'We could go into any restaurant and order anything we liked, or walk into a men's outfitters and buy several suits at one time. We really felt we could do anything.'

John Rostill had joined the Shadows just before Christmas 1963. In essence, life seemed easy; they were all living above deck, port out, starboard home. They dressed the part on stage, too. No one seems sure whose idea it was to start wearing bow ties and tuxes – although, when in doubt, blame management. The image was meant to be Roger Moore going for cocktails at the French consulate in *The Saint,* but – depending on the venue – there was always the danger that they might look more like waiting staff. No longer did they want to look like Elvis, tearing it up in *King Creole*, but rather some kind of two-up two-down rat pack. More to the point, they did not dress anything like the Beatles, or any of their contemporaries. Possibly they were trying to put some clear water between themselves and the beat groups, to show the world they were an older, trusted firm – established 1958.

*

In July 1964, *Record Mirror* reported that 'ex-Shadow man Brian Licorice Locking has formed his own group. And the lineup of Licorice Locking's All Sorts includes a girl, June Presley, on tenor sax and vocals. Others in the group are Dai Bowen, drums and vibes; Mike Drake, lead guitar; and Keith Mansfield, piano tenor and vocals.' June was married to trumpet player Duncan Campbell from the Ted Heath Band; it was Campbell who had introduced her to Licorice.

'This band was nothing compared to my days with the Shadows,' Licorice wrote in his memoir, 'but it was a start to my return to music and I was happy. I had left behind all the hysteria, idolatry and fame. While my work with the Jehovah's Witness ministry was a priority,

I still needed to live and earn money.' Licorice Locking's All Sorts were never heard from again, although Keith Mansfield would go on to an incredibly successful career in production and TV theme writing.*

*

Tony Meehan had recorded 'Song of Mexico' back in November '63, with Joe Moretti on lead guitar; the chances are that it was slated to be the fourth Jet and Tony single. Instead, it was released in January '64 under Meehan's name alone, presumably as a contractual obligation. Once again, it had been written by Jerry Lordan, with Tony sounding comfortable in the control room. The problem was it sounded like a top-three hit from 1962, not 1964. Still, for fans of their continuity Shadows sound, it was another strong single.

Better still was the B-side, Meehan's own 'Kings Go Fifth', a pun on the Sinatra movie title *Kings Go Forth*. There was a high, floating string line and solo clarinet to carry the middle eight, while Moretti again played the main melody. It was an excellent, deeply filmic single, but released in the same month as the Searchers' 'Needles and Pins', Bessie Banks' 'Go Now', Georgie Fame's 'Do the Dog' and the Impressions' 'Talking About My Baby', it sounded out of touch, out of fashion. An appearance on Granada TV's *Scene At Six Thirty* couldn't push it higher than a miserable number thirty-nine. Less than a year earlier,

---

* After arranging the Love Affair's 1968 number one 'Everlasting Love' and Marmalade's first hit 'Lovin' Things', Keith Mansfield went to work for the KPM music library where he wrote themes for a bunch of TV sports shows, including *Grandstand* and *The Big Match*. He would also rub shoulders at KPM with Brian Bennett.

'Diamonds' had vanquished 'Dance On!' as the number-one record in the country, but the arrival of the Beatles had changed everything. Now here was Tony, struggling to make it into the top forty, while Jet – who had somehow been coerced back into the studio in January '64 – couldn't even reach the top fifty with 'Big Bad Bass'.

In spite of Jet's unavailability, Tony still had contractual obligations and he was forced to continue touring alone. He put together the Tony Meehan Combo from the basis of their existing backing group, with Joe Moretti switching to lead and John Paul Jones on bass. Added to this was Glenn Hughes on baritone sax, Chris Hughes, who played soprano sax and clarinet, and a clean-cut Ivy League-suited rhythm guitarist called John McLaughlin.

'He also turned out to be a massive talent,' remembered Chris Hughes of McLaughlin, the future Mahavishnu Orchestra leader and foil to Miles Davis. 'We now had a very nice group, which played out the remaining bookings and promoted 'Song of Mexico'. In the middle eight, I provided a trio of soprano saxophones, courtesy of Ampex multi-track recording, and I had a few bookings from other producers on the strength of that sound.'

Joe Moretti – who, in Jet's absence, had at least been promoted to the same-size hotel rooms as Tony – was understandably pissed off about playing lead on 'Scarlett O'Hara', 'Applejack' and 'Song of Mexico' without getting any credit on the label. He later told Dave Nicolson about the disintegration of the Tony Meehan Combo: 'Oh, what a change came over that band. Within a month [of John McLaughlin joining], we had transformed our repertoire, apart from our two chart hits. Jazz took over ... Of course, the kids came to hear pop music and when they didn't get it, they started to stay away. Within a couple of months, there were no more bookings. The band folded soon after that.'

*

Hank was on a Belgian TV show in 1964, trying to explain how none of the comings and goings in the Shadows made any difference, really. 'Well, it presents certain problems,' he revealed, getting his tenses all knotted. 'For instance, when Jet or Tony Meehan left, the fans may not like it. And at first they didn't. But they soon grew to accept the new member, you see, and we found that it didn't really affect us. Then, of course, Licorice left and John Rostill is now with us. And, again, there's been no upsetting of the fans. They still find it okay.' It was okay, said Hank B. Marvin. It was all alright.

This jovial complacency was understandable. In late 1963, the BBC newsreader and journalist Peter Woods had asked George Harrison if he thought it was possible that the Beatles could settle down to a life in showbusiness. 'Well, we're hoping to – not necessarily a life in showbusiness but at least a couple more years. I mean, if we do as well as Cliff and the Shadows have done until now, we won't be moaning.'

The Shadows had seen 1964 in with the exemplary 'Theme for Young Lovers', written by Bruce. Marlene Dietrich thought so much of it she commissioned a lyric and sang it as 'Ich Werde Dich Lieben'. 'I will love you, will love you until death, will love you until the end of the world,' she sang. It was hard to picture Hank and Bruce singing this in Stockton.

'Theme for Young Lovers' had a sweeping, yearning melody and Bruce must have been gutted when it failed to reach the top ten in early '64. Sweeping and yearning weren't in. What was definitely happening in London – in opposition to the Mersey Beat – was a return to the R&B that the nascent Shadows had cut their teeth on.

John Rostill would get to announce himself as a player to be reckoned with on the Shadows' next 45, May '64's 'The Rise and Fall of Flingel Bunt'. Mr Bunt was not a real person – or even a fictitious one – but a phrase bordering on profanity, something Richard O'Sullivan used to say in lieu of a swear word. The other Shads put it down to *Goon Show* humour. The topline bore some similarity to the Miracles' 'Shop Around'; over a basic twelve-bar jam they had cut on 25 February, Norrie Paramor switched on the light, joined in on piano and it was completed in one take. It sounded entirely contemporary and the reward was a top-five hit.

'You can't help but be influenced by what's going on,' said Hank. 'You listen to things, absorb things, try them out ... It often doesn't come out as a copy, because what you're doing is interpreting. You try to incorporate without losing your own style. It could be jazz, folk, it seems to go in ... It becomes a catalyst, whether it be the Beatles, or R&B, whatever.'

Rostill lifted the band. He was an original musician, and a composer to boot. Great as Jet and Tony were, Brian and John would evolve into the best rhythm section the Shadows would ever have. It looked like a way forward.

*

February '64 saw a mammoth Shadows studio session to nail down their third album. Their new Burns Marvin guitars – in white, with faux tortoiseshell pick guards – gave them a much fuller sound. Content-wise, Norrie called the tune and picked the numbers. His mind-set was still 'Quatermasster's Stores'; he was an old-world animal. This was a pity. The album opened with 'Chattanooga Choo Choo', a true showbiz horror, and included such antiquated tunes as 'Zambezi', a hit for bandleader Lou Busch in 1956; Bing Crosby's '30s hit 'Temptation' (via the Everly Brothers); and Glenn Miller's 'In The Mood' (via Ernie Fields' rock 'n' roll-ish 1958 recording).

Like its predecessor, *Dance With the Shadows* would be a transitionary album, with Licorice still present on half of its tracks. He played on the standout 'Blue Shadows', a tough blues track that – recorded back in August '63 – had been well ahead of the game, and dug out his harmonica for 'Dakota'. Listening to the latter and its twist-friendly yet wistful feel, you have to wonder how the Shadows weren't commissioned for more film or TV work – heck, even the Tornados had recorded the theme for crime writer Edgar Lustgarten's series of cinema shorts, *The Scales of Justice*. John Barry, cutting Shads-alikes with his septet not long ago, was now hypnotising viewers with the theme to *The Human Jungle*, in which psychologist Herbert Lom used his skills to solve mental mysteries (Tony Meehan's thoughts on the show were sadly not recorded).

Maybe one reason for this is that, despite London having become the world's undisputed cultural hotspot by 1964, the Shadows still looked westward to the mythical America of their childhood. While the Tornados focused on the otherworldly ('Telstar', 'Robot', 'Life on Venus') or the English everyday ('Dragonfly', 'The Ice Cream Man', 'Hot Pot'), the Shadows were still stuck hard to their James Dean dreams. Bernstein and Sondheim's 'Tonight' was given the 'Sleepwalk'/'Midnight' treatment, the spotlight resting on Hank and the remainder of the group melting into the darkness of a New York alley. Tex-Mex exotica came from 'The Lonely Bull', Herb Alpert's 1962 hit, which saw the Shads replace brass with booming guitar, while 'Big B' was a perversely downbeat, understated space for Brian Bennett to revisit the drum solos of 'Little B'.

There was one big-screen commission – the theme for director Ken Russell's *French Dressing*. It was Russell's debut and he was given a Brian Bennett tune. 'It's another kind of *Summer Holiday*' ran the movie trailer, 'a delicious mixture of sauce and good old-fashioned cheek'. The theme was jolly, country-flecked and clean, with Licorice on bass, but it was no *Human Jungle*. Brian would graduate to far better cinematic material.

At least the brace of vocal tracks, both Marvin/Welch compositions, sounded *du jour*. 'That's the Way It Goes' could have been a Searchers album track, though its roots were most likely in Buddy Holly's 'I'm Gonna Love You Too', while 'Don't It Make You Feel Good' was strong enough to have made it as an A-side if they'd wanted to chance their arms. Bruce and Hank's harmonies rang strong and true on this ode to simple pleasures: 'You're sitting sipping coffee and your girl walks in / You go to a dance and the music swings / To dance and swing with your girl by your side / Instead of staying home by the fireside.' Both songs were covered by the Swingin' Blue Jeans, one of the hottest groups of 1964, and in the top three with their well-judged covers of Chan Romero's 'Hippy Hippy Shake' and Betty Everett's sensual 'You're No Good'. Still, this didn't encourage Bruce and Hank – itching to do more harmonising – into persuading Peter Gormley and Norrie Paramor that vocals could be a way forward. Were the Ventures, or Duane Eddy, or Johnny and the Hurricanes still on the chart? Even Jet and Tony? No, they weren't. The world kept turning and the Shadows couldn't turn away.

*

The hard groove of 'Blue Shadows' was not released as the next Shadows single, in spite of 'Flingel Bunt''s popularity, and neither was either vocal track. You do wonder if Norrie Paramor was still the force at Columbia that he had once been. There were plenty of Columbia singles in the top ten in 1964: Manchester's clown-beat exemplars Freddie and the Dreamers were produced by junior producer John Burgess, who also took the reins for Peter and Gordon's half-whispered recording of Lennon and McCartney's 'World Without Love' and rode it all the way to number one. And there would be two more Columbia number ones in 1964, Herman's Hermits 'I'm Into Something Good' and the Animals' influential 'House of the Rising Sun', which would convince folk guitarist Bob Dylan to reacquaint himself with an electric guitar. Where was Frank Ifield? He was nowhere to be seen. Did Norrie Paramor have his fingerprints on Herman's Hermits or the Animals? He did not. Both singles were produced by a cat who had been on the bill with Cliff, the Drifters, Eddie Calvert and the Kalin Twins back in the scrabbling days of 1958; he was one half of the pretend Most Brothers, who had unwittingly directed Jet Harris into becoming a Shadow. By 1964, Mickie Most had realised that the real money was to be made in the producer's chair and not behind the microphone. These were his first two number-one production credits. There would be plenty more.

George Martin was laughing up his sleeve. For many years he'd been in Paramor's shadow, but now not only did he have the Beatles and the homely Billy J. Kramer at number one, but he was taking Cilla Black – a cloakroom attendant! – to the very top of the hit parade not once, but twice. To rub it in, he even gave ex-Goon Peter Sellers his first hit in years with a Shakespearean reading of 'A Hard Day's Night'. John Lennon came up with a nickname for Martin's erstwhile nemesis: Noddy Paranoid.

Wonderful Life was in cinemas across Britain in June 1964. 'Flingel Bunt' was in the top ten the same week, as was Cliff's sumptuous Italian ballad, 'Constantly'. Number one was the former cloakroom attendant with a more successful Italian ballad called 'You're My World', but the Shadows didn't let that bother them. The storyline of *Wonderful Life* featured a film within a film – about a director with loftier aspirations, struggling to make a genre movie in the desert with Susan Hampshire; this was a little on the nose. Sad, shy Susan received Cliff's first screen kiss, but black-bobbed Una Stubbs – looking not unlike Billie Davis – would have been a much better fit for him.

The movie's lead single was 'On the Beach', a song that – more than any other in Cliff and the Shadows' canon – seemed custom-made, eager to please. It was as if they'd got the British Market Research Bureau in to come up with lines like 'You can do the dance that you want to, with anyone that you meet'. Was that general enough for you? The references to 'Twist and Shout' were flat-out embarrassing, sounding at odds with the already dated line 'If the bossa nova don't get you, the twist will have you on your feet'. The twist? In 1964? Keep up, Grandad! As usual, a stinging intro from Hank saved it from complete failure. But where *Summer Holiday* had produced three number-one singles, 'On the Beach' – the only Cliff single to be taken from the *Wonderful Life* soundtrack – got bogged down in the sand at number seven.

As with *Summer Holiday*, seven of the numbers had been written or co-written by Cliff and the Shadows, while the arranger (Stanley Black), script writers (Ronnie Cass and Peter Myers) and backing vocalists (the Mike Sammes Singers) were all exactly the same. It just felt as if everyone was working at a half-cocked pace, no more so than with the perilously weak title song which, unlike its two predecessors, wasn't even released as a single, let alone reaching number one: 'Fish in the sea were all born to be free / Yes, they all agree / It's a wonderful life' wasn't going to provide Bruce or Brian with a path to an Oscar.

One of the Shadows' tracks on the soundtrack album, 'Walkin'' – written by Bruce, Hank and Brian – was rock-solid, with Bruce and John tightly meshed under Hank's bluesy topline, while 'Theme for Young Lovers' was starry-eyed and gorgeous, but had already become familiar as a single. Beyond that, Cass and Myers' tunes sounded more like *Easter Parade* rejects than ever, rooted in another era.

Wonderful Life was woeful. They had been sleepwalking and, much as Elvis did in the mid-'60s, delivered a film that possibly appeased the hardcore, unquestioning fanbase, but was never going to win any new converts. A harsh light was cast on *Wonderful Life* when the Beatles' first movie *A Hard Day's Night* opened just a few weeks later. 'Give ush a kish!' leered John Lennon to an uptight businessman in a bowler hat, the same kind of character Richard O'Sullivan had played in *The Young Ones* and now reprised in *Wonderful Life*.

Whose side were Cliff and the Shadows on now? Was the beat boom anything to worry about? Were their careers at stake if they didn't keep up? You could have asked Cliff's sister Donella – she was a fully paid-up Beatles Fan Club member.

Director Sidney J. Furie had presumably had his mind on other matters. By the time *Wonderful Life* premiered, he was already shooting *The Ipcress File* with Michael Caine, working on experimental long shots with cinematographer Otto Heller while creating the best breakfast scene ever filmed, and essentially inventing the noir-ish, anti-Bond, Cold War thriller. Furie turned to John Barry for the score this time rather than the Shadows; he loved them, but he knew this would be more big time than *The Boys*. Brian Bennett, John Barry's number one fan, understood.

Besides, the Shadows had their own film to make.

*

In the end-of-year *NME* annual, a beaming Derek Johnson summed up the Shadows' 1964. 'Their contribution to Cliff's *Wonderful Life* movie received its just applause. But it is the work which they have completed in their own right this year which has really boosted their reputation. First, they topped the bill in a lengthy summer season at

Great Yarmouth. And they succeeded in attracting capacity crowds, who seemed quite oblivious to the fact that Cliff was not appearing. Secondly, they starred in their own short colour film, *Rhythm and Greens*, which was shot largely on the sands at Yarmouth during their residency there, and proved to the critics and public that their specialized type of zany humour was on a par with the Goons or the Beatles.'

'We don't want to get too far off the beaten track,' Brian Bennett assured Johnson. 'We are, first and foremost, a pop group. This is how we made our name, and this is how we like it. But, of course, if any opportunities like the film or pantos crop up, we jump at them. They are good for our image, they keep our minds alert and above all we enjoy doing them.'

'I expect the future will follow much the same sort of pattern,' John Rostill chipped in. 'Though we still have one outstanding ambition to be realized, and that's to play cabaret.' They'd get there soon enough.

They dealt with the rumours that Cliff might eventually want to move on without them. 'I honestly don't see what we would gain by going our own way,' said Hank. 'We have shown that we can work separately, and we shall doubtless continue to do so when we have independent commitments. But when we have a tour or TV or something of that nature, it's great to get together again. Both Cliff and we ourselves realise that we are good for each other.'

'Clearly the old firm intends to remain in partnership,' concluded Johnson. 'The Shadows obviously have no cause for concern about what lies ahead with the abundance of talent to which they have displayed in recent months, their future is assured.'

*

The subject matter was suitably small-scale: a brief history of Britain's beaches, from the Stone Age, through the Victorian bathing boom, to the transistor radios and bikinis of 1964. *Rhythm and Greens*, in its own sweet B-movie way, was the perfect Shadows statement.

The movie saw Hank and Brian combing their hair forward, while, for now, Bruce and John still stuck to their circa '59 Everlys' look. There was no dialogue as such, just a narration from Robert Morley, mocked up as a Home Service radio programme, explaining where Hengist and Taillefer fitted into the history of Britain, while the Shadows – and their cute female counterparts – got to dress in various period costumes and play lutes in Bodiam Castle.

On the Great Yarmouth beach of 1964, there would be no twisting or 'bossa nova played with soul', just pensioners in deckchairs and teenagers on towels tapping their toes to the 'Main Theme' once the Shads had turned up in their short shorts. Brian, in a Dennis the Menace stripy shirt, looked like a cheeky burglar.

Hank was still wearing his NHS specs for the Stone Age sequence, as the boys knocked out the powerful, Sandy Nelson-like 'Drum Number'. Then, dressed as Romans, all four brushed their hair forward and – togas aside – looked more contemporary than they usually did in their suits and quiffs. A bearded Cliff had a cameo, playing King Canute and getting his legs wet. From a present-day vantage point, *Rhythm and Greens* predicted the Monkees much more than it felt like an offcut from a Cliff movie. It was cheerful, colourful and, in its gentle silent surrealism, also anticipated British '60s movie shorts like *The Sandwich Man* and *The Plank*. 'We all felt that it would be tremendously good experience for us,' Bruce told the *NME*, 'and we liked the script, so we thought we'd have a bash. After all, we've got the taste for filming after working with Cliff on his three. We really had a ball making it.'

Just thirty minutes long, *Rhythm and Greens* was succinct and witty where *Wonderful Life* had been overlong and a bit of a drag. All of the music was self-composed – co-credited to all four Shadows – and released on a five-track EP in November '64. It was a major improvement on much of *Dance With the Shadows*, pushing their way forward into the post-Beatles world by using 'Flingel Bunt' as a launchpad.

Although it had been made as a B-movie, for some peculiar reason *Rhythm and Greens* was shown as a support to *King and Country,* Joseph Losey's stark and extremely downbeat First World War film starring Tom Courtenay – a year on from the big-screen version of *Billy Liar* – as a shell-shocked private in the British army accused of desertion. The officer assigned to defend him at his court-martial discovered that it was far from an open-and-shut case. 'The most intense excitement you have ever experienced in this shock-filled story!' screamed the poster. The backdrop was incessant rain. The film, of course, was in black and white.

In the US, Judith Crist praised *King and Country*'s 'deadly tones of realism', while the *New York Times* called it 'an intense, compelling picture – taught and devastating'. So you have to wonder what they'd have made of Hank Marvin as a warm-up act, in full Merry Men garb, playing a lute to a buxom blonde Maid Marian.

The only thing you could say was *wrong* with *Rhythm and Greens* was the title track, which was placed over the end credits and saw the Shadows playing it dressed as cavemen. The backing track was fine, a tough-enough R&B workout to put most of George Martin's charges to shame. The issue was that the Shadows – overcome by Goon fumes – screamed 'Yeah baby!' over the whole thing, along with swanee whistles and all manner of clown-car sound effects.

Over the end credits, this would hardly have mattered. But either Norrie Paramor – not known for his great taste in A-sides – or Peter Gormley had the dreadful idea of making it the Shadows' next single, their first since 'Flingel Bunt' had restored their fortunes and put them front and centre in the British R&B boom. It was released in the last week of August '64, before anybody had seen the film to put it in context. As such, 'Rhythm and Greens' stank the place out. The only possible way for fans, or radio, or the press to read 'Rhythm and Greens' was as a piss-take. Rhythm and blues? Stupid! Just stupid! Rolling Stones? Stone-age wankers, more like! Eat your rhythm and greens, Sonny Jim!

On the flip side was a classic slice of Shadows Americana, with a lush, sympathetic brass-and-strings Paramor arrangement, called 'The Miracle'. But radio didn't get pushed in the direction of 'The Miracle'. The 'Rhythm and Greens' single was an incredible misstep, and even made local paper headlines: 'The Shadows dig at rhythm and blues' tutted the *Rugeley Times*; *Record Mirror* described the single as 'a bit like a Mersey group gone wrong, and certainly not like the Shadows'. It became their first single to fall short of the top twenty since 'Saturday Dance' almost five years earlier.

10

PRETEND YOU'RE HAPPY WHEN YOU'RE BLUE

It isn't so hard to see where the Shadows lost their relevance in the mid-'60s – pop music is ephemeral by nature. Also, it isn't hard to see why. That comforting taste, their home-baked cake of Jerry Lordan's melodies and Hank's panoramic tone – why would you give that up? Sweet and beautiful and safe, it had made them rich and famous, and influential too. Why would you bother looking further down the menu?

The Beatles did.

'I deplore the passing of the smile on stage and the current trend for downturned mouths and lantern jaws,' complained Hank in 1965. 'How can you entertain other people if you don't look entertained yourself? I think groups of the calibre of the Barron Knights might well have an important function to play, the way they send up other artists on their records. If today's groups can't be laughed with, then they must be laughed at – laughter is the criterion.'

The Shadows ended 1965 writing a panto; the Beatles did not. The Beatles started 1965 at number one with 'I Feel Fine', a record that began with an intentional, extended hum of feedback before it raced into a taut rewrite of Bobby Parker's 'Watch Your Step'. It was a small step into the unknown, but the Beatles weren't concerned about watching their step. Their *Beatles For Sale* album, number one that Christmas, was more acoustic than anything they had done before, openly hymning their love of country with 'Baby's in Black'. In 1965, they would test the folk-rock waters with the twelve-string drone of 'Ticket to Ride' and the softer folk-pop of 'You've Got to Hide Your Love Away' (where the lyric skirted the taboo of homosexuality). They would bid farewell to their roots with an ear-splitting version of Larry Williams' 'Dizzy Miss Lizzy', before embracing the sounds of the Indian subcontinent on 'Norwegian Wood'. Maybe they even took heed of Hanks's advice, because their second album of the year, *Rubber Soul*, began life as a comedy album: 'Drive My Car', 'Norwegian Wood', 'Girl' and 'Michelle' were all skits to some degree. But the Shads? If you were looking for clues on their records as to where their career might go next, how they might haul themselves back into relevance, you'd need patience – and possibly a magnifying glass.

*

Pantomime is a tough one to explain to anyone outside of Britain. It's nothing to do with mime, for a start; essentially, pantomime – or 'panto' – is the last hold-out of music hall. The modern pantomime dates back to 1843 when theatres were allowed to put on performances that included dialogue for the first time, without the need of royal decree. Prior to this, 'harlequinades' had been bringing European fables, folk stories and fairy tales to the English theatre, but with the possibility of actual speaking parts, and singing too, panto really took off in the music halls around Britain in the late nineteenth century, with Christmas being their main season. The panto was a chance to introduce children to the stage to help them catch the theatre bug.

What did you get in a panto that made it different from a regular musical? They were drawn from a fairly small, select number of stories: 'Jack and the Beanstalk', 'Puss in Boots', 'Mother Goose', 'Beauty and the Beast', 'Babes in the Wood', 'Aladdin', 'Cinderella'... They included stock characters, variations of which go back centuries, including the principal boy (always played by a girl) and the dame (always played by a middle-aged man). The late Victorian era introduced 'guest stars', who could be singers or actors, and they were never there to be the stars of the panto; they had to fully invest themselves in the zaniness and the physical comedy. There would be innuendo, designed to go over the heads of children. And there would be audience participation – oh yes, there would.

In 1964, there were 300 different pantos being staged in theatres around the country.*

And it was in 1964 that Peter Gormley informed Cliff and the Shadows that they had been asked to become a part of this centuries-old tradition. Not only that, they had been asked to write all of the

* In 2025, pantos would still be bringing in 20 per cent of the annual revenue of British theatres.

music for *Aladdin and His Wonderful Lamp* at the London Palladium, which would run from the end of 1964 into 1965. Hank, Bruce, Brian and John wrote for *Aladdin* as if it were a regular musical and had the whole thing completed before the end of the summer season in Great Yarmouth. 'I remember Mick Jagger came to see the show one night,' Hank later claimed in an interview with the Arts Desk. 'He thought it was charming and said, "You guys are really lucky – you can be here for weeks while we're schlepping around doing one-nighters." Look, it was fun. But I have to be honest... doing two shows a day for three and half months, five or six numbers a show... after a while you think, *This is not what we signed up for*. We wanted to play music instead of fooling around. The novelty wore thin after a few weeks, but then you look at your bank balance and it's okay. The positive side was it really stretched us to write songs that would carry the plot along. We also wrote things like "In the Country", so we had a few hits from it too.'

This wasn't the wry social comment of *A Hard Day's Night*; it was pure escapism. There was a flying carpet with no visible strings. Instead, the idea was to blow the kids' minds. *Aladdin* was also seen as an opportunity to get these kids into Cliff and the Shads, the ones who may not yet have been bitten by the Beatles. Just imagine!, cried Peter Gormley. *Aladdin* could conjure up a whole new generation of fans! Meanwhile, poor Brian Bennett was thrown through a mangle by Arthur Askey for the thirty-seventh time and starting to look for the exit door.

Just as Brian was being dunked into a bucket of soapy water for one last time in February 1965, one of the Shadows' old bosses had been setting up shop in the top five. John Schroeder had left Norrie

Paramor and Columbia to set up the Piccadilly label, a subsidiary of Pye. Flexing his creative muscles, he formed an instrumental act called Sounds Orchestral. With Johnny Pearson on piano and Schroeder bossing the ghostly strings behind, they scored what had to be one of the quietest hits of all time. 'Cast Your Fate to the Wind' somehow cut through on Radio Luxembourg's intermittent signal to reach number five. It was haunting and unlike anything else on the chart.

It was far from the only instrumental hit that year. The summer may have belonged to the Stones with '(I Can't Get No) Satisfaction' and the Beatles with 'Help!', but they had to make room for German pianist Horst Jankowski and 'A Walk in the Black Forest', a jaunty piece that received weekly plays on *Two-Way Family Favourites*. Just twenty years after the end of the war, it was a symbol of forgiveness as much as anything and a big hit on BFBS, the British Forces broadcast. But it also went top twenty in the US and top three in Britain. There was more. Marcello Minerbi took his fast, faster, fastest-train-on-the-track bouzouki instrumental 'Zorba's Dance' to number six on the UK chart in the summer of '65, just as Herb Alpert and the Tijuana Brass sauntered into the US top ten with their upbeat take on the theme from British kitchen-sink film *A Taste of Honey*.

Alpert was a phenomenon. A brown-eyed handsome man who had set up his own successful A&M label in 1962 with Herb Moss, he had no need to become a star in his own right, but he did it anyway by creating dozens of faux-Mexican instrumentals with softly parping trumpets. These sold like crazy. The 1965 album, *Whipped Cream and Other Delights*, outsold everything else in the US the following year. 'Spanish Flea', an insanely catchy thing which became the theme for

US TV show *The Dating Game*, reached number three in Britain in 1966. Herb parped his way through three instrumental albums a year and became richer than Paul McCartney. Beatles Schmeatles! Viva los Tijuanas!

Cliff Richard had gone his own way in August 1964 – and that was towards the US. Epic Records – who had finally scored Cliff his first US top-thirty hit with 'It's All in the Game' – invited him over to record a whole album. He went to New York and recorded Burt Bacharach songs with the great arranger Garry Sherman, previously responsible for the Drifters' 'Up on the Roof' and 'On Broadway', before going to Nashville to record with future Tammy Wynette and Charlie Rich producer Billy Sherrill. These were producers and arrangers at the top of their game in studios which, no matter the high regard in which George Martin and Norrie Paramor held Abbey Road, produced some of the biggest hits in the world. Cliff wasn't messing.

The results of the New York sessions were released in 1965, including 'Look in My Eyes Maria', a Bacharach obscurity that became the lead track on an EP, while Nashville produced the countrypolitan brace 'The Minute You're Gone' – a UK number one – and 'Wind Me Up (Let Me Go)' which would have repeated the feat and been the Christmas number one but for the Beatles' double A-side of 'Day Tripper'/'We Can Work It Out'.

The Shadows stayed home for all of this, unwanted by the Americans and apparently unneeded by Cliff. Bruce chewed his nails. Hank invested in some new gear. Maybe that would help? And they worked on their harmonies. If you can't beat them, thought Bruce, then why not join them?

*

'Mary Anne' was a Jerry Lordan song. It was simple, entirely acoustic, but its fragility was gorgeous, along the lines of the Everly Brothers' 'I'm Afraid', 'Crying in the Rain' or 'Love Her'. Taking a rare risk, it became the Shadows' first vocal A-side since 'Saturday Dance' a full five years earlier. Maureen O'Grady interviewed them for *Rave* magazine after the single came out in February 1965. She used un-pop words like 'professionalism' and 'mature'.

'In general conversation with the Shadows, you cover a lot of ground,' O'Grady wrote. 'They laugh a lot, they talk a lot: saying exactly what they think, never pausing to be evasive ... A surprising thing is that the Shadows admit they have no more actual ambitions left.' She quoted Bruce as saying, 'We've done just about everything now except for straight acting, and that's being covered this year ... When the big beat boom happened in Liverpool, we didn't try to compete with the Beatle-type records. We did the exact opposite. We kept exactly to our own style and recorded "Atlantis". Its success proved we could still compete.'

'Songwriting is our main hobby actually,' said a more optimistic Brian. 'We don't get time for much else, anyway. We all usually chip in together. I write on the piano, and we all add bits. But Bruce and Hank usually get all the credit – which is why they've both got Rolls-Royces, and John and I have Minis!'

They talked about 'Mary Anne'. 'We first heard it about three years ago,' said Bruce, 'but it wasn't right at the time. And then, a couple of months ago, we thought of it again. We asked Jerry Lordan – the composer who's written quite a few of our hits – if he still had it. We knew the time was right now.'

The usually modest Hank came up with a vainglorious quote for the ages. 'We're not being bigheaded, but it's only the ones with talent who last … We've seen everything come and go and we're still here. There was Bill Haley, Skiffle, Rock 'n' Roll, the Twist. The thing is, all these things were trends and fads. They died out.'

'The Shadows give the impression that everything they do is calculated,' wrote Maureen O'Grady.

It sounded like the group needed to let their hair down. They weren't old: Brian was twenty-five, Bruce and Hank twenty-three and John was just twenty-two. Still, to O'Grady, they seemed mature, a little out of the loop. 'The Shadows themselves have the feeling that they aren't quite with-it. This shows when they can discuss TV programmes freely, yet are quite in the dark about top night clubs, like The Ad Lib. It doesn't worry them – but they know they are different. Within the framework of their very personal kind of music, the Shadows have woven brilliantly the essence of current trends. They have remained true to themselves yet echoed – shadowed? – all that is right up-to-date. This is the way of a Shadow.'

Their confidence would not have seemed misplaced at the start of 1965. A *Billboard* magazine survey in January 1964 had concluded that Cliff was 'world champion' of pop, with Elvis in second place and the Shadows in third. But time waits for no one.

'Mary Anne', its acoustic guitars backed by little more than by sandpaper blocks and finger cymbals, received a terrific review from *Disc*. 'A vocal, yet, from the Shads who are certainly spreading their wings versatility-wise. Top side is a composition of considerable charm and the boys treat it folksily, with some expressive guitar sounds behind their four voices. Must be a hit, of course – and it could strike fear and trembling into the hearts of certain other established vocal groups.'

Shadows die-hards weren't so sure. Six months earlier, the Searchers had released the stylistically similar 'What Have They Done to the Rain' and reached number twelve, but 'Mary Anne' couldn't go higher than number seventeen, the exact same position 'Genie With the Light Brown Lamp', their single from the *Aladdin* score, had reached at the end of '64. What to gauge from that? Who knew?

They played safe, sort of, by releasing another instrumental single called 'Stingray' in June. It was not the theme from the contemporaneous Gerry Anderson TV show (which the Tornados handled instead), but had been written by Claus Ogerman, a giant of arranging, who had worked with everyone from Billie Holiday to Antônio Carlos Jobim and who, by early 1965, was arranging Lesley Gore hits like 'Maybe I Know' from his office in the Brill Building. The most noticeable thing about the Shadows' 'Stingray', though, wasn't Ogerman's melody but Hank's guitar tone. *What the hell was that?*

Hank laid down his Burns for 'Stingray' and picked up a six-string Fender bass which he then fed through a fuzz pedal. The sound was fresh, invigorating, something new and more aggressive. But, looking back in 2004, Hank seemed a lot less confident than he had appeared to Maureen O'Grady. 'In the mid-'60s, I just lost it totally, style-wise. I was trying to get away from the echo, thinking it was old fashioned. [On "Stingray"], I used some fuzzbox that sounded like a wasp in a bottle. Terrible. I was trying to find myself but just losing myself. It was a bad move.'

Given the Byrds were breaking through with the Rickenbacker twelve-string jangle of 'Mr Tambourine Man', it actually made a lot of sense for Hank to push forward, to try new effects, new pedals, new sounds. And *Record Mirror* liked 'Stingray' a lot more than he did. 'The highly professional gents have a hit sound to this new, deliberately rhythmic instrumental. Lots of bass, persistent percussion and interestingly laid down. The melody really gets a hold of you after a couple of plays. But there is this point: we played the disc to the rest of the RM staff and they found it hard recognizing it as the Shadows. Flip, with that fine title ["Alice in Sunderland"], is a Shadows composition, jangle rhythm, with loads of Hank's lead.'

George Harrison enjoyed 'Stingray', too, even if Hank didn't, and employed the same distorted bass sound on *Rubber Soul*'s 'Think For Yourself' later in '65. He also enjoyed their next single, another vocal: this time the Shads produced a tough cover of Barry Mann and Cynthia Weil's 'Don't Make My Baby Blue', which had been a minor American hit for Frankie Laine. There was a grungy guitar break and some prominent piano, but Hank sang lead, double-tracked, and it took them back into the top ten for the first time in more than a year. Maybe this was a sign.

'Bruce found a copy of Frankie Laine's latest single,' said Hank, 'an unexpectedly contemporary-sounding 45. We thought, *Yeah, let's record it*. We decided to take a punt and it was top ten. At Abbey Road one day, George Harrison came in and we started to have a chat. He said, "I like 'Don't Make My Baby Blue', it's great. You really should pack in the instrumentals and concentrate on vocals. You can sing. With the right choice of song material, you should go for the singing." And we thought, *Yeah, he's probably right*. But we didn't follow his advice, we kept on doing instrumentals … which is kind of stupid, really. Because the writing, quite honestly, was writ very large on the wall. The instrumental fashion was just tailing off. It was going.

'We had a name, the band was still successful, we'd just had a vocal hit. Logically, anyone with any brain would have gone "Right, let's do another vocal. Follow it up. Get a good song." That's what we should have done, but we didn't.'

They ignored George's advice, for whatever reason, and followed their fresh top-ten hit with 'The War Lord', the theme from a current Charlton Heston film. It was impressive – great drumming and Hank on mildly distorted lead – but impossible to dance to. Recorded at the same October '65 session was an Arnold/Martin/Morrow song called 'One Way to Love', another vocal and an absolute belter, the best kind of material that 1965 had to offer and which swam in similar waters to the Who's 'The Kids Are Alright' and 'I Can't Explain'. How could they have casually dumped it, leaving it to eventually surface on the 1966 *Shadow Music* album? 'One Way to Love' – clangourous, with gorgeous vocal harmonies, tricksy minor chords and superb vibrato-heavy support from Hank's Burns – sounded like a guaranteed hit. Here was a fork in the road and the Shadows went with the safer option: another instrumental. 'Don't Make My Baby Blue' would turn out to be the final Shadows top-ten hit of the '60s.

*

The Beatles had always pretended they hated Cliff Richard and the Shadows, that they represented everything they wanted to overturn. In the other camp that counted, that of the Rolling Stones, was manager Andrew Loog Oldham whose opinion was a little more nuanced. Oldham had recognised the power of the Shadows from the word go, especially when Jet Harris was still involved. He reckoned the Shadows would always have a place in pop because they were 'intelligent'.

Having set up his own label – Immediate Records – in 1965, Oldham gave his old Hampstead neighbour Tony Meehan some production work. As he had with 'Diamonds' two years earlier, Tony thought he could do better than his old muckers. He cut a single with Glyn Johns; usually the Rolling Stones' engineer, Johns was now on the other side of the studio wall. His singing voice was nothing like you might imagine from the man who would go on to produce the Beatles' 'Get Back' sessions and, a little later, the Who's *Who's Next*. He sounded much closer to Tennessee Ernie Ford than Mick Jagger. And the song he was given for his Immediate debut was… 'Mary Anne'.

The press release was weaselly. '"Mary Anne" is a Jerry Lordan composition that some of you may remember by the Shadows, who had a minor hit with it. Glyn's version of the song is so different in arrangement that it won't hurt those of you who already have the Shadows version to get this as well. This is certainly the best that he's ever done, and with this release he reveals himself one of the talented few.' Glyn's version was rotten, and sank without trace.

Around the same time, Columbia release the unimaginatively titled *Cliff Richard* LP, with a sleeve that looked like a typography catalogue mulched by the rain. It was a mopping-up exercise, scouring the vaults, but significantly it would be the last conventional Cliff and the Shadows album. Everything after this would be a special project – a soundtrack, a panto, a farewell album, a live reunion. No one knew it at the time, but the album marked the end of an era.

At least the Shadows didn't have to spend Christmas 1965 in another pantomime. 'I really wanted to be a serious arranger, so I ducked out of the Christmas pantomime in 1965,' explained Brian, 'and the other guys obviously felt the same.' Still, they were talked into writing *Babes in the Wood* for their none-less-cool, yodelling management stablemate, Frank Ifield. Brian took it on as a challenge in arranging to a deadline.

Not wanting to put their feet up for too long, the Shadows recorded a new single between Christmas and New Year's Eve in 1965: 'I Met a Girl' was written by Hank, another vocal but this time very slight, a country-ish lope that was compared in one review to a *Rubber Soul* outtake. That was generous. On the flip, 'Late Night Set' was a push into the future, with Hank using his Maestro fuzz unit and colouring the tone like Tommy Tedesco of California's super-session men the Wrecking Crew.

'I Met a Girl' came out in March 1966. A week before its release, Columbia had issued twin bolts of lightning: 'It's Just a Fear' by the Answers was the latest sound from Newcastle-upon-Tyne, an exercise in wailing, feedback-ridden paranoia with their ace guitarist Tony Hill burning holes in Dansettes across Tyneside (although it gained little national exposure); and the Yardbirds' 'Shapes of Things', the definitive hit from the Londoners, both warping minds and elliptically warning of the growing Cold War, with Jeff Beck playing off the top of his head and doing wild things to a guitar that people had literally never heard before. Both singles made the Shadows' latest sound very tame indeed. 'I watched Jeff Beck of the Yardbirds at *Ready Steady Go!* and he gets a fabulous sound,' said Hank. 'I'm all for anything that creates new ideas for guitars. I've got a few fuzz boxes lying around. It's a great sound, but you must use the box sensibly otherwise the effect is lost. I first heard a foot pedal being used by Big Jim Sullivan and realised how fabulous it was. There are so many good players around ... It gets me worried.'

The week after 'I Met a Girl' arrived in the shops, Columbia released the Tornados' 'Is That a Ship I Hear', the salty farewell from a group who had once challenged the Shadows' imperious standing as Biggest Group in Britain. Seabirds cried over the intro, the sea grumbled like a stormy March night in Felixstowe and the melody – thanks to producer Joe Meek's electrickery – sounded like it was performed by a trio of seagulls. The tide then rolled out and the Tornados were lost from sight. A year later, Joe Meek would be dead.

*

It's easy to think that the Beatles were always the Beatles, from another world, ruled by the gravitational laws of a different dimension, and that you can't compare any other group to them; it's just not fair. But, back in 1964, the Beatles had had a dozen close rivals in beat world: the Kinks, the Searchers, the Pacemakers, the Swingin' Blue Jeans, the Nashville Teens, the Hollies, the Dakotas and the Dreamers, the Fourmost and the Four Pennies, the Applejacks, the Tremeloes, all of them in the top ten, the whole A-plus to C-minus spectrum of British beat groups. Some of them started like a train but quickly derailed (the Searchers); some of them started like dray horses and ended up like stallions (the Kinks). There was no telling where any of them might end up.

There was no blueprint, just as there had been no blueprint for the Shadows in 1960. It was all about letting yourself become unmoored, risking the waters without a rubber ring. In the outside world, there was chaos, there was horror, violence flaring, bullets loading; according to folkies from Bob Dylan to Barry McGuire, it was the eve of destruction. So, having built a world for themselves, having created a safe, loving family of their own, why would the Shadows want to engage with the sorrows of the world, the ridiculous, the hypocritical and the transient? Why would Bruce – from a toxic and turbulent background full of mistreatment and abuse and whispers behind cupped hands –want to take a chance on losing all that, all on a whim? Bruce did not want to take that chance; he would not let his boat become unmoored. He was a stubborn bugger. And, in a twelve-month span, the Shadows' anchored boat was left behind. By 1966, it had become a dot in the distance.

*

Eyes were more often cast westward these days, away from England to the States, and to the West Coast where the Beach Boys' Brian Wilson had forsaken live shows to spend more time in the studio. The result had been *Pet Sounds*, released in May 1966, an album of unimaginable colour and range in its production, with Brian's imagination made tangible by the Wrecking Crew and his bandmates' beautiful harmonising. The lyrics were a song cycle about a love affair, nothing wildly new, but musically it was a phenomenon. Suddenly, pop shifted up three gears. Paul McCartney thought *Pet Sounds* was the greatest record he'd ever heard. In the very same month, the Mamas and Papas' harmonic marvel 'Monday, Monday' would be in the British and American top three, and civil rights campaigner Muhammad Ali knocked out cuddly cockney Henry Cooper in six rounds to become heavyweight champion of the world. London was losing its cultural crown.

The Shadows, just two and half years after *Billboard* magazine had anointed them biggest group in the world, must have felt a creeping sense of panic. Still, although 'I Met a Girl' had failed to reach the top twenty, they did at least share a place with *Pet Sounds* in the top ten of the album chart. *Shadow Music* was also issued in May 1966. A year earlier, they had released *The Sound of the Shadows*; while it included absolute A-grade Shadows material like 'The Lost City', 'Santa Ana' and 'Breakthru', parts of it had sounded so square it was almost a cube: a cover of Xavier Cugat's 'Brazil'; another of Burl Ives' wretched, folksy 'A Little Bitty Tear'; those tuxedos and frilly shirts. So maybe they thought Frank and Dino and Sammy were the bee's knees? This was still no way to get fifteen-year-olds on your side.

Shadow Music was an improvement. The limp folk influence that had hampered *The Sound of...* was gone. Seven of the twelve songs were self-penned and the album's highlights were largely those of Brian. Three of the songs were written by Chris Arnold, David Martin and Geoff Morrow, a writing team who were published by Shadam

Music, a company set up by the Shadows' management as a bulwark against the group's declining popularity. Along with the superb 'One Way to Love' was the pub piano-led 'I Only Want to Be With You', which was almost as strong, with 'Stay Around' also pretty decent. The path to the future should have been obvious.

Two of the album's tracks – 'Magic Doll' and 'Maid Marian's Theme' – were melodies rescued from the *Babes in the Wood* panto, while Brian's 'Benno-San' was apparently inspired by James Bond novels – although what sounds like a Heath Robinson mechanical contraption doesn't have much in common with John Barry. 'Now That You're Gone' and 'A Sigh' were filmic and quite beautiful, 'the sound of the Shadows' fully intact. 'Don't Stop Now' sounded like a Latin number from a Joe Brown picture – not very 1966 – while 'March to Drina' seemed to be going for the Greek package-tour coin, for which there was no real excuse. Still, *Shadow Music* was solid, if slightly frustrating.

*

In February 1966, the Shadows would be the cover stars of musicians' bible *Beat Instrumental*, hogging the limelight from 'Ray Davies Speaks Out', 'Stones Add Keyboard', 'The Sound of Brass' and – goddamit – 'The Ventures'. Well, at least other instrumentalists were still making the news.

Walter Wanderley's 'Summer Samba' and the Bob Crewe Generation's 'Music to Watch Girls By' flew the flag for instrumentals in 1966, both becoming top-thirty US hits and radio staples. The

Beach Boys – the biggest group in the world according to *NME* readers – had included two instrumentals on *Pet Sounds*. You'd think this was heartening news for Shadows fans who yearned to see the boys challenging in the top ten once again. There was one small problem; like the instrumental hits of 1965, none of them featured a guitar/bass/drums set-up. Only the title track from *Pet Sounds*, and the T-Bones' top-three 'No Matter What Shape (Your Stomach's In)' – an extended jingle from an Alka Seltzer commercial – even featured a lead guitar. Brian Wilson's 'Let's Go Away for Awhile' included assorted Hawaiian instruments, oboe and vibraphone to carry it into the ether; Wanderley used a squeaking mouse-organ; Crewe took Alpert's lead with a muted brass section.

Oh, but wait. Something was stirring in that haunted house on the hill. The Castle, as it was known locally, was on Cedarhurst Circle in the Los Feliz area of the Hollywood Hills. It had once belonged to silent-movie actress Norma Talmadge, was rumoured to have been owned by Bela Lugosi and now – looking in a parlous state – was home to a five-piece, inter-racial rock band who hung out there partying with Bob Dylan, Nico, Jim Morrison and a new-in-town Canadian guitarist called Neil Young whose primary influence was Hank Marvin. This rock band were caught between gentility and insanity, either about to become the biggest band in the world or a niche LA concern. They were called Love.

The first Love album was issued in 1966 and it tore through folk-rock, R&B and – with guitars set to max on the jangle-o-meter – a fledgling psychedelia. They closed their debut album out with a song called 'Emotions', which was an instrumental and sounded like the day after some California apocalypse, with deep Hank-like guitar and light, near-military, Meehan-like drums. I know they were from California, and I know that was the home of surf music, but one look at these boys and you knew they hadn't been to the beach since they were six years old. No, the influence on 'Emotions' was clearly that of the Shadows. The most shadowy Shadows, at their darkest and most ominous, like 'The Frightened City' at 16rpm. Love sounded like they loved the Shadows. And Love sounded like the future. There had to be hope.

*

For Hank, there was something of a disconnect in his life. 'There's a lot being said about Indian music in the pop scene, so I went to see Ravi Shankar playing his sitar. I think it was the most moving performance, musically, that I've ever attended.' Days later, he was singing something called 'Paella'.

In 1966, Elvis Presley lay on the grass with his hairdresser Larry Geller and saw faces in the clouds. He saw Stalin. He saw Jesus. He cried. Then he got up, went back to the MGM set and sang 'Smorgasbord': 'Some take just apple pie / Some take just cake / I'll take the dish I please / And please the dish I take.' There was a disconnect here, too. A deep spiritual hole, in fact. Elvis had four movies in British cinemas in 1966 – *four!* – and each had its own soundtrack album. If you stuck them all together, and then pared them back, you could get one halfway decent album. But the films were all rank, rotten, empty experiences.

Cliff and the Shadows had two films on release in 1966. Neither was boring, but neither exactly hit the zeitgeist. 'The nearest we've got to Indian music is something we've written for the new film with Cliff, *Finders Keepers*,' said Hank, still reeling from his Ravi Shankar experience. Presumably he was talking about the explosive 'My Way', a proto-psych gem which stood out from a bunch of songs even Elvis would have flatly turned down; 'Paella', 'Oh Senorita', 'Fiesta' and 'La La La Song' sounded like refugees from a Tommy Steele movie. Instead, they all featured on the soundtrack of the fourth, and the least, of the Cliff and the Shadows films, *Finders Keepers*. 'This Day' was the classy Cliff ballad and 'Washerwoman' had a hint of Elvis's 'Crawfish', with added Beach Boy harmonies and Brian's deep-groove drumming. The peculiar 'Time Drags By' – 'an easy going jog-trotter' according to *Disc* – was the lead single. It scraped into the top ten.

The storyline was *moderne*, all right, but not exactly *Summer Holiday*. The group were booked into a Spanish hotel where they were due to play for the season, but quickly discovered that the management couldn't pay them. So they made the most of the situation, became friendly with the locals and then heard that the traditional fiesta was threatened by a clutch of bombs which had been dropped in error by an American aircraft. Not any old bombs, either – nuclear bombs. 'The beat is the wildest, the blast is the craziest!' read the poster.

NME reader Mary Maynard of Richmond was less than impressed: 'Although I admire much of Cliff Richard's work, I can only deplore the proposed story for his next film. The lost nuclear bomb is hardly a suitable story for a "lighthearted musical comedy". Surely Mr. Richard realises that this serious and dangerous situation is not fitting for any kind of frivolity. Nuclear bombings are no laughing matter.' *Monthly Film Bulletin*'s review was inclined to agree, writing that *Finders Keepers* had 'a clockwork joviality that makes no demands on anyone involved, least of all the actors ... in a mood of determined merriment that never changes. The whole idea of centering a musical comedy round a mislaid nuclear bomb (based on an actual incident) seems, to say the least, a little ill-conceived.'* *Variety* noted that 'it could have had a good astringent and satirical tang', but it didn't. The Shadows' movie career stuttered to a halt once the film reached cinemas on 8 December 1966.

But it wasn't the only Shadows cinema release that month. The Shads as Thunderbirds puppets? Frankly, it was too easy to imagine. John looked like he'd modelled his entire image on Scott Tracy, but Brian's mischief was harder to shape from wood and plastic. They would appear as themselves in *Thunderbirds Are Go*. Brian took his son Warren to the studio while the film was being made and the boy was presented with a scale model of Tracy Island, especially made by Mike Trim and the Century 21 production team. Unsurprisingly, it became one of Warren's most treasured possessions.

In the film, presumably for legal reasons, the group were billed as Cliff Junior and the Shadows. They played a song called 'Shooting Star' written by Hank, Brian and John. The trio also wrote a theme for the glamorous, ice-cool Lady Penelope and, along with another two

---

* The real incident, in which a B-52 bomber dropped some H-bombs in the Mediterranean, had resulted in several deaths. Miraculously, no bombs exploded and the area was cleaned up, though traces of radioactivity linger.

songs ('Zero X' and the theme from *Thunderbirds* itself), they made up an EP which sold so poorly that it became a collector's item.

Most likely, Shadows fans simply couldn't keep up. Their wretched schedule also involved another panto – *Cinderella* – and this time they saved an absolute corker for the soundtrack. 'In the Country' was a Home Counties take on the new West Coast sounds, all ba-ba-ba-ba's and silver streams and waving goodbye to the fume-choked city. There was an understated, percussive string section and a palpable *joie de vivre*. It went to number six and saved their Christmas.

*

Without Cliff, the Shadows had not troubled the top twenty in 1966, not even for a solitary week. 'A Place in the Sun' was a dusky, melancholic piece of exotica and was geographically non-specific (Hawaii? Barbados? Benidorm?), like all the best exotica. It had been written by Petrina Lordan, wife of Jerry, and was nudged into a proper production piece with its judicious use of marimba, Hank's DeArmond pedal and a children's toy that Brian Bennett wheeled around Studio 2 on the middle eight, creating the impression of dazzling sun rays hitting a parasol. It was all rather beautiful, switching from F major to minor, with more than a hint of darkness. Was the place in the sun some kind of a hide-out? Were the Shadows on the run from their own uncertain future? On the flip was 'Will You Be There', a riotous piece of jangle-pop that leaned on the power of the Everlys' comeback hit 'The Price of Love'. Aggressive playing – not angry, but aggressive – and memorable.

With Cliff on lead, they released 'Blue Turns to Grey' – a Jagger/Richards outtake they allegedly stumbled across – and, on the flip of the 'Visions' single, 'What Would I Do (For the Love of a Girl)'. Both were terrific pieces of tough teenbeat with Hank and Bruce acing the harmonies. But both were essentially carried into the top twenty by Cliff's attachment.

Hank's own 'The Dreams I Dream' – released as a single in October '66 – was the real jewel and seemed to channel the Beach Boys both in its complex harmonies and John Rostill's brief bass solo that suggested close attention had been paid to *Pet Sounds*. Maybe there was stuff going on behind the scenes that we weren't privy to: 'She loved me and I was a king.'

'I'd just bought a Revox tape recorder,' said Hank, 'and I was trying to write things on it, to get some ideas. I'm sure in the back of my mind was "God Only Knows". It must have been, with the general feel. And I had this thought, the dreaming idea, when people have dreams of doing something, or ambitions, and it all falls apart. Just these little concise vocal phrases. Some girl came up to me one day and said "I really like that song". The verse structure reminded her of Chinese poetry. I was flattered, I didn't know how else to feel.'

The 'other guys were knocked out by it' and chose it to be their next single. On the flip, 'Scotch on the Socks' was just as strong in a very different way, a 'Flingel Bunt'-style raver with ferocious bass and drums from a totally in-sync Rostill and Bennett, and Hank's mind-melting guitar line threatening to burst from your Dansette. It evoked a party scene from, if not a Peter Fonda movie shot in Love's LA Castle, then at least something with Hywel Bennett wigging out.

There was whooping and laughing, just like the Beatles on 'Yellow Submarine', or Donovan and famous friends on 'Mellow Yellow', two totems of 1966 pop.

Nineteen sixty-six had given us some of the best Shadows recordings in years. 'The Dreams I Dream' b/w 'Scotch on the Socks' was released to radio and press as a promo double-B-side, with a big red 'B' replacing the big red 'A' that was there to explain to people who were far too busy to read a press release which song was the A-side. Classic Shads humour! Those boys! It was the definition of a self-fulfilling prophesy. They had stayed too long at the fair, had become too intertwined in the public imagination with instrumentals. 'The Dreams I Dream' – poignant, exquisite vocal performance though it was – hobbled to number forty-two and died. They would never play it live.

*

Apostolic intervention! Maybe that's what was needed.

Cliff just came right out and said it. One week he was with the Shadows, appearing on the 400th edition of the BBC radio show *Saturday Club*, chatting to Brian Matthew alongside Billy Fury and Marianne Faithfull, the next he was declaring that God was the most important thing in his life. It was unimaginable. Didn't he want to live on a red double-decker bus and drive around Greece for the rest of his days? Apparently not.

He took the stage at a Billy Graham crusade meeting in Earl's Court on 16 June 1966 and sang 'It is No Secret (What God Can Do)', which he presumably knew from Elvis's 1957 *Christmas Album*. Not only that, but in front of 25,000 people, Cliff announced he was a Christian and that once the next panto was over, in April 1967 he would embark on a three-year divinity course.

He talked to the *NME* a week later: 'I feel great all the time and know it is because of my beliefs. I've felt this way for two years now and it has relieved me of the petty jealousy I get in show business and helped me to help others. I did a Billy Graham study course of about five weeks, and found it stimulating.'

By the end of the year, he was seriously thinking about giving up showbusiness to become a religious studies teacher. 'I just want to be an ordinary teacher in an ordinary secondary school. I don't care if some people think I'm a phony, they're entitled to their opinions. I just want to get out of this business because I feel I have to.' It was all over.

A pop star declaring their devotion to God seemed like an outrage in 1966. Three years later, you couldn't move for Jesus freaks, but in 1966 most right-thinking people sided with the Beatles when American fans started making funeral pyres of their albums – and just because John Lennon had claimed that, right then, they were more popular than Jesus. The churches were empty; what John said had been a statement of fact, not arrogance.

'There was a lot of religion in there,' reckoned Warren Bennett. 'It's not trendy religion, it's not Hare Krishna. It's not hippie religion – it's other religion. So it was all very well for George Harrison to be religious, buy a temple, but if you're Cliff and you say "I'm a Christian", everyone goes, "Oh". I think he just lives his life as a Christian person. I don't really see what's wrong with that.

'They weren't managing a rock 'n' roll persona. It was brave.'

Maybe if Cliff had grown his hair, grown a beard, started wearing sandals and started to actually dress like Jesus, then things might have panned out differently. Instead, what he did in 1966 was to cut himself off from the pop continuum, to isolate himself as an exception. Down the line, he would record a single called 'Jesus', which was one of the best he ever made, with a phased groove, fuzzbox-down-a-telephone guitar lines and a lyric about the imminent apocalypse ('Save us from the destruction of happiness, the destruction of the world'). Released in 1972, it sounded twenty years ahead of its time, like the spirit of *Screamadelica*, only imbued with real fire and brimstone.

But Cliff did not record 'Jesus' in 1966. Instead, he chose to start dressing like the RE teacher from a provincial school he was hoping to be. He started to wear NHS specs, even though no one had previously noticed that his eyesight was going. He was talking about retiring from music, giving it all up and working as a schoolteacher. And he seemed genuinely happy. Relieved, even.

Bruce must have lost his mind. All this work he'd put into the Shadows, all the years of discipline and tight control, and sodding religion was going to come and take it all away from him! He needed an apostolic intervention of his own. This soon came in the form of a seventeen-year-old from Australia called Olivia.

11

GOODBYE JET, HELLO OLIVIA

Olivia Newton-John had won a competition on the Australian TV show *Sing Sing Sing*, the first prize of which was a trip to a recording studio in London. She arrived and recorded a tremendously loud and exciting single for Decca called 'Till You Say You'll Be Mine', written by Jackie DeShannon, with a backing group called the Kytes. 'It sounded like it was cut in someone's bathroom,' she later said (which was true; Joe Meek's bathroom, specifically).

Olivia had been born in Cambridge in 1948. Though she would go on to become a superstar, her family had one or two other claims to fame. Her maternal grandfather Max Born was a major figure in quantum physics, who had moved to Cambridge in 1933 to escape the Nazis; he won the Nobel Prize for Physics in 1954. Olivia's father Brin was originally an opera singer. He could speak perfect German and so was signed up by MI5 during the war – Brin would be one of the soldiers who captured Rudolf Hess after he bailed out of his plane in Scotland. He had also worked on cracking the Enigma code at Bletchley Park. You could say, all things considered, that Olivia was the under-achiever of the family.

The Newton-Johns moved from Cambridge to Melbourne when Olivia was six years old after her dad took a professorship at the University of Melbourne. Her first group was formed when she was just fourteen; the Sol Four, formed with three school friends, would sing at a local coffee shop run by her brother-in-law. Australia's pop scene was still in its pupa stage and this was enough to get her noticed, with a bunch of TV shows featuring her: there was *The Happy Show* on which she performed as 'Lovely Livvy'; *The Go Show*, where she met singer Pat Carroll and they became tight friends; and, most importantly, *Sing Sing Sing*, on which she won a talent show by singing 'Anyone Who Had a Heart' and won her trip to London. Olivia delayed the trip by almost a year, but was still just sixteen when she cut 'Till You Say You'll Be Mine' in 1966. It sold very poorly.

Homesick, she would repeatedly book trips back to Australia, but her mother would cancel them all, telling Liv she should stay and make the most of the opportunity. A few months later, Pat Carroll also won a talent contest which enabled her to move to England. It was all alright – the pair quickly formed a nightclub folk act called Pat and Olivia. Tapping into the Australian ex-pat community, they soon came under Peter Gormley's wing. 'We opened for the Shadows in Bournemouth,' remembered Olivia, 'which is how I first met Bruce. I loved singing with them!'

Olivia had long hair, a fringe, ridiculously large blue eyes and wore cotton shirts and tartan skirts that came from Marks and Spencer's children's department. In 1966, she was living with pal Pat in a flat in Earl's Court, which in the '60s was an enclave of Australians. Neither of them could cook; Pat had never even boiled an egg. They got by eating mashed potatoes and sausages pretty much every night.

'She was over here with her singing partner Pat Carroll,' Bruce later told Mike Read, 'but I got her alone one day and asked her out. To which she replied, "I don't mind going out with you, but I'm not going alone." So Pat had to come with us.' Bruce was only twenty-four, but he seemed to have lived several lifetimes of anxiety. He was a married man, his group were beginning to dip in popularity and their lead singer was thinking of retiring. He was throwing caution to the wind – a mid-life crisis in his mid-twenties. 'I desperately wanted Olivia to audition for our third pantomime, *Cinderella*, which was lined up at the Palladium at Christmas, but she declined and flew back to Australia and her steady boyfriend in November. They were troubled times for me. My wife Anne had found out about Olivia, Olivia had gone back to her boyfriend and there was a lot of squabbling going on within the group.'

Bruce had just met a girl who would have a huge impact on the Shadows' future career. 'I wasn't proud of what I did, walking out on my wife and family,' he revealed in 1989. 'I just fell in love and it was sad and unfortunate that two other people should get hurt – my wife Anne and my son Dwayne, who was only six. Looking back, I realise I was selfish. Everything I had promised myself in the past, to keep my family together, was destroyed ... I was hardly ever at home, I was always away on tour or recording. I broke up the family I had always wanted and ruined two people's lives.'

Bruce wasn't alone in his domestic upheaval. During the making of *Finders Keepers*, Hank had started spending time with one of the dancers in the film, Carole Naylor. She was also appearing in *Hello Dolly* in the evenings; when Carole had a night off, Hank took her to the Pickwick Club where organist Roy Phillips and his hip jazz trio the Peddlers were playing.

The first Mrs Marvin and the first Mrs Welch would now simply melt into the shadows. Trying to find information on them, either before or after their splits, is surprisingly difficult. Hank's explanation for his separation from Billie was that they had grown apart and mutually agreed they no longer had anything in common. Maybe this was true, but it was easy for him to say when he'd just met a saucy dancing girl and his wife wasn't asked for her side of the story. Billie would be left to bring up their son Dean, his twin brothers Peter and Paul, and sister Philippa alone. These things happen.

*

By 1966, Jet Harris was ready. Cliff Richard had given him £700 to buy himself some decent gear and Tony Meehan had agreed to be his manager. Everyone wanted Jet back. Cliff's gift was generous enough, but soon afterwards Jet also – finally – received £11,000 in damages from Midland Red buses for his career-destroying car crash. Of course, it wasn't just a question of money.

'I tended to like stuff a bit harder. Not being snide to the Shadows, but I liked something with a bit more balls to it than "Foot Tapper".' Jet was still a popular face around Soho, a real hero to the younger set, and getting other players around him wasn't a problem. 'I was in a pub on Tottenham Court Road. Upstairs in the rehearsal room was myself, Viv Prince on drums from the Pretty Things, Rod Stewart and Jeff Beck*... Tell me about it. Then we went downstairs for a drink ... and that was the end of it. Because of the drink. Yeah, that could have been something.'

He was now living with his girlfriend Julie Bucknall in Dolphin Square in Pimlico, a swish residential block with its own bar and theatre ticket kiosk. One night, in January 1967, they went to see Jimi Hendrix at the Brady Club in Whitechapel. Supporting were a group called the Sloane Squares whose singer, Pete Gage, had invited Jet along with an eye to the future. Jet needed a singer for his new group and, a couple of days later, Pete auditioned for him and Tony Meehan in the Dolphin Square flat. He sang 'Summertime' as Tony strummed a guitar and he was in. Keeping his distance, Tony was now managing the group from his home in Hendon; part of his management deal was that Jet would go into a detox programme in a Hampstead clinic.

Meehan engineered a one-single deal with Fontana and found a song called 'My Lady' for the A-side. It was written by Reg Presley of the Troggs, one of the hottest groups in the country. Big Jim Sullivan came in on guitar, Ray Cooke was on drums and Pete Gage sang lead, with Jet providing back-ups. It was a peculiar drone of a song, with a two-note riff played on a flute.

* In another quote from Jet, the drummer was Ray Cooke.

A *Juke Box Jury* panel that included Adam Faith and Anita Harris voted it a unanimous 'hit' and it made it into Radio London's airplay-led chart. But up against extraordinary new 45s like Traffic's 'Paper Sun' or the Move's 'I Can Hear the Grass Grow', 'My Lady' sounded half-hearted. All the goodwill in the world couldn't make people buy the thing.

No matter, the line-up of the Jet Harris Group soon formalised. Pete Gage was still on vocals, but the rest of the players were hijacked from R&B band Sonny Childe and the TNTs – Billy Adamson on drums, Mike Vaughan-Jones on Hammond, Ernie Hayes on guitar.

The problem now was the travelling – unsurprisingly, Jet hated it. No one was talking about post-traumatic stress disorder in 1967, but given the hell he'd gone through, Jet was a classic case study. The first show for the new group was at the Top Hat in Spennymoor in County Durham, several hours up the A1 and then down a weaving mess of back roads that linked small mining towns. Jet was found by Pete Gage slumped in the toilet at home on the morning of their first gig, paralytically drunk before breakfast.

They drove up to Spennymoor, Jet was given some speed and – remarkably – he made it through the set. It was the first of six nights at the Top Hat. Their set included Booker T and the MGs' 'Red Beans and Rice', Howard Tate's 'Ain't Nobody Home' and Chris Farlowe's 'Good to Me', with a segment for Jet and Tony's three hits. By now, 'My Lady' had made it to number twenty-eight on the Radio London chart. Jet made 'mistakes on each and every performance', according to Gage, but the WMC crowd were surprisingly forgiving. Manchester's Palace was less understanding. They were booed off. 'This is showbiz,' Jet told the crestfallen Gage. 'It happens sometimes.'

In September 1967, after a show in Sunderland, the rest of the band told him they'd got a contract to back PP Arnold. The Jet Harris Group was over. Returning home to London, Jet discovered Julie Bucknall had gone too. He wouldn't make another record for almost a decade.

12

SUNDAY FOR SEVEN DAYS

Regrets were beginning to unfold, to pile up like recurring flashbacks. Why hadn't they listened to George Harrison and switched to vocal A-sides? How did they lose their sense of timing so badly? Why were they still doing that dance, like it was 1960 and not 1967, like Merseybeat and R&B and folk-rock and psychedelia had happened elsewhere, and not in their world?

Cliff was still there, clocking into the top ten, biding his time at the EMI factory until he could finally fulfil his dream. This dream was to stand at the front of a classroom and talk in front of thirty gurning teenagers about the Bible: in reality, the boys would all be thinking about what they'd like to do to the fragrant girls, while the girls were all thinking about the best way to avoid the unwashed boys. None of them would be thinking much about Jesus (apart from one boy, who was thinking about how his name sounded like 'cheeses', which made him think about lunch). Cliff wanted to do this day after day. But, for now, he'd just have go through the motions of being a pop star and record Hank's new song, 'The Day I Met Marie'.

It was quite something, multi-part, unlike anything Hank had written before. A sun-dappled meadow of a verse, lazy and a little unsettling, led into a chorus that sounded like a riot in a mechanical toy museum, before a slightly threatening coo of 'Baby, go to sleep now' wrested the listener back to the meadow. Cliff thought it was the best record he'd ever made.

If it hadn't been Cliff – newly Christian and thus cut adrift from pop's secular heart – then it would have gone higher than number ten. But if it hadn't been by Cliff, the BBC might have seen their way to banning it. It sounded a lot like D.R.U.G.S. were involved – surely not, if it was sung by Cliff? – rather like that worrying new single by Hank's heroes, the Everly Brothers. 'Clouds so sweet cloud my mind' ran the opening line of 'Mary Jane', another terrific mid-'60s Everlys record which few people bar Hank actually bought. But 'The Day I Met Marie' wasn't about drugs at all; it just – like the Flowerpot Men's 'Let's Go to San Francisco' and Keith West's 'Excerpt From a Teenage Opera' – gave that impression, because any good pop records made in the summer of 1967 were bound to have been at least glanced or lightly bruised by the magic of 'Strawberry Fields Forever' and 'A Day in the Life'.

*

In Los Angeles, acid-tinged folk rock sensations Buffalo Springfield were releasing their extraordinary second album, *Buffalo Springfield Again*, to unanimous acclaim. Fronted by twin threats Stephen Stills and Neil Young, they covered the entire back cover of the record with a dedication: 'We wish to thank the following friends, enemies and people we don't know from Adam for their influence and inspiration.' The list included Chuck Berry, Tim Hardin, Judy Collins, Jimi Hendrix, Bert Jansch and Chet Atkins, but the very first dedication was to 'Hank B. Marvin'. The US may not have cared about the Shadows, but Neil Young was Canadian and that meant Hank was a touchstone for guitarists of his generation, just as he was in Britain.

In Bradford, the Shadows were California dreaming. They were on the cabaret club circuit by 1967, the one John Rostill had told *Fabulous* that he was really looking forward to. It was lucrative, but hardly conducive to musical experimentation or progression. A typical night for the Shadows now would be one in Laisterdyke, an industrial district on the southern outskirts of Bradford, at a place called the Lyceum Rainbow club. There were tables at the front instead of a dancefloor. There was chicken grease on the checked table-cloths and Tetley ale in dimpled glasses. Brian flicked a thimble in the air during the washboard number, 'Putting on the Style'; they were so close to the audience that it could end up in someone's pint.

In Laisterdyke, they opened with 'Dance On!', their milkiest number one, and followed it with 'Lara's Theme' from *Doctor Zhivago*. Then came a couple of vocals, the George Harrison-approved (though probably not in this setting) 'Don't Make My Baby Blue' and an Everly Brothers song, 'Let it Be Me'. 'Nivram', 'Apache' and 'Foot Tapper' got the old fans going before 'the washboard number' and Burl Ives' feeble 'A Little Bitty Tear'. 'Flingel Bunt' saw them play as hard as they would all night and would be followed with one of the slower vocal hits of the day – Scott McKenzie's 'San Francisco', or Dave Davies's

'Death of a Clown', or Cliff's 'It's All Over' – before they closed with 'Somewhere' from *West Side Story* and then brought out the big finale with 'FBI'. That, essentially, was their set from 1965 until 1968, by which time – decent pay or no – they must have been heartily sick of it. They never even played 'Wonderful Land' or 'The Frightened City' or 'Man of Mystery' or 'Kon-Tiki'.

To the outside world, the Shadows' new releases still represented some kind of English exotica, a heroic globetrotting sound as if they were a musical version of International Rescue. Film work still seemed an obvious move, with a spy movie called *Maroc 7* looking like a possible entry point. It starred Gene Barry as a jewel thief, with eye-catching support from Cyd Charisse, Elsa Martinelli and English rose Angela Douglas. *Maroc 7* had a similar Anglo-continental feel to TV shows like *The Saint* and was co-produced by Leslie Phillips, who appeared on screen as a fashion photographer.

The theme from *Maroc 7* had been written by Paul Ferris, a friend of Hank's who had written Cliff's 1966 hit 'Visions' and who would end up playing the occasional substitute's role in Shadows shows when somebody was ill or unavailable. It was a bewitching melody that smacked of foreign intrigue; the recording featured some muted brass and high, eerie strings, with Hank on rapidly strummed mandolin and twin-tracked guitar. Beginning with 'A Place in the Sun' the previous year, their singles had started to become more experimental and the group were now engaging with Abbey Road's 1967 spec. *Sgt Pepper* had been recorded there! Quite rightly, they were trying a little harder.

The group had initially agreed to score the whole of *Maroc 7*, but somehow ran out of time and only cut the theme, which wouldn't even be used in the film. EMI stalwart Ken Jones spared their blushes and completed the score, while a *Top of the Pops* appearance at least helped to push the single to the brink of the top twenty.

On a rare night off, Hank and Brian went to see Gary Burton, the American vibraphonist, playing with Larry Coryell. 'It was all different,' raved Hank, 'early jazz fusion I suppose. The use of vibes and voices.' Burton's influence imbued their next single, 'Tomorrow's Cancelled', with a very different atmosphere. The high wordless vocal sounded a little like Olivia, but Hank later claimed, 'I think it's my voice! Brian and I liked ["Tomorrow's Cancelled"] a lot. It didn't really sound like the Shads I suppose, with the jazz and South American influence.'

It was a lovely recording but, issued the same month as the Beatles' 'All You Need is Love', the Rolling Stones' 'We Love You', the Jimi Hendrix Experience's 'Burning of the Midnight Lamp', the Small Faces' 'Itchycoo Park' and Traffic's 'Hole in my Shoe', 'Tomorrow's Cancelled' sounded completely out of step. Not dated, but just nothing to do with what was happening in paisley-and-patchouli 1967 Britain. With its portentous title, the single didn't even register on the charts. 'That wasn't unexpected,' admitted Hank years later. 'Even at the height of our success, I thought, *It's got to stop*. It happens to everybody, unless you're the Beatles or Elton John.'

The title track of their *Jigsaw* album, released in July 1967, moved like an E-type, with a power-pop drive that looked forward to '80s guitar bands like REM and the Smiths. Bruce's electric rhythm guitar had a sharp tang and they were clearly enjoying making the most of the studio. *Record Mirror* gave *Jigsaw* a lead review, describing it as 'gutsier', with the headline 'BEST SHADS LP FOR A LONG TIME'.

The opening chord of 'Tennessee Waltz' rang out like the opening of 'A Hard Day's Night', unsettling and foreboding, but the track was rather undermined by a herky-jerky rhythm based around John Rostill's single fuzz note on the off-beat, like a duck attempting ska. It built up to a fine dissonant, metallic ending, which only makes you wish they'd ditched the fuzzy duck (warning: it will reappear). 'Prelude in E Major' was filmic and Brian's drums were given a decent work-out. The rhythm guitar almost sounded like a Fender Rhodes piano and Hank used his whammy bar to good, tearful effect.

Up to the minute, song-wise, were the quartet of songs that closed Side One and opened Side Two: Manfred Mann's 'Semi-Detached Suburban Mr James', Burt Bacharach's 'Trains and Boats and Planes', the Easybeats' 'Friday on My Mind' and the New Vaudeville Band's Grammy-winning trifle 'Winchester Cathedral'. There was no great effort on any of them, save the gormless comedy opening to 'Winchester Cathedral'.

An album that began so strongly petered out into Music For Pleasure easiness and novelty. The only stand-out on Side Two of *Jigsaw* was 'Waiting for Rosie', a drizzly, cool, British jazz number that could have accompanied a contemporary London-set movie like *Morgan – A Suitable Case for Treatment*; you can picture David Warner kicking his heels in the city's back streets.

Cool jazz film scores weren't much in evidence on the 1967 tour dates, though. Instead, they were still playing the wretched

'A Little Bitty Tear' and, worse yet, had added 'Green Green, Grass of Home' to their set. What on earth were they thinking?

*

With falling chart positions, Hank and Brian branched off into side projects. Brian's 1967 solo *Change of Direction* LP signalled his move into film and TV work; he used John Rostill on bass, former Krew Kat Jim Sullivan on guitar, former Checkmates keyboardist Alan Hawkshaw and flautist Alan Skidmore. Now, here was a sign of where the Shadows could be heading if they wanted to. It was much more jazz-inspired than *Jigsaw* – jazz, after all, was where Brian's heart remained. But it was intriguing to see how a current Shadow (Rostill) and a future Shadow (Hawkshaw) slotted so easily into Brian's arrangements while remaining under Norrie Paramor's watchful eye. Here, effectively, was a parallel Shadows, one in which Hank and Bruce had gone their own ways. You could hear the sense of release and relief on tracks like 'Canvas', bravely released as a single in November, which was more avant than anything the Shadows had tried in years: flute and piano solos over abstract block chords, with an intense duet between the Shads' rhythm section. It also showed they didn't need to compete with Traffic or the Small Faces or the Herd. They were talented enough and popular enough – if they'd only just take that step.

Instead, the Shadows seemed incapable of getting off an early-'60s treadmill – recording an album a year, writing pantos, getting thrown through the mangle year after year. At least, in 1967, they got to play more alluring destinations than Laisterdyke.

They were pictured in Japan wearing what were apparently called 'happiness jackets', with their first names written vertically one side. They also picked up a bunch of excellent tunes to record when they got home: 'The Wild Roses' appeared on their next album, while 'Omoide No Nagisa', 'Kimi To Itsumademo' and 'Gin-Iro No Michi' would be released on a Japanese-only EP alongside, for no apparent reason, 'Londonderry Air'.

While playing in Australia, they met Melbourne group the Strangers and Bruce clicked with their guitarist John Farrar. 'It's obviously good for the ego to see groups still following what we do,' Hank told the *NME*. 'If you see local star outfits standing in the wings, well, you feel you're not going out of date or something. This, right now, is really the first time ever that we've been able to look upon ourselves as a group in our own right.

'Playing cabaret by ourselves in Australia helped build the confidence. We've worked into a real group – you know, in the way we think together. It's a matter of complementing what each other is doing.'

Australian journalist David Frith wrote that 'in 1961 they were a quartet of weedy youngsters playing pulsating rock 'n' roll to a shrieking teenage audience. Now they are four smooth, well-dressed, mature young men, playing to predominantly middle-aged audiences at Chequers night spots and drawing a standing cheering ovation. Strangely their repertoire includes many of the same numbers that made the kids squeal six years ago. Their secret? "We play the same old rubbish mostly," says Bruce Welch, "just play it a bit slower and turn the amplifiers down halfway."'

Reviewer Sydney Mann observed 'four young men sartorially elegant in the style of pseudo Regency Bucks, wearing boots fashioned from delustred satin, no less. They played on wafer-thin guitars and by the time they had finished their first number, I, if I may use the modern American idiom of our literary giants, had egg all over my face. They were killin' 'em … these fellows are not the shadows, they are the substance.'

Hank sounded rejuvenated by the tour, telling the *NME*'s Peter Jones that 'each country we visited did us good, notably in record sales. It's a sort of revitalising process. And each country we visit gives us some new ambition to work on.'

He also revealed some peculiar plans for future Shadows shows. 'We saw Peter, Paul and Mary in a one-group show and this has made us want to create a two-hour act for ourselves. We already do about an hour but to extend it means we can show off different aspects of us as individuals … We'll throw in comedy at greater length, we can switch instruments, explain more about the different effects we use … really tell people about things like a fuzzbox. We know that fans are interested, but in a normal sort of act you haven't got time to talk much.'

It sounded strange, and it never happened.

*

A second album of 1967, *From Hank, Bruce, Brian and John*, emerged in time for Christmas, and built on the promising aspects of *Jigsaw*. Titles like 'The Tokaido Line' showed what a mark Japan had left on them. There were also a few vocals this time – they tore into the Box Tops' sleepy southern soul stew 'The Letter', with an intro so abrupt and abrasive it sounded like it could have been cut live in an all-night, uppers-fuelled session. Hank's solo at the end – replacing the Box Tops' smooth flight of strings – was equally jagged and wild. More of this sort of thing, please and thank you! The only weak spots were a couple of perfunctory instrumentals of contemporary hits – although at least the Monkees' 'Last Train to Clarksville' and Lee Dorsey's 'Holy Cow' were fairly unusual choices, and the good easily outweighed the average. They were tight as a drum – and beginning to flex their creative muscles too.

'Let Me Take You There' was John Rostill's venture into pastoral psych-pop, a truly gorgeous thing, with wordless hummed backing vocals and a touch of Pentangle in its structure. It was also released on a very rare promo single; the other side was an instrumental by Graham Gouldman called 'Naughty Nippon Nights', which he was at pains to point out was not his title. 'I don't think I gave it a title,' he said, years later, 'but I hope they had some naughty Nippon nights. The Shadows version was very different to mine. The verse was the same, but they added the intro. I was delighted. I was a massive fan of Cliff and the Shadows.'

Here's the surprising and slightly depressing thing. The Shadows never played any of this material live – nothing at all. There was no real chronology to their shows, just a groundhog day existence of donning tuxes and bow ties, playing the same three or four hits – even though they had two dozen to their name – doing their leg-kicks and bowing at the end.

'We'd started playing the working men's clubs instead of theatres,' Brian Bennett observed. 'You'd go on at midnight in front of loads of pissed blokes going, "Give us 'Apache'" and "Is Cliff a poof?".'

*

The new year rolled around with the Beatles at number one ('Hello Goodbye') *and* number two ('Magical Mystery Tour') in the chart. New kids in town the Bee Gees had 'Massachusetts' and 'World' in the top twenty, while the Monkees' 'Daydream Believer' and Gene Pitney's 'Something Gotten Hold of My Heart' showed that ballads didn't have to be dripping in Engelbert ghee to sell. In January 1968, Hank, for the first time, tried his hand at solo work with a single called 'London's Not Too Far'. It was a cute tale about kids running away from home, not in any kind of gritty way, and it wasn't hard to imagine Val Doonican or Vince Hill singing it. Pop pickers were unmoved. It was quickly followed by 'Dear Old Mrs Bell', a Shadows vocal 45 which fitted into the current trend of toytown psychedelia.

While the American psych was based around the Vietnam War and looking for real alternatives to the military-industrial complex, the parameters of British psychedelia had been set out by the influential BBC screening of Jonathan Miller's woozy *Alice in Wonderland* in December 1966, followed a few months later by the Beatles' *Sgt Pepper* and Pink Floyd's *Piper at the Gates of Dawn*, Character sketches like Cat Stevens' 'Matthew and Son' and the Kinks' 'Autumn Almanac' dealt with the day-to-day in 1967 with an oddly heightened sensibility;

Keith West's 'Excerpt From a Teenage Opera' told the story of Grocer Jack, aging and overworked, while hymned by a children's choir, harpsichords and ornate orchestration. 'Dear Old Mrs Bell' was the Shadows' contribution to the genre – 'she enjoys her little visits to the zoo' – with a Hank vocal, pretty harmonies on the chorus and a truly lovely baroque string section. Again, it failed to even trouble the top fifty.

*

Bruce had followed Olivia on a trip to Australia where she and Pat Carroll were doing a TV special. He openly declared his love for her, which caused some embarrassment on set, and Olivia was abruptly fired from the TV show because of what the producer called her 'entanglements'. She was mortified and felt bad for unintentionally ruining Pat's big night.

Worse yet, when they tried to fly back to London, they discovered that Pat's visa had expired. She insisted that Olivia return to London without her, telling her she was more than ready to go out on her own. Olivia wasn't even sure if she could sing without Pat; like Hank and Bruce, they had been joined at the hip for so long. But, back in London, she would move in with Bruce and the couple lived in bliss with two Irish setters called Geordie and Murphy. Pat's enforced stay in Australia turned out to be a blessing in disguise. She re-met writer/singer/producer John Farrar, whose group the Strangers had begun to splinter. Pat and John – like Bruce and Olivia – decided to marry.

In 1968, solo Olivia was quickly signed up to join a new four-piece group assembled by James Bond producer Harry Saltzman and the bulldog-faced pop mogul Don Kirshner, the man who had put the Monkees together – and subsequently been fired by them.

They would be called Toomorrow, one in the eye for Columbia's psychedelic act Tomorrow of whom Kirshner was presumably unaware. Kirshner described Toomorrow as 'the best-looking total group that ever existed'. They were to make a movie (about aliens needing Earth's pop music to survive) and their debut album would be the soundtrack. It was a big deal. David Bailey did a photo session with them, which weirdly was not used on their album cover.

'We filmed at Pinewood Studios outside of London and Val Guest was our director,' wrote Olivia in her memoir. 'I worked with the clothing designer and had approval of my clothing, which was very mod for the time. We were being moulded to be the next Monkees. Of course, when you do anything, you hope it's going to be successful… it was certainly a fun experience.' *Toomorrow* was fun to watch, too, but a daft film even by 1968 standards – and, as ongoing problems would delay its release until 1970, it sank without trace. Olivia frequently got to show off her legs in high Carnaby Street fashion, but was otherwise badly underused on screen. The obvious star of the film was seen cooking bacon and eggs for the rest of the group more often than she was singing.

So the *Toomorrow* film was a dud. That wouldn't have mattered so much had the soundtrack album not been similarly weak. All of the songs were written by Brill Building writers Ben Raleigh (author of pop classics like 'Tell Laura I Love Her', 'That's How Heartaches Are

Made' and the *Scooby-Doo, Where Are You?* theme) and Mark Barkan (Manfred Mann's 'Pretty Flamingo', the Banana Splits' 'Tra La La Song'), but none of them sounded like a hit. Olivia's new boyfriend Bruce offered to write another soundtrack using his contacts in Britain, but that would have been too expensive. In the end, the *Toomorrow* film took two years to complete, but disappeared much more quickly. Olivia later told the *NME* that 'our film died a death and it was all a bit of a shambles'.

The album was released on RCA in Britain, where Toomorrow's press officer was a brusque but sharp-witted East Ender called David Martin. 'Olivia and I met in 1969. I got this call saying we want you to meet these people from the new Donnie Kirshner and Harry Saltzman movie. Into my office came Liv – we became instant best of friends. And then I moved to Pye, just after the Toomorrow project.' It hadn't been a promising start, but things were beginning to fall in to place for Olivia.

*

On New Year's Day 1968, the Shadows were in the West End appearing at the Talk of the Town's cabaret venue. John Rostill, always the quiet man of the group, collapsed and was unable to perform. Licorice Locking stood in for him; this was a line-up of the Shadows that hadn't been on stage since 1963. Before the season was over, though, Brian was taken ill with appendicitis and the Shadows had to find a substitute drummer – Tony Meehan agreed to step in. Forgetting the animosity of six years earlier, it must have felt like a school reunion.

For just over a week, the Shadows line-up would be Hank, Bruce, Licorice and Tony.

Brian had one eye on the exit door by now. Bruce, for once, seemed happy and settled, living with Olivia in the Hertfordshire village of Hadley. Hank, on the other hand, was struggling; at home things weren't great. Though he'd met Carole in 1966, the separation from his wife Billie was drawn out and they wouldn't divorce until 1971. Much later, he opened up to the *Daily Mail*: 'Having success early had a big impact on my young family as I was away touring so much. I was just nineteen when my first child was born. I was way too young to get married and I didn't fully understand the implications of it all, and probably was far too young to be a father.

'Suddenly, you're hit with this young child to consider and to look after and feed and clothe and educate, and try to make them into a decent human being. I've got four children from my first marriage; our first son, Dean, died [from pneumonia aged thirty-four in 1997, after years of drug and alcohol abuse]. It tore our hearts out, but you just have to learn to live with it as you would with any loss. The grieving eventually stops.'

John was also having serious mental health issues, though he bottled them up and tended to keep his problems very much to himself.

In 1967, he had been interviewed by *Fabulous* in an article entitled 'This Shadow Is Cast for Bachelorhood'. 'The home life of the other Shadows knocks me out,' said John, 'with kids and all that. I tend to think I'm missing out.' Still, he seemed to have no plans to settle down. 'It means I can do what I want, when I want. I would miss that if I were married.' But, within months, he met a girl called Lynn Waller;

although he never confided in the other band members, it seemed he was truly in love. Big Jim Sullivan became close to him during their time playing with Tom Jones in 1969, 'as close as anybody ever got, I reckon. He actually poured out some of his worries, which was unusual for him. The Shadows toured Australia and the Far East during 1967. John said he had been going with a girl called Lynn Waller. He really missed her during that long tour. He was really in love with her. Something happened to John on that tour, which I'd rather not talk about. Suffice it to say that it put a further strain on his relationship with Lynn and, early in 1968, she ended their liaison. It was a bad blow for John, a very bad blow. He was devastated.'

Talking to Rob Bradford, John's old friend Bruce Baxter recalled how John would fall into bouts of depression. 'No one ever knew why, even though we were desperate to help him. I remember John, one time, sitting on the bed rocking backwards and forwards, sobbing quietly. I did my best to comfort him. "John," I'd say, "what is it? What's bothering you?" All he could ever reply was "I don't know." It was dreadful. A day or so later, he'd be fine. Sometimes these moods just came over him.'

The Shadows' workload remained insanely busy. But there was no one looking out for the mental health of pop groups in the late '60s. The Beatles escaped to Rishikesh to refuel between *Magical Mystery Tour* and the *White Album*, and Traffic began the craze for 'getting it together in the country'. But the Shadows would spend their downtime at John Rostill's house in Radlett, Hertfordshire, in the home studio he had built from scratch, writing and demo'ing on their days off before the next inevitable tour. 'John was the first of us to get a home studio going,' said Brian Bennett. 'John was a real electronics wizard. His demos were good enough to release as they were, but we still used Abbey Road to record. We used to call John's studio Radlett Notown! John was really into the technical side of things. He rigged up banks of Revox and Brenell type machines. He became an expert at bouncing tracks.'

Hank, like most people in Britain in 1968, put something on the clinical depression spectrum down to 'mood swings'. 'John was a moody person. When we were in Australia, we never saw John except for on stage. He just used to disappear every day. The joke between the rest of us was that we reckoned he sellotaped up all the windows of his hotel room and just sat in there with a carton of 200 Rothmans. He'd adopt a very aggressive attitude, picking on things I did, splitting hairs and generally being uncooperative for no particular reason. It's not enjoyable working with people when they're like that. I remember one day, during the Palladium season, John sat there with his face black as a thundercloud and suddenly spat out "I despise you, Hank! Everything that Bruce does, you do." I bit my tongue and asked him what he meant. John seemed to think that if Bruce were to sneeze, I'd catch a cold.

'The atmosphere in the group was definitely getting far worse. We were working a lot – too much, probably. We were together virtually the whole time, doing live appearances, writing and recording. I think really we were getting increasingly disenchanted with the music, as we felt we weren't going anywhere. [There was] little room for new expression.'

Brian Bennett, keen to escape this claustrophobic situation now his solo career was underway, described 1968 as 'the worst of times.

Silly things, really silly things used to happen. We went to Korea and some crazy fan banged on the door and asked for an autograph, and Hank asked John for a pen. So he signed the thing and gave him the pen. John said, "You've just given him my pen." And Hank said, "But it was a Bic." And that went on for about an hour … If you put four creatures in a small room, *Lord of the Flies* is going to happen.'

In August 1968, the *NME* ran a story with the headline 'Shadows will not disband', quoting their manager Peter Gormley. 'Bruce has been talking about settling down for some time and now that Brian is going and the group is having to be reshaped, Bruce feels that this might be an opportune time for him to leave too. But nothing will be decided until the boys return from holiday at the end of August. If Bruce does leave, he will probably go into music publishing and management, but whatever happens the Shadows will continue – both Hank Marvin and John Rostill are quite determined about that.'

That October, to celebrate ten years together, Cliff and the Shadows released *Established 1958*, a low-key collection with a sleevenote that said the Shadows would still be around when men landed on the Moon. Not quite.

It was an extraordinarily downbeat album, with virtually every song implying separation and, in its happier moments, confusion. It started with Cliff's recent hit 'Don't Forget to Catch Me', a gentle stroll with a horn line holding Cliff's hand – it was never an A-side, however. Reviewing it in *Disc*, Penny Valentine wrote: 'Presumably because he's celebrating his tenth anniversary in pop, though I hardly find this a good enough cause or excuse, they've issued this track from Cliff's LP *Established 1958*. I find it a bit pointless and sad. Lately, Cliff surprised me by coming up with some quite good records, "Marianne" being one of his best, and it's a shame that this is reverting back to the corny, boring stuff of years gone by. A waste of time, talent and people's ears.'

From 'Don't Forget to Catch Me''s gentle start, things only got slurrier, blurrier. 'Voyage to the Bottom of the Bath''s descending chorus melody was a ship, slowly becoming submerged, with Hank's fuzz guitar (echoes of the troubled Stingray) sounding niggled; the comic title was less than a sticking plaster.

Cliff's 'Not the Way That it Should Be' looked forward to 'Miss You Nights', with a neat Hank solo going through a Leslie cabinet, as Cliff was left 'sitting, talking to the wall'. Likewise, the pretty instrumental 'Poem' painted a picture of isolation; we imagine Hank in his room, gathering his thoughts as a cotton curtain billows by an open window. Cliff's take on 'The Dreams I Dream' was delicious, while the tempo barely lifted for Hank's 'The Average Life of a Daily Man', an elegy to a loser with hints of Deram-era Bowie: 'She's gone away forever, wonder if she knows he'll never make it.'

This state of affairs couldn't be kept up for a whole album. Side One ended with Cliff's perkier but quite peculiar 'Somewhere by the Sea', a very Shads variation on 'Norwegian Wood': 'We said all the usual things that you say at a party / I told her some real funny jokes – she broke down and cried.' What was the subtext here? Irritation with his contemporaries? 'We were drinking Scotch and cola, and the smoke was far too much.' It was hard to tell from the lyric exactly what was getting on Cliff's nerves, apart from him ending up with a hangover.

The second side opened with a stinker. 'Banana Man' sounded like a failed kids TV theme, the most joyless circus music you've ever heard; the image was of Harpo Marx in a launderette watching the spin cycle, wondering where his career went. 'Girl on the Bus', despite its title, was a country mope written by John Rostill, which suggested Cliff was in love with a ghost, a 'beautiful stranger' who appeared at very specific times of day. The punchline was a precedent to 10cc's shaggy dog story 'I'm Mandy Fly Me'. Warming to the country theme, 'The Magical Mrs Clamps' had a *Beverly Hillbillies* feel and featured the return of John Rostill's quacking fuzz bass.

Bruce and Hank's Beach Boys-influenced 'Here I Go Again Loving You' was a stand-out, with keys centre-stage and a heartbreaking chorus that reached for the piquancy of the Beach Boys' 'Caroline No'. There were breakdowns and miscommunications on 'What's Behind the Eyes of Mary'; Cliff can't read her at all, but that doesn't stop him imagining all kinds of worlds where they might be together. It's pure projection; Cliff was the blank slate for his fans and would be at pains throughout his entire career to keep it that way.

With the closing 'Maggie's Samba', everyone relaxed and slipped into Brian's cosy Latin instrumental, which again featured a keyboard break. They audibly pour themselves a Scotch each. It wasn't enough, though. There was clearly little left in Cliff Richard and the Shadows' tank.

Tim Rice's sleevenote for *Established 1958* may have been meant to suggest permanence, but instead read like a death sentence: 'In August 1958, Harold Macmillan was Britain's prime minister, the first manned space flight was nearly three years away, the farthing was still legal tender, Elvis Presley was in the US army, beetles were insects and

Columbia records were instantly recognisable by their bright-green label.' Yet the Shadows were still around?

It should be said that there was no sign of despondency on a London Weekend Television special called *Cliff at the Movies* to promote the album, which included Hank dressed as Carmen Miranda and much larks on a skit for 'The Magical Mrs Clamps', with cowgirl Olivia chased around a farm in Hertfordshire by an enthusiastic Bruce.

*

Bruce had solved his tuning trouble back in 1963 by paying John Rostill £10 a week to do it for him. Five years later, Rostill was, sullenly, still doing it. He had suffered a nervous breakdown after splitting with his girlfriend in 1968. Months later, Bruce quit, again temporarily, on another Australian tour. Clearly, they were working too hard. 'We were like rats in a box,' said Brian. 'Hank was thinking of giving up playing. He wanted to be a comedian. The new Woody Allen. I couldn't understand it.'

When had the sweetness soured for John Rostill? When he had first played 'Apache' alongside the other Shadows and within three minutes realised that all of his youthful dreams had been entirely fulfilled? Or when he tuned Bruce's guitar for the millionth time while its owner frolicked with the divine Liv upstairs? Or when he realised that *Established 1958* only included one of his songs because, deep down, the public still missed Jet and didn't think of John as a real Shadow? Or when Hank gave his sodding biro away, the unthinking git?

The bitter end, when it came, wasn't in a Hollywood-friendly locale. There was no blazing sunset behind them as the four horsemen went their separate ways, just a red-brick wall that separated the Talk of the North from all the other red-brick buildings, the acres of terraces and factories and mills and warehouses that made up Eccles in Cheshire.

Who was the Talk of the North, according to Eccles? In April, it would be another star on the wane, Dusty Springfield, whose sequins and mascara provided a West End glamour to compete with Bet Lynch, the recently departed resident of *Coronation Street* currently on a sabbatical after giving Lucille Hewitt a black eye. In March, it would be Freddie and the Dreamers, once thought of as Shadows usurpers, the ever-smiling Mancunian beat group whose relentless lack of seriousness had inevitably led them down the path to the children's TV show *Little Big Time* and its unintentionally psychedelic adventure story, 'Oliver in the Overworld'.

In February, it would be the Bonzo Dog Doo-Dah Band, who may have skirted the top five with 'I'm the Urban Spaceman', but weren't so famous that they didn't need a disclaimer: 'This is not a dog act' ran the Talk of the North's programme, to avoid disappointment. In the cold, early winter of 1968, though, it was the Shadows who made their way to Eccles, a group who not so long before had played the London Palladium for weeks on end. Now here they were in the town's converted Majestic cinema, a building which had seen some crazy paving glued to the front wall and been glamorously renamed just three years earlier.

That night, the Shadows would be staying at the Piccadilly Hotel in Manchester, a slab of other-worldly '60s concrete that could have been conceived by Gerry Anderson. In their Thunderbirds hotel rooms, the Shadows put on their tuxedos before making their way west, over the flatlands of Salford, to the very non-futuristic Eccles. John arrived at the venue first, as usual. He tuned his bass, then Bruce's guitar, and then Bruce's spare guitar (just in case). Hank would always arrive second, but not this time. This time John sat in his tux, in brooding silence, alone.

'I trusted John totally,' said Bruce, 'and never questioned his tuning like I'd questioned my own. Hank would always arrive second, and Brian and myself would turn up next, and all the instruments were in tune. The night we played at the Talk of the North, we were arriving at 11.15, virtually ready to be on stage by 11.30. John was alone in the dressing room and his face was black – he was fuming and he demanded to know where Hank was. Brian, Olivia and I hadn't seen him for hours, and had imagined he'd already be there. He turned up with five minutes to go, breezed in with a "Hi fellas!", picked up his guitar and said "Give us a D, John." John told him he was late and flatly refused to cooperate, and even Brian, who never caused any trouble or aggression and was always one for shrugging things off, muttered "You should really have been here, Hank." I heard the Rolls running outside and, as the fur flew in the dressing room, I yelled "Fuck it, fuck the lot of you, I'm going home." John just glowered and Hank burst into tears.'

'I just broke down,' admitted Hank. 'Bruce was about to run out on us, John had got it in for me and my fuse just went. I ran out of the building and gulped in a mouthful of cold Lancashire air. I went back minutes later, having regained my composure a bit, to find that Olivia had persuaded Bruce not to go home, as we'd got a job to do and a contract to fulfil. As far as I was concerned, it was all over that night. We eventually went on half an hour late and the usual veneer of professionalism that you can summon up when things aren't all they should be was noticeably absent.'

But there were commitments and they were professionals, always professionals.

The late summer saw a ten-day tour of Denmark by British and Danish EMI artists. It was sponsored jointly by EMI (Dansk Engelsk), department store fashion label Shubette of London and Yardley cosmetics, with a line-up of the Shadows, Gordon Waller and the Danish group Keld and the Donkeys; the compere was a Danish comedian called Poul Reinau. Billed as 'Young Britain on a Visit', the tour included a film called *The London Look*, sponsored by Yardleys, with a very fine theme tune written by Graham Gouldman and performed by Herman's Hermits. Schlepping around provincial Denmark, the Shadows did not exactly look or feel like representatives of 'Young Britain'. There was no rest, though. From Copenhagen, they went straight into their second season of the year at the London Palladium with Cliff. Reviews echoed the glumness of *Established 1958*: 'It was a sad night, Cliff's return to the Palladium for his autumn season. Sad, because it marked beyond all shadow of doubt that the era of Cliff, the teenage idol, has finally departed.'

'I felt, it's not giving us anything now, we don't want to do this anymore,' said Hank, looking back on the black cloud of 1968. 'It wasn't happening. There were too many arguments, too many problems. Bruce had already left a couple of times before, anyway, and come back. But he seemed to feel this was a definite termination. I thought it was time to call it a day. So we did the Palladium, it was very successful. We gave Bruce a nice clock.

'I always felt like I'd been the one to patch things up and make excuses, to do shows without Bruce and make an excuse for why he wasn't there. Holding it together. I felt the sense of responsibility. Deep inside, when he said he was leaving, at that stage, it was a relief. It had gone. There was no point in carrying on.'

*

At number one in the singles chart as the Shadows played their final shows at the Palladium in November 1968 was 'The Good, the Bad and the Ugly', the Hugo Montenegro Orchestra's interpretation of Ennio Morricone's spaghetti western movie theme. There were grunts and whistles and strange coyote-like noises, a girl's wordless voice, a staccato trumpet and a lonely harmonica. And there, right in the heart of this grand production, was a chiming guitar break, an echo-laden Stratocaster. It suggested mystery and intrigue, menace and sunsets and unknown futures over the horizon.

In the shops that month was a new single by Fleetwood Mac, heroes of the booming British blues scene, called 'Albatross'. It was an instrumental and it sounded like a walk along the Lancashire seafront, collar turned up to keep the drizzle at bay, looking out towards the grey sea. It was beautifully played by Peter Green, whose first hero had been Hank Marvin, and it would be number one a few weeks later. Both records, without question, had the sound of the Shadows, but came from a place where the Shadows hadn't dared to go. It was a sound that the Shadows themselves had somehow let slip through their fingers.

13

IN THE TWIST OF SEPARATION

In 1970, T. Dan Smith gave a speech to the British Association for the Advancement of Science about how he saw the future of Britain. No time to stand still, said Dan, the white heat of technology would take Britain with it whether we liked it or not. He reckoned there would be 'briefcase computers' by 1975 rather than each machine taking up an entire wing of an office block. He foresaw a country embracing electronic film and music production; he predicted full automation of major industries; and he reckoned there would be a personal computer in every home by the year 2000.

A utopian, social-democratic, technology-filled future was just over the horizon, said Dan. Newcastle-upon-Tyne, the city he had reshaped as a visionary and a seer, was just about to see him unveil his plans for the European-styled metro rail system; it already had his Civic Centre, a Scandi-style post-war beauty that had been opened by Norway's King Olav in 1968. And construction had just begun on the Byker Wall, that continuous block of 620 maisonettes that wiped out the bleak, unsanitary terraces leading down to the polluted, coal-sullied

Tyne. Dan would clean and purify the river. Dan would build palaces for the people. Fiery factory chimney stacks be gone!

*

Hank Marvin was free.

The future, the future. It had now completely opened up for Hank. What would he do? Could he move into soundtrack work, making more of those atmospherics he had mastered? Possibly, but the Shadows' career, their entire writing style, had been based around three-minute pop songs: Buddy Holly lives; Duane Eddy is king. In their heads, Hank and Bruce were still Tyneside's Everly Brothers. The Move got in touch – the constantly splintering Birmingham group needed a new guitarist and would Hank like to join them? He was flattered, but declined; he'd had his fill of being on the road. The following year, George Harrison would contact Hank – he wanted him to play with Eric Clapton on his *All Things Must Pass* album. Hank never made it onto the album, but praise and requests from the younger guitar heroes gave him a warm glow. 'I found it very exciting,' he told the *NME*'s Mick Farren a few years later. 'I liked very much what they were doing. I'd have secretly liked to have done something similar, but I thought it would have sounded phony if we'd started producing big heavy riffs, so we never really got round to it.'

Hank bought a house in the village of Southleigh, near Honiton in Devon, called Higher Wiscombe. He put in a swimming pool and modernised the house for the 1970s, referring to it as his 'Devon estate'. One of the new mod cons he installed was a burglar alarm system: if a door or window was opened, it broke a circuit, which then automatically called the police and played a seven-inch single to them. Sadly, it wasn't an unreleased outtake of 'FBI', just Hank's voice politely asking the cops to come as quickly as possible.

And, free to do whatever he wanted, pretty much the first thing Hank wrote was the post-traumatic, apocalyptic 'Throw Down a Line' in 1969, around the time of the Moon landing: 'See the moon it's getting nearer / But no more clearer than the earth below / What do we really know?' He had originally written it with Jimi Hendrix in mind, but was sidetracked by producer Mickie Most, who gave it instead to the Jeff Beck Group, at that point fronted by a pre-fame Rod Stewart, who sang the hell out of it. Hank later told the Arts Desk that he got 'a call from Mick – "I love the song. What's that funny drum sound?" It was a terrible little Japanese drum box and all it did was go boom-clack-boom-clack. He said, "I want that sound!". So I took it down to the studio and dropped it in. I remember that night very well. It started to snow very heavily and we just made it home. I had a Porsche then with rear-wheel drive. It was going really well unless you had to stop and then you skidded all over. Then I got another call from Mick. He said, "Hank, I really think this is a hit song but not for this band. It's just not happening." Lo and behold, Cliff called me up and said, "Hank, I just heard that song and I think it's great. Why didn't you play it to me?" I said, "I didn't think it was your sort of song." He got all huffy – "I should decide what's my sort of song!" Then he asked, "Shall we do it together as Cliff & Hank?" It turned out pretty well.'

Its air of menace was partly down to the arranger Mike Vickers. 'I'd done "Good Times", "Big Ship" and a few album tracks for Cliff.

With "Throw Down a Line", there wasn't much to it. Low strings. I remember Hank had brought his speaker into Abbey Road Studio 2. He was right in the middle, on a pedestal. This speaker was sort of like a Leslie speaker – I didn't see anything moving, I don't know what it was, but the sound was whirling around the whole studio, which you very rarely heard in an orchestral session. Generally speaking, they kept the local sound down to make sure it didn't leak into the other mics. But it was whirling around ... you can hear it on the single.'

It wasn't like anything Cliff or Hank had done before. With a death-march drum intro, weeping guitar solo and cries of 'Help me', it was an intriguing counter to the blithe 'Hand out the arms and ammo!' revolutionary optimism of Thunderclap Newman's 'Something in the Air' and the Plastic Ono Band's la-la-la-hear-no-evil naivety of 'Give Peace a Chance'. Cliff and Hank were closer in spirit to another 1969 totem, the Rolling Stones' 'Gimme Shelter'. It was also Cliff's highest-charting single of 1969.

Cliff and Hank played 'Throw Down a Line' on a *Top of the Pops* episode that also featured Fleetwood Mac, the biggest British band of the year. Guitarist Peter Green came over to Cliff and Hank, nervously, and told them how much *Me and My Shadows* had meant to him as a teenager. That was the album he'd cut his teeth on, Green confessed.

This post-Shadows world wasn't going to be predictable.

*

Others in the Shadows' world found darker corners.

Licorice Locking had last put his head above the musical parapet in 1965. He had boarded a tube train and noticed his old friend Terry Kennedy – lead guitarist back in the 2i's days when Licorice was working with Terry Dene – was sitting opposite. They fell into conversation. It turned out that Kennedy was now a record producer and he needed someone to play double bass on a recording session with a new singer-songwriter called Donovan. So it was that Licorice played bass on Donovan's first two hits, 'Catch the Wind' and 'Colours'. At the time, he thought nothing would come of it; he remembered drummer Gypsy Dave's kit was literally held together by Sellotape. Years later, even his sister Babs, who put Licorice's memoir together posthumously, admitted she was entirely unaware that her brother had ever recorded with Donovan – who happened to be her favourite singer.

Otherwise, work was thinner than thin on the ground. Licorice moved between various addresses in south London – Herne Hill, Brixton, Peckham – before ending up in a hostel in Paddington. Two Jehovah's Witness friends, Denis and Pat George, would visit him there. They were in a band called the White Liners – Denis on drums, Pat on guitar and vocals – and invited Licorice to join them on bass and harmonica. They also invited him to move into their house in Streatham, which he accepted gratefully. Under the radar, Licorice would play with the White Liners at pubs and clubs around London for, he estimated, fourteen years. They had a residency for three nights a week at the Downham Tavern in Bromley. It was a million miles away from *Summer Holiday*, but he had a roof over his head and his faith to keep him strong.

Jet Harris's career, briefly back on track in 1967, had completely derailed by 1969. 'There was a time in my days of being in the Zambezi Delta, shall we call it, that I had to sign on. They knew who I was. "What do you do for a living?" I said, "Well, I'm a musician." They said, "No, what do you do for a proper job?" And I just sat there and looked at them.

'I was dealing with Harley Street in them days, on first names with the doctor – Bobby. I said to him, "I keep drinking this vodka but I'm not pissed. I can hold a conversation." He said, "You've become immune to it. You're pickled." It went from bad to worse, in and out of nursing homes. They tried everything with me, even those electric shocks, ECT. I was in a nursing home in Highgate – Bethany it was called. It was run by nuns. Me and Jerry Lordan were in there at the same time, about three weeks, drying out.'

Jerry Lordan was, briefly, back in control of his songwriting talent in 1969. He was introduced to songwriter Roger Greenaway – of the Cook and Greenaway team, Denmark Street hit machines – by bandleader and arranger Johnny Keating at the 42 Club on Tottenham Court Road. 'I was a fan of Jerry Lordan,' said Greenaway. 'The meeting led to us becoming friends and writing together. He was a joy to work with and had a knack for strong melodies. He introduced me to fine wines and gourmet food of which he was a genuine connoisseur. And, as he was close to Peter Gormley, Cliff and the Shadows. Once we'd written a song, our first port of call would be to play it to them.'

Lordan wrote 'Good Times (Better Times)', a preternaturally upbeat song for Cliff, which became a top-twenty hit in 1969, with the songwriting help of Cook and Greenaway. 'He had an unfortunate marital situation that really dragged him down emotionally and he dried up', said Hank of Jerry, 'but came back a little at the end of the '60s when we split up.' Jerry approached Hank and said that Cook, Greenaway and himself had written something he should record. It was called 'Sacha'. Why was it called that? Because they had started writing it as a song for Sacha Distel, but 'as it developed, they thought *Actually, this would make a hell of an instrumental.*

'I was very friendly with Jerry, written a few things with him myself, and I loved it. So we did an arrangement on it and recorded it with Norrie Paramor. The annoying thing at the time was that we got a really good response in places like Holland, but we couldn't get airplay in the UK. It was hard work. It just bubbled under for three or four weeks, then disappeared into oblivion.'

Jerry Lordan did much the same. 'He did go through a long bad patch after his split from his wife,' recalled Roger Greenaway. 'He never got over her decision to divorce him.' Lordan retreated to write his masterpiece. 'The Old Man and the Sea' was a postcard from the edge. It took months to create, but was powerful enough that George Martin agreed to write the arrangement and David Bailey took Lordan's publicity shots. The single was an epic, a sea-faring tragedy, a stage show inside three minutes. Spanish guitar and oboe backed his opening lines: 'I can see the future stretching out before me / A path that leads [pause] nowhere.' 'The Old Man and the Sea' also felt like a vortex, that if you listened to it three times in a row, it could pull you into the darkness with it. It was beautiful, but also quite frightening. CBS released it as a single in June 1970 and it sold – according to one story – 286 copies.

The man who had dreamt up 'Apache', 'Wonderful Land', 'Atlantis', 'Diamonds' and now 'The Old Man and the Sea' – which sounded too close to his last will and testament for comfort – would fall into a writer's block so deep that he wouldn't emerge for more than a decade.

*

In Australia, the Shadows were still kings and – given the right material – radio would play them without question. Hank's 'Sacha' was made by its arrangement, the switch from stately acoustic verse to organ and electric guitar bridge with frantic cowbell. New, young arranger Nick Ingman also gave it a strong string counter-melody. 'The Australian public and radio had a sense of propriety, a bit of taste!' reckoned Hank as 2SM in Melbourne and 3XY in Melbourne and Sydney played the single enough to make it a local number one and a top-twenty hit across the country. What was it about Australia? First Olivia, now the potential lifeline of 'Sacha'.

Hank was restless. He was dipping his toe in the waters of a solo career in 1969. First there had been a manic, four-to-the-floor screamer called 'Goodnight Dick', which fell one place short of the top fifty, and then a self-titled album that was very low-energy. It included a bunch of covers like 'Aquarius' (pretty good) and 'This Guy's in Love With You' (less so). Aside from 'Sacha', the highlights were two Brian Bennett songs, 'Love and Occasional Rain' and 'Chameleon', both of which had already been released on *Change of Direction*. Maybe Hank could have roped in some of the people, now the biggest rock stars of the day, who had looked up to him as kids. Maybe he could cut an album with Peter Green and Pete Townshend, stretch out a bit. There were cautionary tales, though, including *Lord Sutch and Heavy Friends*, the unloved all-star album by the former Joe Meek charge. Or P.J. Proby's *Three Week Hero*, on which he was backed by most of Led Zeppelin. Both smacked of desperation and appealed to neither the original fanbase nor the hairier youth market.

Best stick to Plan A. Besides, 'Sacha' had a tweak of modernity; maybe that was all he needed, just a tweak. A beautiful melody, with Lordan's trademark unexpected turns, it was ushered in on a slightly menacing organ hook before moving into an acoustic Hank melody, backed by woodland glade strings and a forested glockenspiel. And that chorus was something else, Hank as untethered as he was on 'Throw Down a Line', teaching those young pups how to make the guitar sing. You only wish there was an uncut version that didn't fade quite so soon.

When Britain snubbed 'Sacha', it also missed out on the phenomenal B-side, 'Sunday For Seven Days', a menacing cello-driven thing that punched through walls. The boredom of a British Sunday in the '60s had previously been taped for posterity by the *Hancock's Half Hour* episode 'Sunday Afternoon at Home' ('I vote we all go to sleep'). Hank's number caught a time when there was nothing to do but go to church in the morning, then sit by the window and watch your neighbour leave the house to visit their sister in Acton or their mother in Tooting. 'Sunday for Seven Days' was meant as a threat, not a celebration, and the sound of the record was claustrophobic. There was a monotone hook and pummelling Bennett drums, with Hank kicking out on the middle eight as the walls closed in.

*

Nineteen sixty-nine saw Brian Bennett enjoying the easy life and easy money of a top session man. 'When the Shadows broke up, I had a really good run. I played on everything from Ella Fitzgerald to Rock Hudson to Ken Dodd … across the board.' He cut a second solo album under the spiritual guidance of Norrie Paramor, though by now Brian had learnt much from his master. It had the splendid title of *The Illustrated London Noise* and featured mates like Alan Hawkshaw, flautist Harold McNair, bassist Herbie Flowers and old Krew Kat Jim Sullivan. Brian didn't miss the psychodramas of the Shadows, not for a minute.

Meanwhile, John Rostill had got himself a gig playing with Tom Jones, probably the biggest solo act in the world at that point. Vegas! That ought to improve his mood. Bruce was busy playing house with Olivia, who was plotting a move after the Toomorrow project had disintegrated.

And what about Tony Meehan? He put out his first single in five years, the genuinely frightening 'Hooker Street', a dark jazz instrumental that combined vibraphone, echoed piano and deep-groove drumming – it gradually built and built until it disintegrated among freaked-out guitar work and human screams that Joe Meek would have been proud of. It was fantastic. The top side of the single, sung by Tony's brother Keith, was 'Darkness of my Life'. Again, it was no 'Good Times (Better Times)', but it was disturbing, a lyrical precursor to Peter Gabriel's 'No Self Control': 'The street lamp shone brightly as I entered the darkness of my life.' Tony's arrangement was epic, leaning on Barry Ryan's 'Eloise' from a few months earlier. If it hadn't been released on Giorgio Gomelsky's Marmalade, a black hole of a record label, then it could have been a hit. It matched the bleakness of 'Throw Down a Line', all right.

*

Could they cut the ties to the past completely? Hank, John and Brian came up with one final Shadows single in 1969, a grand farewell with 'Slaughter on Tenth Avenue', ornately arranged by Brian Bennett. It was elegiac, five minutes long and people barely noted its existence.

The apparently defunct Shadows could also find time to back Cliff singing 'Move It' in January 1970, on an episode of *It's Cliff Richard* that also featured Mary Hopkin and Cheryl Kennedy. They dug out the tuxes and bow-ties for this performance; the only reason you could tell it wasn't 1963 was because of the addition of Alan Hawkshaw on piano, plus John Rostill's mutton chops (presumably he was between Las Vegas stints) and Hank's centre parting. On 3 May, billed as Hank Marvin and the Shadows, Hank, Brian, Paul Ferris and Alan Hawkshaw relived their youth and played the *NME* Poll-winners' Party alongside Cliff, Juicy Lucy, Bob & Marcia, Lou Christie and Marmalade.

The new decade brought upheaval. We weren't just living in a post-Shadows world. We were now living in a post-Beatles world. And because the Beatles were so influential, swathes of their beat group contemporaries broke up too: the Dave Clark Five, Manfred Mann, Herman's Hermits, Freddie and the Dreamers, Dave Dee, Dozy,

Beaky, Mick & Tich. If Freeman, Hardy and Willis had gone their separate ways, no one would have been surprised.

The Shadows, though, couldn't keep away from each other. Hank released a solo vocal single, 'Break Another Dawn' (backed with 'Would You Believe It'), and the producer was Tony Meehan, who steered it some distance from a trad Shads sound. Brian put out an extended groove on a Columbia single, 'Riding on the Gravy Train', under the name Thunder Company.

And then, believe it or not, came a brand-new Shadows album. Its origins remain murky. No one seems to recall exactly how it came about, beyond someone – Norrie? – having suggested it and Hank and Brian having said 'Why not?'*

So, in the autumn of 1970, *Shades of Rock* emerged with only Hank and Brian present: part-timer Hawkshaw played keyboards and dominated the sound, which inevitably meant the album would be given short shrift by Shadows purists. The bass parts were divided between session maestros Herbie Flowers and Dave Richmond, as John Rostill was tied up working with Tom Jones. Aggrieved that they had ever called it a day, John must have been less than thrilled to hear that Hank had got the band back together without him. All covers, it sounded quite unlike any Shadows record that had gone before. The old live favourite 'My Babe' was reworked with backwards drums and droning psych moves and had a strange menace to match the record's moody cover. There were also invigorating run-throughs of 'Paperback

* Norrie had also suggested an album of family-friendly movie songs, and the group had got as far as recording 'Chitty Chitty Bang Bang' before collectively deciding it was a horrible idea.

Writer' and 'Proud Mary', but overall *Shades of Rock* seemed strangely throwaway. No one seemed especially proud of it.

In August 1970, Hank would be back on *The Cliff Richard Show*, playing 'Sacha', only this time instead of a tux he sported a proto-Suzi Quatro bouffant, crushed velvet pants and a Kensington Market waistcoat. He still had to perform a Bonnie and Clyde skit with Una Stubbs, but at least the tux was in the bin. Still, it must have come as a shock to the nation two months later when Hank was on again, only this time reunited with Bruce Welch after two years apart, and with a third singer and guitarist called John Farrar.

They weren't introduced as the Shadows, but as Marvin, Welch and Farrar. They sang a song called 'Faithful' and it sounded for all the world like it had come out of Laurel Canyon. Starting with an acoustic guitar line that summoned up a Spanish coastal scene, Hank sang 'Watch her ride the morning tide, easy as she sways, as the sunlight plays upon the water'. It was poetic, as evocative as they had been with 'Atlantis' or 'Theme for Young Lovers', only this time there was an added sunburst of three-part vocal harmonies on the chorus: 'And as I watch the white of the sails in the sun catch the breeze, I sigh / All too soon she'll be gone beyond the horizon.' It was quite exquisite. Maybe it lacked the kind of hook to make it a hit single, but it was a genuinely new sound, a brave sound, and entirely contemporary.

14

HARMONY IN MY HEAD

'The Shadows used to go to Australia regularly,' recalls Bruce, 'and John Farrar had this band in Melbourne called the Strangers. They were like the Australian Beach Boys. They used to support the Shadows and we used to watch him. First of all, he was a great guitar player, but he has this high, strong falsetto voice. In 1970, Hank and I decided to do something that was not the Shadows, something to do with the new acoustic sound on the West Coast. Hank said, "Wouldn't it be good if we had a third voice?" Olivia was a friend of John's and she said "What about the guy from the Strangers?" I rang him up and asked if he'd be interested in coming to the UK. So John was here ... he taught us a lot. He knew all about open tuning which we didn't. English players didn't tend to know unless you were an actual folkie.'

When he first heard John play the guitar, after the new trio got together, Bruce was astonished. 'He was so good that I just felt totally inadequate. In my mind, compared to him, I was hopeless. I told Hank that I should give up the guitar and just concentrate on songwriting. He persuaded me that Marvin, Welch and Farrar definitely needed the sound of three voices and three guitars. Hank convinced me to carry on playing.'

You wouldn't have said that John Farrar was a natural front-man, with his drowsy demeanour and hair that was straight out of a Playpeople catalogue. He also had the look of someone who might occasionally emit a small quack, but who was never going to out-talk or out-shine either Hank or Bruce.

Shy John Farrar had learned his trade and become as good as he was by playing along to Bruce and Hank when he was a kid in Melbourne: 'The Shadows were huge when I was at high school, absolutely huge.'

He had joined the Strangers, then an instrumental band, around 1964. 'Strangely enough, a lot of the material that we did was Shadows stuff, which was all in vogue at the time. Every group was doing the same thing, every group in Melbourne, and then when the Beatles and the Beach Boys happened then we started to do all their stuff. We were basically doing cover stuff all the time.' They were tight, though, and reliable, unlike young Brisbane trio the Bee Gees whose foul language had seen them kicked off TV shows. So, work came easily to the Strangers, plus John Farrar played guitar beautifully and had a high, pure voice. The Strangers covered 'Good Vibrations' and didn't disgrace themselves. Farrar was no songwriter, though; he contributed nothing more than a solitary (albeit extremely good) B-side – 'Take Your Time' – before leaving the group to become a producer in 1970.

The Shadows had played a hotel in Melbourne 'and we [the Strangers] opened for them. I got to hang out with Bruce a little bit. In the Strangers, I used to sing all the high parts. And I think they wanted a top voice – I mean harmony-wise, not top quality! – because they wanted to do three-part stuff. Not long after they went back, I got a call from Bruce, asking if I'd like to come over and start a vocal group with Hank and him. So of course I said, "I'll be there!"

'I didn't really start writing until I went to England, because of Bruce and Hank. I sort of realised that if I was gonna survive, I was gonna have to write, you know. It was just a survival thing because it didn't really feel like I was a writer. It was always very difficult for me. I had to try and make some kind of impression because I was with Hank and Bruce and Brian, all guys who have had fabulous careers, and so I had to try and come up with something, you know?'

As a songwriter, things would really work out for John Farrar. When he arrived in Britain, he discovered that the Marvin, Welch and Farrar project was being held up by Hank's aspirations to become a stand-up comedian. He had a residency on the Cilla Black show, so the new trio would have to wait. To kill time, Peter Gormley suggested John help out Bruce and produce a few tracks on Olivia Newton-John's first album. That suggestion would change John Farrar's life; he would go on to write 'You're the One That I Want', 'Hopelessly Devoted to You', 'Magic', 'A Little More Love' and several more massive hits for Olivia that made him a millionaire. But on her debut, he was content just to play, arrange and help to choose the songs. 'Between Bruce and me and Olivia, we pretty much picked what we would do. Bruce was more of a song man than I was. I remembered the guitar parts.'

Bruce was the perfect producer for Olivia and helped to shape her distinctive style. 'He told me that he used to listen to music on his crystal radio and that it was very intimate,' she wrote. 'He said,

"Imagine that you're singing to that one young person, me as a boy, who is listening on their crystal set."'

Along with Mike Sloman, Gormley ran the UK office of an Australian record label with a management wing called Festival Records. After leaving the RCA press office and moving to Pye, David Martin had met up with Sloman at the Festival office just off Baker Street. 'I'd been at Pye about three or four months. I said to Mike, "There's a girl singer who's available and a friend of mine. I really think you should sign her. This girl is great." He asked me, "What's her name?". I said, "Olivia Newton-John" and he reached into his briefcase, he took out an acetate, threw it at me and said, "Here's your next record." It was "If Not For You" He had just signed Olivia.'

Martin had helped secure airplay for 'a lot of records at Pye – Mungo Jerry's 'In the Summertime', 'Lola' by the Kinks. So I was doing okay in the record promotion business. Olivia was my friend and I decided this was my pet project. The way I did it was real simple. You take the poster. You take the record. You go into every office at Radio 1. You talk to all the guys. They take one look at the poster and they stick it on their wall. They take one listen to the record and they go, "Oh!" Everybody gave me play time on it, everybody. Terry Wogan, Tony Brandon, *Breakfast Special*... those were all of the plays in the first week for "If Not For You".'

On 8 February 1971, 'If Not For You' was played for the first time on Radio 1's *What's New*. Four days later, it was reviewed by guests on *Roundtable*. Over the next week, it was played by virtually every daytime Radio 1 show. It even made it onto the children's Saturday-morning show *Junior Choice*. 'If Not For You' vaulted into the top thirty and a request to appear on *Top of the Pops* swiftly followed. Olivia was on her way, as Bruce had always known she would be.

*

Looking like a radiant, hippie vision, Olivia had been caught by a *Brighton Argus* photographer as she walked around the site of the 10th National Jazz and Blues festival at Plumpton racecourse near Lewes in Sussex. It's hard to imagine that she picked up many ideas from the acts at Plumpton – Yes, Deep Purple or Black Sabbath – though Island Records' newly signed singer/songwriter Cat Stevens or the Sandy Denny-led folk-rockers Fotheringay might have floated her boat.

In early 1971, Olivia was also appearing as a regular guest on the second series of *It's Cliff Richard*, alongside extremely middle-of-the-road performers like Roger Whittaker, Daliah Lavi, Judith Durham, John Rowles and Cheryl Kennedy. Also making almost weekly appearances was Labi Siffre, newly signed to Festival's roster and managed by Peter Gormley, a hard-to-pigeonhole singer-songwriter whose early albums would benefit from the presence of Brian Bennett and the extended Shadows family.

One weekend, Olivia took Bruce's son Dwayne and Brian's boy Warren to watch Manchester United at Old Trafford, taking the train from London to Manchester and sitting in a compartment with a corridor at one end. Red-and-white-scarved United fans, not known in the early '70s for their fine manners, passed the compartment, caught a glimpse of Olivia through the window and did a goggle-eyed double-take. *Was that her off the telly?* Yes, it was.

'James Taylor, Crosby, Stills and Nash – and the country stuff like Kris Kristofferson and Gordon Lightfoot – she loved that,' remembered Bruce. 'From when I first met her in 1966, she always loved folk music.'

The tracklisting for Olivia's debut album was solid, mostly recent hits which these days are regarded as standards: Lightfoot's 'If You Could Read My Mind', Kristofferson's 'Me and Bobbie McGee', and 'Love Song', which would later be made famous by Elton John but which in 1970 was a beautiful but obscure B-side by its writer Lesley Duncan. 'Yeah!' laughed Bruce. 'Lesley was Hank's ex-girlfriend, so we'd known of her for quite a while.'

What could have just been a collection of rewarmed recent hit records had a feel of new beginnings. John Farrar was excited to be at Abbey Road, Bruce Welch was recording for the first time in almost two years and, of course, Olivia was finally centre-stage, recording songs she wanted to sing, some four years after her initial Decca session. The atmosphere on the album was entirely relaxed and the nimble rhythm section of Dave Richmond (bass), Herbie Flowers (bass) and Brian Bennett (drums) gave songs as unlikely as 'Help Me Make it Through the Night' a lightly danceable feel. The end result was as sweet as mountain water, nothing but blue skies. At the heart of the record, Olivia's voice was outstanding in its softness, clarity and emotional reach.

'I would supervise the vocals,' said Bruce, 'like the breathy vocal on "If Not For You". It was country-tinged and it broke her in America. They thought she was from Nashville.'

Olivia's first record had been released some five years earlier and dispiritingly sold nothing; between 1966 and 1971, she had sung in a folk duo and then been part of her barely remembered post-Monkees band Toomorrow, all with minimal fanfare. Success with her debut album was far from assured. She had a terrific team around her, though, as well as abundant talent and looks to melt. John remembered the first time he had worked with her, on an Australian TV show when he was still in the Strangers. 'Liv and I met on the set. I remember thinking, *She's a very cute girl*. Then I watched as everybody in the studio fell in love with her almost immediately. I knew she had a lovely sound, something that was different and unique.'

*

The real reason John Farrar had come over to England wasn't to work with Olivia, though. It was to sing and play with a brand-new band. The aim was for them to quickly join Liv on *Top of the Pops*.

Marvin, Welch and Farrar needed to distance themselves from the Shadows to give the new act its own identity. One problem was that the very visible presence of Hank and Bruce meant it looked a lot like the Shadows in their weekend casuals. An obvious way of getting around this was via the new group's artwork – no photos of the group, something more other-worldly and evocative was needed. Hipgnosis were the hippest name in town; their sleeve for Pink Floyd's *Atom Heart Mother*, with its solitary dairy cow and no text on the front, was the apotheosis of the new cool and paralysingly 'other' for anyone raised on '50s rock. Hipgnosis were based in a studio on Denmark Street. The walls were painted black, there was a makeshift dark room and at the rear of the studio was a bathroom.

Hipgnosis's sometime assistant Gai Caron remembered that 'it was so filthy, I don't know how they could invite rock stars up there. They had pages of newspaper – not even cut-up bits of newspaper – hanging next to the loo because god forbid anyone would spend money on loo paper.' Hipgnosis founder Storm Thorgerson decided the toilet was so revolting that he recommended his clients to use the dark room sink instead. Hank Marvin was apparently the first person to use this facility. 'To have him in our studio, pissing in our sink, was an event,' reckoned Thorgerson.

The *Marvin, Welch and Farrar* album, with its blue, misty, mysterious cover – the Cornish coast on a foggy day? the Urals from a plane? – emerged in February 1971. It included a harsher recording of 'Throw Down a Line' and the ecological warning 'Silvery Rain' (which Cliff would also cut as an A-side). 'A Thousand Conversations' and 'Wish You Were Here' were ethereal, wispy ballads, two of the best songs Hank and Bruce ever wrote. There was also a tribute to Newcastle-upon-Tyne in 'My Home Town', which sounded like it was written about the city as it used to be, with the London-to-Edinburgh road still blackening the city centre buildings and causing kids to cough. And there was another to Brownie, Kentucky, the Everly Brothers' hometown and an unseen, mystical influence on Marvin Welch and Farrar. They still hung on to their childhood dream of America, using it as a means of moving forward, creating something just beyond the real world.

Another album, *Second Opinion*, would be in the shops before the end of the year. Clearly, the trio clicked; it was an excellent album. The songs were stronger yet, with John fully integrated into the songwriting. 'Ronnie' was a Ray Davies-like character sketch about some poor soul on Tyneside. 'Tiny Robin' was a fragile melancholic ballad with a message of 'I love all the world'. On the other hand, 'Simplify Your Head', in its way, was the toughest thing they had recorded since 'Flingel Bunt'. The lyric was, finally, a way to understand what made them tick. It referenced macrobiotic food, it mentioned Irish munitions – neither very positively. 'Don't overthink it' was the message and it came from John Farrar's pen. It wasn't what Hank and Bruce would ever have come up with without John's presence, shifting them along, shaking them up. 'Simplify your head and damp the circuits down / Let the world go 'round without you.'

John Farrar winced at the memory of it. 'When we were doing "Simplify Your Head", it needed a guitar line in it and Hank said "Why don't *you* come up with the guitar line, John?". So I was in the studio with my guitar and Paul McCartney came in. And they all obviously knew one another. Hank and Bruce were talking to him and they said, "What do you think John should play here, Paul?". And Paul said, "Why don't you just play this?", suggesting this line, and it was the simplest line… and I was so intimidated I couldn't find those notes anywhere on the guitar. It was so embarrassing. He was so nice, you know? But… *Paul McCartney*! Jesus! I couldn't believe it.'

*

Marvin, Welch and Farrar's live shows brought another pair of Australians on board – drummer Trevor Spencer and bassist Alan Tarney, both of whom had been in a group called the James Taylor Move back home. The connection was Dave Mackay, an Australian producer who had been working for EMI Australia, where he was close friends with John Farrar, before coming to the UK as a staff producer. He would soon be given the onerous task of replacing Norrie Paramor, who retired in 1972. Mackay had been encouraged to come to London by Peter Gormley, the quiet ringleader of this whole story.

Mackay initially got Tarney and Spencer together with the James Taylor Move's guitarist Kevin Peek and a second guitarist Terry Britten, formerly of the Twilights. He recorded the four of them as Quartet – a couple of singles came out on Decca and an album was started, before the four of them realised they could do just fine, probably better, as session men. Tarney and Spencer became a rhythm section for hire, in the style of Locking and Bennett, or Harris and Meehan.

Looking back, Tarney was flabbergasted at their nerve. 'To up sticks and come here from Australia, and to think you were going to do something worthwhile ... ignorance is bliss. It's unbelievable that something actually happened. I mean, the whole world was coming here. So why should *we* be able to do something?'

Alan Tarney would go on to play a major role for the Shadows, but especially for Cliff, producing a string of international hits from 1979 to 1987 including 'We Don't Talk Anymore', 'Wired for Sound' and 'Some People'. He was originally from Maryport, an isolated town on the Cumbrian coast, and he grew up under the entertainment guidance of Lord Reith – essentially, no rock 'n' roll. By the time the Tarney family moved to Adelaide when he was twelve, the boy Alan 'knew about Elvis, but only scant stuff. The music in Australia was different to the music you heard here, the radio stations were full of American records. That's how we grew up. John Farrar, Terry Britten, we were all influenced by this American music. And in your early teens, that's when you're most receptive. You hear a record when you're fourteen, you know every aspect of it, you just do. So we were all receptive to this American radio music that you couldn't get here. When we came back here, you sensed that it wasn't the same. Even in the '60s, you had to locate pirate radio stations. Eventually you had Radio 1 in 1967... and even then, you *had* to listen to Radio 1, there were no other options.'

The Australians, then, had learned a secret language that most kids in Maryport, Middlesbrough and Mirfield were – even at the turn of the '70s – largely unaware of. Their grounding meant they had grown up listening to wilder, more exciting, more varied sounds and they brought this knowledge over to England with them. At the same time, as Terry Britten said, 'the Shadows were gods to us'. They couldn't have landed a sweeter gig.

John Farrar, a major name in Australia thanks to the Strangers but still an unknown quantity in the UK, was more than happy to have familiar faces around him. 'Marvin, Welch and Farrar wanted a drummer and a bass player,' Tarney recalled. 'Cliff had a TV show at the time and Hank was on it. He was always funny. He *was* funny! They wanted to do something different, more Crosby, Stills and Nash, I suppose. The thing is that Hank and Bruce really loved to sing.'

Tarney was flattered to be asked. 'I thought, *I'll give it two weeks*, playing working men's clubs up north, a week in Batley. Everybody performed there, they were a good crowd. Everyone loved it. Everyone loves the Shadows. No one has a bad word to say about them. And when those shows came to an end I thought, *Well that's it*. Then I got a call…

'Cliff's playing, would you like to do that? So Trevor, Terry and Kevin, we all got involved.'

*

It was only a matter of time. They might have got through 'Lady of the Morning', 'Silvery Rain' and 'You're Burning Bridges', but they knew it was coming. Some card was going to shout 'Play "Apache"!' It might be in anger, it might be pleading, but there was always one. They did not yield, they carried on with their sweet, flowing, three-part harmonies, avoided any instrumentals, but they knew something had to give.

They hit on an idea. If they didn't go on with their trademark Burns guitars – nothing electric, no symbols of the mouldy, olden days – if instead they took on three acoustic guitars, then people might be more understanding, give the lads a chance to demonstrate what they could do, show the world where they were in the 1970s. It was a good idea. But it made no difference.

They began a residency in Batley, where they wouldn't appear on stage until 11 p.m., by which time the crowd was well-oiled. And there it was, before they'd even played a single note. That noise.

'Apa-cheh!'

Others joined in. The voices swooped and dipped over Marvin, Welch and Farrar, like hungry birds flying over their heads.

'*APA*-cheh! *APA*-cheh!'

They were like seagulls, circling a trawler, unrelenting.

'*APA*-cheh! *APA*-cheh!'

So, one night in Batley, Marvin, Welch and Farrar played 'Apache'. And the following night in Batley, they played 'Apache' again. Then they played it in Sheffield. And every night after that. They played 'Apache', they played 'FBI', they played 'Kon-Tiki'. They knew, there and then, that they would never shake the dust of the Shadows from their clothes.

*

'Marvin, Welch and Farrar ... that gives me a fair amount of pride,' Hank told the Arts Desk years later. 'We did it well, wrote some good songs. It was a rewarding time but a difficult period as we encountered resistance from Shadows fans. On the other hand, a new section of the public opened up saying it was great. They'd like it, then hear it was from the Shadows and some would say, "No thanks."'

In April 1972, a new single came out – 'Marmaduke' – which was written by Alan Tarney and Trevor Spencer, and based loosely on an old Quartet single called 'Joseph'. It had a smooth, locomotive feel to it and a *Top of the Pops* appearance should have nudged it into the top fifty at least, but nothing happened. There would be no third album.

Talking to Mick Farron in 1977, it was all still a little raw for Hank. 'They wouldn't wear it. When we got on stage, they just didn't want to know. We had more success abroad. They could accept that we'd done one thing with the Shadows and now we were doing something different. In Britain, we lost out both ways. We lost out on the old Shadows and we lost out by not getting through to the people we thought we'd get through to. They just wouldn't accept us.'

Second Opinion would enjoy minor success in the US when it was picked up by the fledgling Sire Records, a label run by Seymour Stein who, a short few years afterwards, would sign the Ramones, Talking Heads and the Undertones. But it wasn't enough to quell the sound of seagulls over Bruce and Hank's heads.

'We were heavy underground figures,' laughed Hank, with some bitterness. 'I even grew my hair. Bruce left to become a millionaire. I made an album called *Marvin and Farrar*. It lacked something in direction. It was a bit like Frankenstein meets the Beach Boys.'

*

Bruce, needless to say, did not leave Marvin, Welch and Farrar to become a millionaire. He was lucky to live through the next year. He would later write that 'there have been lengthy periods in my life when I have been wrapped up, totally, in my own self-imposed sadness to the detriment of everything else around me ... [this] sometimes made me very difficult to live with.'

Soon after the release of her first album, Olivia, according to her autobiography, 'went down a path that I would later regret'. Whatever it was, it led to Liv breaking off her engagement to Bruce. He was distraught and moved out of the home they shared in Hadley to a flat in

Soho. 'I always had the utmost respect for Bruce who helped to create my sound,' wrote Olivia in her memoir, 'and I will be forever grateful to him. He was a very funny man with an amazing creative sensibility, and he also knew how to nurture me. Bruce came up with the idea of the bass voice for my first country records. He helped me develop my taste in clothing and opened my eyes to different types of music and food. I owe him a great deal.'

*

Bruce had told his friends that he was going away for the weekend and couldn't be contacted. He'd be all right, he told them, and he'd be back first thing on Monday morning. He cancelled the milk and the newspapers because he didn't want anyone to notice anything different, anything amiss. He didn't want to be found. 'The last thing I remember,' he wrote in his memoir 'was the red sky at night. I thought I had planned it so well. I thought I had covered every eventuality.'

Fortunately, he had forgotten to cancel the window cleaner.

He had taken an overdose of barbiturates, but thankfully, even though the tablets were very strong, he hadn't taken enough of them. When he came around in hospital, he found Peter Gormley waiting at his bedside. His skin was blistered and burned from the effects of the barbiturates. He was in hospital for two months and didn't work for a whole year. 'Maybe Jet had been right after all,' he thought. When Bruce Welch finally got home, he drank and drank.

*

'When Bruce bowed out, Hank was nice enough to want to continue with me,' said the ever-modest John Farrar, now marooned in England with no band and no hits to his name. 'He didn't really have to. I think he was looking after me, you know, to be honest, so I will always be grateful for that.'

Cliff wanted to take the gang with him to Japan in the summer of '72. The tour would include the whole extended Shadows family, with the obvious exception of Bruce. Brian Bennett would be the MD; the 'Brian Bennett Band' were the Shadows in all but name and opened proceedings with the ferocious instrumental 'Backscratcher'. Cliff's set included a version of Barry Ryan's recent hit 'Can't Let You Go', while Marvin and Farrar did a whole set of songs from the two MWF albums, as well as Simon and Garfunkel's 'Keep the Customer Satisfied' and the Everlys' 'Bye Bye Love'. Olivia Newton-John and Pat Carroll provided back-ups, and Liv even duetted with Cliff on Bacharach and David's 'Walk on By'.

The *Marvin and Farrar* album eventually emerged in 1973 as something of an afterthought, the fag end of a failed experiment. The lead single, 'Music Makes My Day', released in July, was a stand-out. By now a confident songwriter, John sang lead and Olivia played a school recorder in the background. It was light as a cloud. But the album lacked a certain spirit – or much of a purpose. The exception was the six-minute 'Galadriel (Spirit of Starlight)'. John's voice was high and feminine, while menacing, phased synth swoops ushered in a chorus that threatened to overpower the song. There were even higher, almost imperceptible string lines and suddenly – around the three-minute mark – it felt like the song was diverted into some cosmic burlesque house. Eventually, it returned to the triumphal chorus for a few spins, then faded to black. Of every song in the Shadows' catalogue, it feels the most remote from a lineage with 'Apache'. It was bold, but confused and confusing. It also suggested Hank and John were looking for mythological guidance from somewhere, anywhere.

15

LIBRARIES GAVE US POWER

'Everybody in Winnipeg was learning Elvis, or learning Gene Vincent, Chuck Berry – but we had a cousin in England that would send us British records: Shane Fenton and the Fentones, Johnny Kidd and the Pirates, Marty Wilde and the Wildcats, Cliff Richard and the Shadows. I loved them because the Shadows were their own band, and then when they backed Cliff Richard they had double barrel shot, right? And so we copied them.

'We were called Chad Allen and the Reflections, just to be like Cliff Richard and the Shadows, and we played all the Shadows music and we were the best band in town. Then another young gun came to town. His name was Neil Young. He was also influenced by the Shadows. We both bought an orange 1957 Gretch guitar that came in the window at Winnipeg Piano – I bought one, he bought the other. So Neil and I were competitors all of that time, in like '62, '63, '64. We were just teenagers.

'He left Winnipeg, met Stephen Stills, started Buffalo Springfield … but when he plays the guitar solo, it still sounds like Hank Marvin from the Shadows. And when I play a solo – like, listen to "You Ain't Seen Nothin' Yet" – the solo in there is pure Hank Marvin.'

Randy Bachman, *We Say Yeah!* podcast, 2025

While they lay low, the Shadows' influence continued to crop up in altogether unexpected places.

Queen had first been introduced to the public in 1973 as an alternative to Led Zeppelin, with more concise songs and more relatable artwork. They had been a bunch of boffins who loved to play and practise, trying to be famous but not starry in any way at all, until they hooked up with a charismatic singer who had arrived in Britain when his Indian parents fled a violent colony for suburban London. Does this sound familiar?

Brian May had watched the Shadows on TV as a kid. He had bought their records, making a note on each sleeve of where and when, numbering them, cataloguing them. They were very important to him.

'I was at school ... you used to listen to everybody you could get your hands on, pick up all the records and copy them. There was competition to see who could play them fastest and earliest. A lot of people at the time were listening to rhythm and blues records, so it was very cool to say "I don't like modern beat music – I like Chuck Berry and I like Bo Diddley." But, secretly, everyone was going home and studying their Hank Marvin licks. He was always there for people who wouldn't even admit it at the time. They were all "How does he do this? How does he get that very individual sound?"

'It was *the* thing in English music at the time. Totally different from the playing on Elvis Presley records. It was much more wiry – you could hear every string, quite sustained. It wasn't just Hank Marvin. Bruce Welch's rhythm style was very, very important, like nothing before it. The way the bass was approached, the drums were miked up – everything about the Shadows was, I'd say, very original.'

Brian wanted to play like Hank Marvin, but there was fat chance of that when he couldn't even afford his own guitar. Maybe, his father Harold suggested, they could build one? That was just the kind of scientific craftsmanship that appealed to indoorsman Brian. It took them a whole year; it was like a musical adaptation of Johnny Cash's 'One Piece at a Time'. A family friend was tearing out a fireplace from their Victorian home, about to throw it in a skip. 'Wait!' shouted Harold, and he salvaged the mantelpiece, woodworm holes and all, for the guitar neck. Brian then plugged the holes with match-sticks. The body was a mix of softwood strips and oak salvaged from an old dining table. The guitar utilised mother-of-pearl buttons and insulation tape. And then Brian stained the whole thing with layer after layer of Rustins Coating – 'Heat, impact, alcohol and solvent resistant,' claimed the bottle. 'Tough as plastic!' – until it turned a deep red.

It was Brian May's own coat of many colours and when he played 'The Rise and Fall of Flingel Bunt' on it, he felt like a star. And, as at the end of all good fairy tales, he did become a star, too – although that wouldn't happen until the Red Special was a full ten years old. It wouldn't happen until EMI spotted that Led Zeppelin were away, spending too much time recording *Physical Graffiti* and that now was a good time to push May's band into the spotlight with *Queen II* and its flamboyant glam single, 'Seven Seas of Rhye'.

Less than a year earlier, EMI had given Queen's self-titled debut the big launch and not a huge amount had happened. They had had the full attention of the press and promotions office at Manchester Square, a floor full of desks with separate panelled booths for the big noises dotted around the edge: promotions man Eric 'Monster' Hall, who would later become football's first super-agent; his boss Ronnie Fowler,, who had eyebrows that could magically split in half, one half going up, the other half staying down; and Colin Burn, a sober, old-school record man and confidante of Norrie Paramor who was also busy pushing his eleven-year-old son Darren's career in a vain attempt to make him Southgate's answer to Donny Osmond. Queen's and Darren Burn's singles would now be released on EMI – a neat, new red-and-tan label designed for the '70s that corralled and replaced the tired old Columbia, Parlophone and HMV subsidiaries. The same label would release the Shadows' *Rockin' With Curly Leads*, just three months after they had released the *Marvin and Farrar* album.

The Shadows were back! In the shops! A new album – and it was *all instrumental*! The line-up was now Hank, John, Brian and – once again – a still-damaged Bruce. 'We decided we had nothing to lose,' he said. 'It gave me something positive to do with my life, to occupy my time, and it was good therapy.' The pesky three-part harmonies that had seemed to alienate what was left of their fan following had been banished. *Disc* magazine had launched a 'Save Our Shadows' campaign in 1972, receiving hundreds of letters from fans – and it seemed to do the trick. Hank and Bruce were nothing if not crowd-pleasers. EMI were happy, too, with the seeming abandonment of the Marvin, Welch and Farrar project. 'There are no plans for live appearances,' reported *Disc* in October '73, 'but the group may do TV shows.' They would if they could. On the week that 'Turn Around and Touch Me' was released as their first single in four years, Blue Mink would appear on *The Two Ronnies*, Roy Wood guested on *Lift Off With Ayshea*, while Darren Burn had a whole documentary devoted to him in BBC2's *Man Alive* strand. EMI acts were doing okay. But there was no room at the inn for the Shadows.

Couldn't Eric Hall conjure up a 'monster monster' piece in the *Sun* or the *Daily Mirror*? Wasn't the return of Bruce Welch and the lack of vocals a big-enough news story for EMI? The answer was no. They had Queen, they had Darren Burn – money spent, sunk investments, and they needed a quick return. The Shadows had been away too long, it seemed. A Radio 1 publication from 1973 described them as 'a sort of bow-tie and tuxedo version of Crosby, Stills and Nash'. Who needed that? The Shadows still had their old fans, thought EMI. They could take care of themselves. They'd be fine.

And so *Rockin' With Curly Leads* emerged to little fanfare, dressed in its black-and-white Hipgnosis sleeve in 1973, a year when Britain was obsessed with the technicolour excesses of glam acts. In the same year that Wizzard had two number ones and Roy Wood scared small children with his garish make-up, releasing a record in a monochrome sleeve – with the boys hidden and shaded behind a Venetian blind – felt like a statement. It wasn't a statement that Canadian EMI were on board with, though; they bizarrely went with a photo of John Farrar and Brian Bennett on the front cover – and a colour one at that.

What EMI did manage to secure for the Shadows, rather unexpectedly, was a Peel session on Radio 1. Alongside 'Turn Around and Touch Me' and 'Jungle Jam' from the new album, they couldn't resist a nod to the past and played 'Wonderful Land' and 'Nivram' too. 'John Peel invited us to do his show, which we did,' Hank recalled in 2014. 'I admired John's approach to radio, finding new bands, giving them exposure. He said to us, "I was a bit of a Shadows fan in the early '60s, but as the '60s went on, it became really uncool to say you liked the Shadows. I want to tell you something – it's becoming cool again. We're all coming out of the closet."'

The session was broadcast on Christmas Day evening 1973. Miners strikes and the ensuing energy crisis meant the government had ordered the three TV channels to close down at 10.30 p.m. You could either go to bed early or tune into something on the radio. EMI were hoping for that latter. 'It's around this time,' said Peel sardonically, 'that we collect a whole handful of listeners that we wouldn't normally get if the television was working.'

There was also a half-page interview with Hank by Shadows supporter Rosemary Horide in the faithful *Disc*. They were still 'more or less the original Shadows, just slightly tarnished!' grinned Hank. He insisted to Horide that Marvin and Farrar would continue as a duo, but wondered out loud if a reformed Shadows was a possibility. 'The act would probably consist of Shadows numbers with a few Marvin and Farrar-type songs. I think that would be a nice compromise that the audience would like.' He tried to explain the volte face, the return to instrumentals after three albums of harmony vocals. 'When I'm using that Shadows sound, I try to make it a clean sound.

I don't turn the amplifier up too loud and thus distort the sound. I went away from that sound for a while, but so many people said that it was distinctive. It can take a lifetime to get your own sound. I had to go back to it.'

Rockin' With Curly Leads would be only the Shadows' third fully instrumental album, after *Jigsaw* and *Shades of Rock*. In some respects, it *was* a return to the olden days and an acceptance of their public perception. There was a lot of competition in the world of vocal harmonies, after all. As an instrumental group, they were number one, no question. The logic wasn't hard to follow.

Marvin, Welch and Farrar had engaged with the here and now – if America, or the New Seekers or even a revived, denim-clad Marmalade could score three-part harmony hits, there was no real reason why MWF shouldn't have been able to. *Rockin'* was another matter. It played well with the still-strong fanbase, as it sounded like an updated late-'60s Shadows. But it had nothing much to do with what was going on in 1973: Bowie's *Aladdin Sane*, Gamble and Huff's Philadelphia soul or even Focus's brace of instrumental hits that year. A Dutch group who had one foot in prog, another in folk and a third in early music, Focus scored simultaneous major hits with the hugely uplifting 'Sylvia' and the yodel-and-riff monster 'Hocus Pocus'. Both – yodelling aside – were instrumentals. They showed that it could still be done.

Guitarist Jan Akkerman breezed his way through 'Sylvia''s near hymnal joy, confident and joyous. He played clean, crisp single notes and chugged out something equally hook-laden on the intro riff. It could have been us, thought Bruce. Hank could have done that in his sleep. The Shadows' only single of 1973, 'Turn Around and Touch Me', had a tree-lined melody and an atmosphere not dissimilar to 'Sylvia', only with Akkerman's fierce confidence replaced by a restrained English grandeur. It was up against not only Hocus Pocus but 'The Jean Genie', 'Blockbuster', 'Can the Can', 'Rubber Bullets', 'See My Baby Jive', 'All the Young Dudes'... the charts of 1973 were no place for restraint. *Disc*'s review damned the single with faint praise: 'Happy memories of such golden goodies as "Apache", "The Rise and Fall of Flingel Bunt" and "Guitar Tango" can be relived with "Turn Around and Touch Me", which I suspect must have been recorded before 1968 when the group broke up. If the song's a hit, then perhaps we could coax them to reform, which would be wonderful.'

For now, *Rockin' With Curly Leads* would be a one-time thing. But they took it seriously enough. 'I have to say that that was one of the most fun recording projects I've ever had,' said John Farrar. 'We all sat in the rehearsal room for about a week ... I know we wrote a lot of stuff together. A lot of laughter and a lot of fun in the studio too, yeah, and that comes across. It's got a really good atmosphere.'

The rehearsal room was a church hall in Finchley, where they rehearsed each song before taking it to Abbey Road. John thought the covers were a deliberate decision after three straight albums of original material. 'Bruce and Hank were always very conscious of what the people would want, you know, so I'm sure that it was based mainly on their knowledge of audience reaction.'

The album found Hank toying with 'Pinball Wizard' and 'See Me, Feel Me', two songs from the Who's *Tommy*, written by Shadows devotee Pete Townshend and a medley that had recently been a middling hit for titans of supper-club harmony, the New Seekers. It was an inauspicious opening track for a comeback album and a poor, misleading choice. Once past it, though, *Rockin' With Curly Leads* would turn out to be one of their very best albums.

Freed from playing back-up, and second fiddle to a vocal blend, Hank now sounded liberated. 'Years Away' was a John Farrar tune dating back to 1971 that had originally been recorded as a solo single in Australia under the title 'John and Mary'. It was elegant and melodic, and it truly soared on the chorus. Bruce didn't play on the track at all; Hank played his white Strat and John's heavier guitar lines came from his Les Paul.

Brian thought the new set-up helped to inspire them and he knew what the secret sauce was. 'Hank and Bruce were being kicked up the proverbial from a playing point of view by an outside force for the first time, namely John Farrar, who was a fabulous musician,' he told *Pipeline* magazine. 'There was competition, no room for complacency. We'd booked the scout hut in Finchley for a fortnight and rehearsed solidly. Then Farrar would get off on something and soon everyone would be improvising around riffs like a proper band.'

Every track on *Rockin' With Curly Leads*, bar the two covers, had a John Farrar writing credit. John's input would change the sound of the Shadows for good; where Norrie Paramor would have included string or horn arrangements, John improvised these lines on his guitar. Occasionally he would play harmony with Hank's lead, creating a denser sound, which wasn't entirely popular with fans of Hank's clean, pure lines. Bruce's old insecurities flared up during the rehearsals, only for Hank to cool them. 'When the Shadows reformed, Hank convinced me that we needed my rhythm playing with John as a second guitarist. After that, we never looked back.'

*

> 'What has happened to all the Shadows fans in Britain? *Disc* brought them together again and now they've got a great new album out, one of their best, and yet it didn't appear in the charts. Shads fans, take your feet in your arms and have a walk to your next record dealer! Or will you let this fantastic album poke its nose in at the bottom of the charts and disappear again like *Shades of Rock*? I really can't believe that you will let the Shadows split up again.'
>
> Arnold Gurtler, Sindelfingen, West Germany
> – *Disc* magazine letters page, 1974

You might have expected John Rostill to be a part of this new set-up, but since 1969, he had remained part of Tom Jones's backing group, along with former Krew Kat Big Jim Sullivan. They had spent much of the last four years with Jones in Las Vegas. John had married Margaret in 1970 and set up home in Radlett in Hertfordshire. He had his home studio, Radlett Notown, and – always the tinkerer – taught himself production. He wrote and wrote, songs that would almost always only end up as one-off acetates.

Soon, Hank and Brian both followed John out to semi-rural Hertfordshire and each of them likewise set up their own home recording studio. In September 1973, Bruce and John met up after an American tour with Tom Jones. They both had deep personal problems. 'You need motivating, Bruce. What you need to do is work,'

Rostill told him; that was clearly his chosen road out of depression. Bruce went out to the Notown studio and attempted to write with John. It took time, but soon they wrote the keening 'Please Mr. Please', inspired by Bruce's break-up with Olivia. This would become the one and only Bruce Welch solo single when EMI released it in April 1974.

John played Bruce a few of his other new songs and asked for an honest opinion. They included 'Let Me Be There' and 'If You Love Me (Let Me Know)', country-pop of a very high calibre. Bruce was impressed. Despite the break-up and the heartache, he was still in regular contact with Olivia Newton-John – they had even spent Christmas 1972 together – so he took the demo tape to Peter Gormley. As soon as Gormley heard them, he knew the songs were perfect for Olivia and wanted John Farrar to produce them. Farrar and Bruce ended up co-producing 'Let Me Be There', which was released on Pye in Britain in June 1973. It sold a paltry 8,000 copies.

John Rostill started to prepare for a season at the London Palladium with Tom Jones. Outwardly the failure of 'Let Me Be There' didn't seem to bother him, not at all. Why should it? When had he ever written a hit? No emotion at all. Just the black moods, the black stares – they were the only clues to the constant electrical storm inside his head.

On a Sunday in November 1973, Bruce turned up at John's house for a writing session. When he arrived, he was met at the door by Rostill's wife Margaret, who told him that there had been an argument the night before and that John had locked himself in the studio and drawn the curtains. Bruce wasn't too surprised; John had been a terrible sleeper right through his time with the Shadows and often stayed up working through the night. What Bruce found when he forced his way into John's studio was a slumped figure on the floor; he was dead. It was horrific for both Bruce and Margaret. At first, they thought he'd been electrocuted. Bruce had to stay at the house all day to answer questions from the police and doctors, and wait for an undertaker to come and zip up John's body in a black plastic bag. It seemed incredibly degrading to him, completely unreal. John had helped Bruce through a lot of his troubles and now he was gone. The post-mortem revealed he had taken a deliberate overdose of barbiturates.

If John Rostill had only known it, he had everything to live for. 'Let Me Be There' would become a hit that same month in the States, eventually reaching number six at the start of 1974 and reinvigorating Olivia's career. Within weeks, Elvis Presley would be including it in his live set and it would feature on his *Elvis Recorded Live on Stage in Memphis* album in the summer of '74. By then, Olivia was at number three in the Billboard singles chart with 'If You Love Me (Let Me Know)'; John and Bruce's 'Please Mr. Please' would be another number-three hit for her in 1975. All three singles sold in excess of a million copies. In Britain, Liv was still regarded as the cute girl on *The Cliff Richard Show*; in 1974 America, she was a bona-fide star. But John Rostill didn't live to see any of this.

*

Rockin' With Curly Leads had arrived in the shops alongside Cockney Rebel's *Human Menagerie* ('The group's name sounds more applicable to a greyhound,' quipped the *NME*, 'but don't let it deter you from buying or borrowing this wonderful record'), John Lennon's *Mind Games* (savaged by the press) and Black Sabbath's *Sabbath Bloody Sabbath* ('not exactly a group of the moment,' said *Disc* in a mopey, two-star review), as well as another all-instrumental album, *No Pussyfooting* by Robert Fripp and Brian Eno. This was an experiment in sound collages and dreamy drones, so subtle and experimental that John Peel – handed a reel-to-reel tape of the album rather than a vinyl copy – accidentally played the entire album backwards. Still, Peel described the album as 'magnificent ... well worth having'. With Mike Oldfield's *Tubular Bells* selling by the truckload, there was clearly a growing appetite for a more adventurous instrumental music, something Eno would label 'ambient'.

Brian Bennett was bewitched by this new music. He was now doing session work as the Shadows were on/off and his job as musical director for Cliff Richard had finished. He had itchy feet. In 1973, he wrote an ambitious piece called 'Metropolis Suite' and recorded it in Abbey Road's Studio 2. He was thrilled with the results and played it to Norrie Paramor who, diplomatically, noncommittally, told him, 'That's very nice'.

'I couldn't get arrested for it,' moped Brian.

By a happy coincidence, a new avenue suddenly opened up for him to explore both this new music and his arranging skills. Middlesbrough-born Steve Gray was an old friend of Brian's, a British jazz pianist who had played in Phil Seamen and Mike Cotton's combos before becoming a well-respected session player. In the '70s, he would go on to work on albums by Olivia Newton-John, Sammy Davis Jr, John Barry, Quincy Jones, Peggy Lee, Lalo Schifrin – the biggest of the big. But Steve Gray also wrote and recorded music for a company called KPM, who pressed records that were never sold to the public. They all appeared in uniform, olive-green sleeves and were given away to TV companies, film companies and advertising agencies.

Gray approached Brian and said he had been asked by KPM to find composers who would write music for television – not just TV themes but incidental music, written to order. This was the shadowy, invite-only world of library music. The apprenticeship Brian had served with Norrie Paramor would now come into its own and his work at KPM would give him kudos well beyond the sphere of the Shadows.

'I met Steve Gray doing session work – he was a great pianist – and he said [KPM boss] Robin Phillips was looking for a five-piece band that could play and write for each other. And we formed this little band of session guys called Wasp. And we were prolific.'

Robin Phillips had the idea to put together five musicians who could read, compose and play music – the top players. If one of them wrote a piece, the other four would be able to play it together in a heartbeat. It was a beautifully economic model. Steve Gray hand-picked the group: Dave Richmond on bass, who had played on Serge Gainsbourg's 1971 album *L'histoire de Melody Nelson*; Clive Hicks (Elton John's self-titled debut, the *Jesus Christ Superstar* score) on guitar; Duncan Lamont – who had written the Sherlock Holmes Suite, with Spike Milligan, for the Festival of Britain, as well as the music for *Mr Benn* – on saxophone and woodwind; and Brian Bennett on drums and percussion. The combination was a huge success. TV themes flew out of KPM – *Grandstand*, *Ski Sunday*, *News at Ten*, *Nationwide*, *Mastermind*, *Grange*

Hill, *All Creatures Great and Small*... Every other show you watched seemed to feature something that involved Brian Bennett or another KPM name.

The KPM studio used by Wasp was in the basement at 21 Denmark Street – only a small place, but with a full, clean sound created by engineer Dave Clements. 'We went on until we dropped,' Brian told writer Kieron Tyler. 'Ten hours, probably an album of about sixteen tracks. If you couldn't sight-read, you wouldn't have been able to do it.' Orchestral parts were usually recorded in Brussels, with the Brussels Opera Orchestra, because the synth-wary, progress-allergic Musicians' Union banned library music – and because the KPM musicians had to be members of the union to get work anywhere else in Britain. The whole thing was a secret wrapped up in an enigma.

'We spent two weeks in Brussels with a ninety-piece orchestra,' said Brian. 'This was my first-ever orchestral arrangement! The session was finished and it was two songs short. Everyone was asked if they had anything – I had the arrangement for "Image" in my bag which I had been working on in my own time. If I hadn't have had it with me, how hard would it have been to get into orchestration? I owe a lot to that moment.'

When Robin Phillips had first brought Brian into the KPM team, he'd said 'Don't tell anyone.' He knew it was a wonderful secret, but he was also aware that KPM's exclusivity – De Wolfe was the only comparable-size music library in Britain – had a time limit. The bigger beasts in the music industry were bound to start catching on at some point: where was all this music coming from that was on the telly? What was that incredible, floor-shaking piece of music in the Denim aftershave advert? (Answer: 'Confunktion' by Dave Richmond, from *Rock Spectrum*: KPM 1163). And, eventually, that's exactly what happened. By the '80s, there would be dozens of other music libraries fighting for the same royalties.

Once, while Brian was having lunch with Alan Hawkshaw in an Italian restaurant in 1974, the Hawk – having previously kept schtum as instructed by Robin Phillips – admitted he had been writing and recording music for KPM since 1970. To an extent, it was frowned upon by 'serious' musicians. But not by John Cameron, Herbie Flowers, Alan Hawkshaw, Alan Parker and other top-of-their-game jazzers and session players.

Brian loved the short pub breaks, the swift halves while there was some overdub or edit going on in the studio. He loved the long lunches with fine wines – 'Chateau Latour at ninety quid a bottle' – which were hosted by Robin Phillips. He would be quite the raconteur, but it always came down to the job at hand: eight, ten, twelve titles, sometimes more, built around a theme and recorded in a single session. Brian didn't expect praise or encouragement. Phillips was no Paramor. 'He'd just say "Nice writing. No playback. Next!" And it was great. Then he'd send people up to Central Television and Anglia Television, take the new product up, buy them all lunch... It was that personal contact with the client that mattered.'

The result of Phillips' largesse was the spreading of KPM's recordings all over the background of shows like *The Sweeney*. Brian's first contributions to the library had been two titles, 'Sunset' and 'Our Valley', which were both included on an album called *The Human Touch* at the end of 1973. Straight off, the pastoral, piano-led 'Our

Valley' would be used on the soundtrack to a triple-X rated film called *The Story of Joanna* (synopsis: a millionaire begins a sado-masochistic relationship with a naive young woman. We were a long way from *The Edgar Wallace Mysteries*). Brian's slo-mo solo material seemed to lend itself to the booming 'blue movie' sector – 1976's widely distributed *The Opening of Misty Beethoven* featured both 'Bourbon' and the eerie 'Glass Tubes' from Brian's growing KPM catalogue.

'People would write complex, fabulous arrangements,' said Brian, 'and Robin would say "It's all about the picture. It's not about your music – write to picture." And he'd type out these very specific briefs.

'Robin would come up with the album title. And the descriptions on the sleeves. You'd come in with some arty-farty title and say, "What do you think?" He'd say, "It's for a news programme, just call it 'News News News'." You'd say, "Really?" But when a client came in and said "We're looking for something for the news", they'd see a track called "News News News" and that was it! He understood how the whole thing worked. He understood that an editor had filmed an advert and needed some music. Looking at hundreds of KPM albums, he had to start with a title like "News News News".'

No matter how prosaic the music's origins, the results could be hypnotic and beautiful – like 1976's 'Reflections on a Misty Morning' – or unlikely floor-filling material. Brian worked well under pressure: in 1974 alone, he recorded an entire album, *Synthesis*, with Alan Hawkshaw, as well as writing four tracks on *Childhood*, one on *Great Expectations*, one on *Image* and six on *Jingles*. On top of that, he drummed on dozens of other KPM tracks.

KPM required a different kind of focus to the Shadows; Brian's work had to reflect music that was currently being played on the radio, or in TV shows, or at the movies. 'Usually it would be something coming out of America, *Ironside* or *The Streets of San Francisco*,' he told Kieron Tyler. 'Once *Shaft* came out, everything had to have wah-wah guitar.' The vaguely 10cc 'Honey Days' and the 'Nutbush City Limits'-alike 'Keep Truckin'', both from *Chartbusters*, reflected hits of the day, while 'Glass Tubes' – on the perfectly, blankly named *Industry Vol. 2* – had more than a suggestion of *Tubular Bells*.

Decades later, the top musicianship and sense of adventure on library records would make them great source material for sampling. A track by Nas sampled Brian's 'Solstice' and made him thousands of pounds; Drake did likewise by sampling 'Glass Tubes' for his 2016 hit 'Summer Sixteen'. Kendrick Lamar would release his *Untitled Unmastered* album in a plain, olive-green sleeve as an homage to KPM.

The other Shadows largely left library music to their drummer and their keyboard player. Hank would only dip his toe into this world once, composing two pieces with Alan Hawkshaw for a 1985 album called *Top of the Range*: 'Brian's very talented,' said Hank, gallantly. 'I'm not in that bracket of composition.'

Warren Bennett would follow his dad and eventually record dozens of library pieces. He is proud of the long reach of Brian's music, but does find it gently amusing that 'if you go on YouTube and look up "Solstice", there's all these comments going "Man, this is deep! Who is this guy? Brian Bennett's a spaceman!"' Like 'Apache', Brian's KPM output has shaped a lot of twenty-first-century music in ways its creators could never have foreseen.

*

Split screen. On the left, we have the Shadows recording 'Apache' in 1960. On the right, we have the Incredible Bongo Band cutting Jerry Lordan's song in 1973.

The Incredible Bongo Band was the name of a studio group put together to create a theme for a movie called *The Thing With Two Heads*. The film was successful enough that they recorded a whole album of tracks called *Bongo Rock*, an album featuring a version of 'Apache' which would become as significant to the development of popular music as the Shadows' version. It is one of the most sampled tracks of all time.

The chorus, blasted out by a brass section, was a sassy variation on Hank's ad-libbed intro, with Jerry Lordan's main melody – now played on a Hammond organ – becoming the Incredible Bongo Band's verse. The bongo player was King Errisson, a Bahaman percussionist who had moved to Los Angeles when he was eighteen to become an actor. He kind of got his wish, appearing with his calypso band in the 1965 James Bond movie *Thunderball*. But he was a gifted conga player, cutting eight albums with saxophonist Cannonball Adderley and playing on various Motown records – that's him on the Four Tops' 'Reach Out I'll Be There' and 'Standing in the Shadows of Love'. The drummer with the Incredible Bongo Band was Jim Gordon, whose first gig had been with the Everly Brothers and who played on such seismic records as the Beach Boys' *Pet Sounds* and Mason Williams' *Classical Gas*, a big favourite of Hank Marvin.

The second life of 'Apache' began when the Incredible Bongo Band's sole album was dug up by DJs in the Bronx area of Manhattan in the late '70s, got played at street parties and provided a perfect soundtrack for breakdancing. The Sugarhill Gang would then release a rap version of 'Apache' in 1981, which neglected to credit Jerry Lordan in the writing credits at all. This version would then inspire the West Street Mob's 'Break Dance – Electric Boogie' in 1983, which looped the bongos from 'Apache', added scratching and vocoder, and used Hank's hook as the chorus to create an electro classic. Also released on Sugarhill, the entire writing credit was now given to label boss Sylvia Robinson and her son Joey.

The West Street Mob twelve-inch was a monster. 'The youth of today will never understand the savagery of this tune in a dance-off battle,' says one YouTube commenter in the twenty-first century, 'NEVER.' Another reckons that 'with the exception of the Jazz era, there has never been and never will be a musical era as influential and far reaching as the early hip hop and electro era'.

'Break Dance – Electric Boogie' would be coming out of every boombox in the Bronx, Brooklyn and beyond in the summer of 1983. It had the sound and smell of the Bronx – the Bronx River, Jerome Avenue, White Plains Road, Mott Haven... impossibly romantic names to pubescent British breakers. It was as evocative of a romantic Americana as Elvis, John Wayne and James Dean had been to the teenage Shadows, with kids across shopping centres and precincts from Newcastle to Newquay popping and locking to it like crazy.

The Incredible Bongo Band's 'Apache' would go on to be sampled by Madonna, Kanye West and Amy Winehouse, among many others. Whether Jerry Lordan or the Shadows were even aware of its existence in the '70s is unlikely, but it went on to become a foundation stone in hip hop. When a three-minute single has a ninety-minute Netflix documentary made about it, you know it's special.

'Apache', thanks to this unlikely cover, would continue to cast a long shadow over popular music.

*

Olivia got the gig of the Eurovision Song Contest in 1974. The Cambridge-born English rose was asked to represent the United Kingdom and sang a different potential entry each week on *The Cliff Richard Show* before the public voted for their favourite from six songs. Ultimately, she came in fourth. ABBA won that year with 'Waterloo', so no matter what Olivia sang, it was pretty unlikely to win. It wasn't a particularly happy experience. She described her personal life at this point as 'a shambles' and, for a short time, she got back together with Bruce. For a second time, it didn't work out. This time, at least, Bruce found some sort of closure.

Alan Tarney recalled how all the Australians would congregate in the Festival Records office at the top of Harley Street. 'They were trying to break Olivia here. They were trying to establish Olivia, but they couldn't. They released a few records and nothing much happened.'

When she was chosen for Eurovision, it must have seemed that the Shadows' extended family had the whole thing sewn up: Cliff had sung 'Power to All Our Friends' – his second attempt to win the contest – in 1973; even the New Seekers' 1972 entry, 'Beg, Steal or Borrow', had been co-written by Olivia's brother-in-law and produced by Dave Mackay. But Olivia was done wrong by the British public in

1974, who ignored her takes on Tony Macaulay's 'Angel Eyes' and Ben Findon's Brian Bennett-arranged 'Hands Across the Sea'. Instead, they plumped for Valerie Avon (co-writer of 'Dance On!') and Harold Spiro's 'Long Live Love', which sounded more like a First World War call to arms than a '70s pop song. The year before, Spiro had written 'Nice One Cyril' and performed it on *Top of the Pops* with a bunch of his Spurs-supporting mates as the Cockerel Chorus.

This was all Olivia seemed to be worth to the great British public: a support act to the Cockerel Chorus, eye candy on Cliff's next Saturday-night variety show. Her former Pye promotions man David Martin called 'Long Live Love' 'a horrible piece of rubbish'.

Meanwhile, in the States, they did not see Olivia performing this knees-up terrace chant on Eurovision. Instead, they saw Olivia for what she was, a country/pop crossover star in the making. John and Bruce's 'Let Me Be There' and 'If You Love Me' were classy, clever songs, reaching out across the divide between the Opry and Johnny Carson in a way that even stars like Tammy Wynette and Loretta Lynn couldn't manage. Alan Tarney, like the rest of the Shadows circle, knew something had to give. 'Bruce and John recorded them with Olivia, they released them here and nothing happened. But in America they were huge hits ... She was contracted here to play these working men's clubs, Talk of the North, places like that. She was number one in America while she was contracted here to play Southend-on-Sea! Can you believe that?'

Just after Eurovision, in the spring of 1974, Olivia got a call from the head of her American record company, UNI. In 1961, Russ Regan had taken California hopefuls the Pendletones and renamed them the

Beach Boys. In 1974, he was on the phone to Olivia Newton-John, telling her that she shouldn't ever tread the boards in Southend again; she needed to be in the States to capitalise on her growing success. 'Honey, you got a hit!' he roared. 'You gotta get over here!'

Russ Regan's phone call made up her mind. With nothing to lose, apart from possibly upsetting the BBC light entertainment division, Olivia packed her bags and decided to continue her adventure in the US. The Shadows family were about to lose a key member, the one who had given them new aims, new ambitions. The new old gang was beginning to break up.

16

COOL CLEAR AIR

In late 1974, Cliff Richard and the Shadows were brought back together for a one-off performance. BBC producer Colin Charman had died unexpectedly and this was to be a benefit concert for his widow. Watching in the audience was the BBC's Bill Cotton Jr, son of the 'Wakey wakey!' radio legend who had strong-armed the country into grinning through the immediate post-war years, the age of Eddie Calvert and Ruby Murray. Bill Cotton approached Hank and Bruce after the performance and asked if the Shadows would like to represent the UK in the 1975 Eurovision Song Contest.

Did they have much else on? Not really.

The Geordie saviours of British pop were barely in employment.

The main problem with doing Eurovision was that the Shadows didn't really exist anymore; *Rockin' With Curly Leads* had been seen as a one-off and Brian was now busy with KPM and session work. But they decided to give it a go. Alan Tarney would be brought in on bass and John Farrar on guitar. The first step was *A Song For Europe*, which would involve them singing and performing six songs on Lulu's TV show, with the public then picking a winner. Amusingly, Brian had written his own entry – 'This House Runs on Sunshine' – before he was aware that he'd be performing it. Oh, and so had John Farrar! The BBC somehow glossed over this jobs-for-the-boys gaff, but unsurprisingly neither entry won.

Guy Fletcher and Doug Flett, a songwriting team who had been introduced by Tony Meehan in the late '60s, came up with 'Cool Clear Air', an opportunity for Marvin, Welch and Farrar to show the UK and maybe the rest of Europe what they'd been missing by not buying more copies of their harmony-laden MWF albums. Better yet was 'Don't Throw It All Away', written by Gary Benson – who had been slogging away as a singer-songwriter unsuccessfully for seven or eight years – and David Mindel, who would go on to write jingles for Bisto, KFC and Ryanair. It was a beautifully constructed '70s ballad, the kind of thing David Cassidy could have taken to number one a couple of years earlier (it would go on to be recorded by Stacy Lattisaw, Barrington Levy and Barry Manilow). Benson himself would even, finally, have a top-twenty hit with it in Britain. But no. The British public, who had picked the execrable 'Long Live Love' a year earlier, chose a different song to go head-to-head with the best in Europe.

'Let Me Be the One' was written by Paul Curtis and that's what the Shadows would perform in Stockholm in April 1975. As they'd have to play it live, Hank and Bruce decided to play six shows to get the feeling back, to play together in front of an actual live audience, as the Shadows, for the first time in seven years. The first show was at the Fairfield Halls in Croydon, where the crowd stood and applauded for five solid minutes before the group were able to even play a note.

The same thing happened at the next five venues. It was going to be all right.

For Hank and Bruce, the daunting task of playing the Eurovision Song Contest, live on TV, must have taken them back to their battle-of-the-bands days, up against shit-hot skifflers and Malaysian opera singers at the Granada in Edmonton. They were nervous for the first time in years. It was Bruce's time to shine! Don't blow it, he thought to himself, you've gone through enough shit recently. The curtain rose and the sherbet fountain of harmonies jumped out of people's monophonic speakers across the continent. It sounded great! They were going to win! But, hold on, they'd devised some awkward little knee-bend dance to emphasise the slight oompah of the verse; it was a bad move to look like you're taking the piss out of your own song. No matter. Bruce grinned at Hank – he was absolutely loving it, the old gang back together. 'Let me be the one who's loving you tonight,' he sang, clear and true. 'Let me be the one who leerily holds you tight,' he bumbled. WHAT? On live television. In front of several million viewers. His brain was now on fire. 'I knew it,' he thought, and his thoughts came out, into his microphone, into the homes of millions of people watching from France to Finland to Faro. *I knew it*. He pictured Bill Cotton's bald, rapidly reddening head in the audience – 'WELCH! *I KNEW IT.* You're finished, lad!'

Somehow, he got to the end of the song. Had Bruce's fluffed line cost them the competition? Possibly. 'Let Me Be the One' came in second behind the Dutch entry 'Ding-a-Dong' by Teach-In, a flowery piece which had a similar number of bomb-proof hooks. The Shadows nearly won. The Shadows neerily leerily won.

*

Having recorded six whole songs as potential Eurovision entries, it seemed a terrible waste not to release them. Besides, the reaction to their warm-up shows – plus an additional sold-out performance at Paris Olympia – had been as good as they could have hoped. People wanted to shout out for 'Apache'? That was just dandy. The Shadows decided to add another six tracks and *Specs Appeal* was released immediately after Eurovision. The bulk of them had already been recorded in April and May of 1974, as part of an aborted sequel to *Rockin' With Curly Leads*.

Alan Tarney couldn't make all the sessions as he had an intriguing job on the side. 'We [Tarney and Spencer] did sessions, as a rhythm section. We worked with Kate Bush. She had a development deal with EMI. She must have been ever so young. Remember when EMI were in Manchester Square, the famous *Please Please Me* cover? We recorded there with Kate Bush because Dave Mackay was the EMI in-house producer ... I'd love to know which songs we recorded. It's so long ago.'

Of the Eurovision songs included on *Specs Appeal,* 'This House Runs on Sunshine' – written by Brian and Mike Redway – was the weakest, being rather *Seaside Special* and trying too hard to fit the Eurovision template. 'No No Nina', however, written by John Farrar and Peter Best (who would go on to score *Crocodile Dundee* in the '80s), had definite hit potential; it was punchy, classically mid-'70s and you could imagine Badfinger or Pilot doing it.

Unsurprisingly, the cobbled-together nature of *Specs Appeal* gave it something of a split personality. There was great production throughout, and the new instrumentals were pretty special, but again there were covers that added little to the originals and were nothing more than a sop to their less questing fans. There was no instrumental version of 'God Only Knows' that was ever going to approach the perfection of the Beach Boys original.

But the album also included the West Coast-influenced 'Cool Clear Air', with a MWF open hillside feel, more County Durham than Orange County and none the worse for it. Of the new instrumentals, Brian's 'Colorado Songbird' – written on the piano while he'd been staying with his family at Hank's home in Devon – had a suggestion of snow-capped mountains in the melody and a full-spectrum production, not unlike his KPM material. 'Honourable Puff Puff' was a workout with a stuttering funky keyboard and rooting, booted-monster bass from Dave Richmond. Brian gave the toms a time of it, there were phased drums and – intriguingly – maybe as little of Hank and Bruce as any Shads track ever. But with his own composition 'Spider Juice', Hank made up for it, played in various guises including a fizzing Hendrix-like pair of solos and a garage band fuzz run in the middle; John provided the neatly phased underlying guitar. The song's title came from Hank's daughter Tahlia who had an aversion to orange juice, giving it the most disgusting name she could think of. The track switched into a mellow, silky jazz at the end, not unlike Brian's work at KPM. Hipgnosis were called in once again, but came up with a disappointingly literal sleeve. And, with Eurovision out of the way and *Specs Appeal* in the shops, the Shadows were once again on hiatus.

*

Before she left London, Olivia Newton-John had phoned publisher Artie Wayne to see if he had any suitable songs to record – she wanted to be prepared, not kicking her heels in California. He suggested a cover of 'God Only Knows' – big deal. But he also had a new song co-written by Brill Building veteran Jeff Barry and new kid Peter Allen, another Australian who had moved to England and then on to the US.

Olivia and John Farrar listened to the acetate of 'I Honestly Love You' in her London flat and they decided to demo it immediately. Alan Hawkshaw provided the piano intro and, in a tiny, cramped space on Denmark Street, Olivia delivered an incredibly heartfelt vocal that *Billboard* would later call 'empathetic and clear-eyed'. She would land in the US with a future number one in her suitcase. After she performed it on *The Tonight Show*, with a tear escaping down her cheek, the US had completely fallen in love with her. 'I Honestly Love You' was top of the Hot Hundred in October, just eight weeks after release. With this, Olivia was lost for good from the Shadows' orbit. When the follow-up, John Farrar's 'Have You Never Been Mellow', also made it to number one in the States a few months later, he took his cases down from the top of the wardrobe. 'Well, Olivia was going, and Peter Gormley was her manager and the Shads manager as well … After we did Eurovision, Olivia decided that she wanted to go and Peter encouraged me to go too. He said "You should really be with her over there." So we packed up and went.'

'Please Mr. Please', Bruce's bar-stool ode to his ex, was then brought out of the cupboard by John and Olivia; it gave Rostill and Welch a writing credit on an American top-three single in the summer of 1975. This was the fantasy world of the Geordie Boys made real, a genuine

American hit single, written by Bruce Welch! No matter that it had been written about the woman who had shattered his heart to pieces, the woman who was now singing the damn thing and that it was her voice on the jukebox: 'Don't play B17... No, actually, it's cool, I'm okay with it now.' 'Please Mr. Please' was huge, the huge American hit Bruce had always dreamed of.

Nashville remained snooty about this run of hits, but Olivia Newton-John's country-pop crossovers would work in both directions. They legitimised Dolly Parton's jump into the mainstream with Barry Mann and Cynthia Weil's 'Here You Come Again' in 1977; and Dolly, in turn, helped to make Taylor Swift's step from country into international superstar possible. The Shadows' attempts to rebuild their own career had resulted in million-selling American singles and no small measure of Stateside influence. John Rostill hadn't lived to see it; Bruce Welch had almost slipped away too. But it had finally happened.

*

Cliff Richard was not figuring on any chart in the summer of 1975. He had reached the point of no return. He could go on prime-time BBC1, any Sunday, singing songs about Jesus, that was not a problem. But having singles that landed in the top twenty, that was his raison d'être. *More Hits By Cliff*. More and more. He needed them. And they'd stopped some years before: in 1969, he'd managed four top-twenty singles and all seemed good. In 1972, 1973 and 1974, he registered just one per year. And then came 1975, annus horribilis, when nothing charted at all, not even in the top fifty. Even more than spreading the word, Cliff knew that he had been placed on Earth to make hit records, ones that appealed across the board. In 1975, the stats showed that he seemed to be appealing to no one at all.

The year before, he had taken the plunge and made an album almost entirely comprised of songs he'd written himself. It was called *The 31st of February Street* and, for anyone vaguely interested in digging under the surface of Cliff's showbiz persona, it remains a key text.

For some reason, EMI in Britain took no singles from it. The beach-ready, driving-through-the-Alps breeze of 'Nothing to Remind Me' was sneaked out as a promo single and obtained a full release in Belgium, for some reason, but what a waste. Here was a record that could have repositioned Cliff, encouraged him to write more; he could have shed his light entertainment garb for good and rebuilt his career. EMI sat on it. And the two singles that followed – 'Honky Tonk Angel' and 'It's Only Me You've Left Behind', blow-outs both – were a public humiliation.

In times of stress and creative impasse, Cliff could always call on the Shadows. They had almost won Eurovision while he was in his slough of despond and they had scored *their* first top-twenty hit in ten years. In 1975, finally, they were doing something right. Peter Gormley decided to throw Cliff's next album open to Hank, Bruce, Brian, John, Alan: whoever could source the best material would have the opportunity to produce it.

Bruce missed being a producer – his work with Olivia had made her name, after all, and he knew he was more than capable. Gormley's bait had him working flat out. He called everyone he knew in publishing. He flew to the US to meet Lionel Conway, head of Island Music, who gave him a cassette of two long-forgotten songs that he was convinced would be hits for Cliff. Back in England, Bruce had a long hard listen to them, trying to hear what Conway could hear, but it was no use. Then he flipped the cassette over and, on the other side, was a song by little-known writer Dave Townsend called 'Miss You Nights'.

'Thinking / Of my going / How to cut the thread and leave it all behind.'

'I couldn't believe it,' wrote Bruce in his memoir. 'It was such a great contemporary ballad, with a magnificent lyric.' Bruce got a package of half a dozen songs together, then whittled them down to just three before taking them to Cliff's home in Weybridge. 'When he heard "Miss You Nights", he very nearly fell on the floor. The hair stood up on his arms.'

Bruce got the job of producing the album that would eventually be called *I'm Nearly Famous*. Cliff then told him he had some other songs lying around that he had not done anything with. One of them was a song called 'Devil Woman' by his sometime guitarist Terry Britten, which he had been sitting on for more than eighteen months, worried it might be a bit much, too red-blooded for his fanbase. Bruce rolled his eyes; he knew it was the perfect vehicle to gently reposition Cliff in the public eye.

Like Arif Mardin with Barry Gibb, Bruce located a falsetto in Cliff's range that neither had realised he possessed. 'I feel just like a slave that has been freed,' he sang on 'I Can't Ask For Any More Than You' and the greasepaint of ten years in light entertainment was wiped clean. Most significantly, 'Devil Woman' took off in the US, reaching number five. As a result, *I'm Nearly Famous* became his biggest selling album to date.

17

LOVE WILL KEEP US TOGETHER

'Down one place to nine go Marmalade who are still "Falling Apart at the Seams". And climbing two to this week's number eight, here are our old friends the Beatles.'

What year was it? 1976, allegedly. Bruce listened to Tom Brown counting down the new top twenty at 6 p.m. that April Sunday, sussing out the competition. The Shadows had just recorded a new single called 'It'll Be Me Babe' – no, not the old Cliff single from 1962, he would emphasise – and Bruce thought it had a chance. He and Brian had written the B-side, 'Like Strangers' – no, not the old Everly Brothers single from 1960 – and he was pretty proud of it. The feel was contemporary. He was attuned to 1976 and he understood how to get the best out of a studio – hadn't 'Miss You Nights' proved it? Hadn't 'Devil Woman' crept its slinky way across American airwaves, coast to coast? He felt in touch with the modern world. He felt in love with the modern world.

Hank and John Farrar had written 'It'll Be Me Babe', with a rhythm section that sounded like a car entirely made of bubbles, rolling slowly down the road, and a guitar line that mewled like Custard the cat from current TV smash *Roobarb*. It also featured a fine, high vocal line from John on the chorus. But John wasn't there to promote it. He was in Los Angeles, producing Olivia. He'd gone. Alan Tarney subbed for him on bass in the promotional video, a straightforward affair which looked like a TV performance. Hank wore a red-and-white hooped rugby shirt and played his legendary Strat, by now in fully customised mode – gold parts, Fender WRHB, Gibson humbucker, wiring changes – but Bruce was reduced to miming John's impossibly high 'In case there's any doubt, it's you I'm talking about' on the chorus. He hoped people wouldn't notice, dazzled and distracted by the bling on the Strat.

But that single was still a month away. Here was Bruce, listening to the chart in April 1976, with the Brotherhood of Man's Eurovision entry 'Save Your Kisses For Me' at number one (only eleven places higher than 'Let Me Be the One' had managed a year earlier, he noted drily). Barry White's 'You See the Trouble With Me' and Billy Ocean's 'Love Really Hurts Without You', floor-fillers both, made up the top three. But there too were the Beatles – back in the top ten, a full six years after they'd waved farewell with the ponderous 'Let It Be'. After a couple of false starts, Paul McCartney's Wings had finally become one of the biggest groups in the world, with a massive American tour booked and a new album, *Wings at the Speed of Sound*, to promote. So who on earth was buying a single of 'Yesterday' in 1976?

The entire Beatles' singles catalogue had been re-issued in February 1976 in natty green-and-black sleeves and collected in a box of their own; it sold out in seconds. So EMI put out a second box a few weeks later, this time adding 'Yesterday' (backed with 'I Should Have Known

Better') and letting that go out as a single on its own for the first time in Britain. When this box also sold out and 'Yesterday' reached the top ten, EMI issued a third box, with 'Yesterday' *and* 'Back in the USSR' b/w 'Twist and Shout', another first-time 45rpm release. 'Back in the USSR' gave them *another* top-twenty hit. No doubt, it was a big win for EMI, who didn't incur any recording costs by recycling old material. Money for old rope. Maybe they should do this more often – it was a lot cheaper and easier than plugging new acts.

EMI had created a TV Advertised division in early 1976, headed by Brian Berg. For the last four years, a bunch of upstart labels – K-Tel, Arcade and Ronco – had been stealing a march on the majors by licensing tracks and cobbling together compilation albums, then flogging them on TV with exactly the same fast-talking technique they applied to the Buttoneer, the Hair Magician and the Veg-o-Matic. 'NEW! From RONCO! Just ONE NINETY NINE!!' There was *Twenty Star Tracks Volume One*. There was *Twenty-Two Dynamic Hits Volume Two*. There was *Twenty Fantastic Hits Volume Three*. With sleeves that no one would mistake for the work of Peter Blake or Richard Hamilton, they included T. Rex, Slade, Joe Cocker, Chicory Tip, Hot Butter, the Delfonics, Olivia Newton-John, Labi Siffre and the Royal Scots Dragoon Guards, all thrown randomly into the same pot of melted vinyl. Give the people what they want. Colin Ashby, K-Tel's sales manager in the late '70s, had 'come from the food industry. We were marketeers who happened to be marketing black plastic. There was no desire to win prizes or ad campaign-of-the-year awards – no desire at all. Our TV spend in the '70s was as big as Heinz's.'

For strap-cashed teenagers and lovers of socio-historic time capsules alike, these albums were kind of wonderful. For the likes of EMI, they were an embarrassment. From time to time, the TV-advertised albums would be excluded from the official album chart so that their presence didn't embarrass the sales of the latest release by Bowie, Led Zeppelin or Diana Ross.

When Arcade managed to somehow license Elvis's *40 Greatest* from RCA in 1974 –and, unsurprisingly, score a massive hit with it – a threshold had been crossed. Were the majors throwing money in a bin for the sake of a relatively small percentage from a licence and some dignity? Of course they were. Four years after K-Tel's *20 Dynamic Hits* had shown them up as slow-moving and even snobbish, EMI took matters into their own hands. If TV advertising was the way forward, they would join in. But it would be done stylishly.

That summer, EMI would release the Beach Boys' *20 Golden Greats*, with the catalogue number EMTV1. It had only been five years since the *Beach Boys' Greatest Hits* with an almost identical, though slightly shorter, tracklisting. But this time there was no picture of the Californians on the cover. Instead, EMI's Brian Berg commissioned an illustration of a silvery alien figure on a surfboard. It looked like 1976. They advertised the album on TV, like K-Tel or Ronco. And it worked. The Beach Boys' *20 Golden Greats* would outsell *Wings at the Speed of Sound* and Queen's *A Night at the Opera* and ABBA's *Arrival*. In fact, it would outsell everything in 1976, bar ABBA's *Greatest Hits*. It was a phenomenon. Peter Gormley paid close attention. Bruce Welch paid close attention.

*

On 3 April 1976, while Bruce listened to the Beatles' 'Yesterday' with a furrowed brow, Jet Harris was in Gloucester prison. He was recording a live album there called *Inside*. His playing was sweet and the DIY production gave the recording a raw quality that the Norrie Paramor sheen had rarely allowed room for. The gig and the recording came about because, a few months earlier, he had got chatting to a pub landlord in Gloucester called Jim Budd. By the time Jet left the pub, Jim Budd was his manager.

There was a logic to the album. Jet was a brooding pop legend like Johnny Cash. And Johnny Cash had recorded not one but two huge-selling albums live to a crowd of prisoners. The most obvious difference was that Cash was straight when he recorded those albums, knocked into shape by his wife June Carter. Jet was still struggling. No big surprises, but he lacked Cash's easy patter. 'Anyone know where the bar is?' he joked. No one laughed. 'This album tells more about Jet Harris than mere words ever can,' wrote Tony Hall in the sleevenote. 'It shows a man and a performer who has come through fire, not unmarked, but with a determination rarely seen.' The bookings picked up, which involved more travel, which led Jet to panic... By September 1977, Jim Budd had thrown in the towel. Jet was in retirement once again.

*

'Apache' would be on a top-five album in the summer of 1976, but it wasn't the version by the Shadows. It appeared on a compilation called *Instrumental Gold* and was played by an unknown act called Terry

Walsh and the Phantoms. *Instrumental Gold* was on another upstart, TV advertising-based label called Warwick, which seemed to focus on the pre-rock era of Frankie Laine, Guy Mitchell and Doris Day. The album featured the likes of Mantovani's 'Moulin Rouge', Leroy Anderson's 'Blue Tango' and Eddie Calvert's 'Cherry Pink (and Apple Blossom White)', all given 1976 revamps by session musicians.

The album was produced by the Shadows' old mate Brian Matthew, formerly host of *Saturday Club* and *Thank Your Lucky Stars* – he used his Rolodex of contacts to find some decent jazzers who could knock out an impressive 'Apache' in no time at all. Among the players on *Instrumental Gold* were trumpeter Stan Roderick, who had played with Tubby Hayes and Nelson Riddle, as well as on one of Norrie Paramor's Big Ben Banjo Band albums. There was also jazz trombonist Don Lusher, the first person in Britain to ever stick his head above the parapet and release a single called 'Rock and Roll', back in 1955.

Brian Matthew's first stab at production was so successful that Warwick asked him to create a follow-up. The result was Bert Weedon's *22 Golden Guitar Greats* and it went to number one in November 1976. Bert Weedon, whose *Play in a Day* book was still on sale in every musical instrument shop in Britain, played his interpretations of 'Dance On!', 'Kon-Tiki', 'FBI', 'Sleepwalk', 'Man of Mystery', 'Diamonds', 'Scarlett O'Hara' and – naturally – 'Apache'. By now fifty-six years old, Weedon put his own rough, improvisational stamp on 'Apache', bringing in some unexpected brass, the kind of thing Tony Meehan might have done. Hank's intro was nowhere to be heard. You had to admire Bert's cheek.

Suddenly, surprisingly, in the news again, Weedon was interviewed in *Record Mirror*, sporting bushier hair than he'd had in 1960 – and even a Zapata moustache.

'I used to do quite a few rock'n'roll shows, and today I still get groups of original Teddy Boys coming to my concerts. I became a cult figure with them,' smiled Bert. 'And, at the same time, I have collected the biggest following of middle of the road fans in the country. I never try to compete with the Jimmy Pages or Eric Claptons. If I played on stage with Zeppelin, I'd feel a right berk. I know my market and stick to it.'

Bert Weedon? *Bert bloody Weedon?* He was old enough to be my dad in 1960, thought Bruce, and now he's number one? *In 1976?* That line haunted Bruce: 'I know my market and stick to it.'

He got EMI's Brian Berg on the blower. Berg had Glen Campbell down for EMTV2, but if Bruce could fiddle with the old mono tapes to try to make the Shadows more 'with it', do some 'electronic re-processing' so that they sounded like stereo recordings, then the Shadows could be up next.

*

As with the Beach Boys album, there was no picture of the Shadows on the cover of *20 Golden Greats*. Instead, there was Jeffery Edwards' illustration, little more than a line drawing of a bare, brown wall revealing the shadows of three guitars propped up close by. The cover was more skirting board than anything else. To add to the starkness, the title was written in a typewriter-like font. It needed no more embellishment; it was minimal, it was clean-lined and it was perfect.

The cover was one reason that the Shadows were about to sell a million albums. The advert, directed by filmmaker Alan Parker, would also seal the deal for EMTV3.

A kid in a tank top – maybe fifteen, sixteen – puts the album on and picks up a cricket bat. He sees himself in the mirror, hears the opening to 'Apache' and does the Shadows walk around his room. Warming to his theme, he jumps on the bed imagining thousands of screaming girls. We see an almost subliminal cut to the Shadows at the Simpkins Youth Club in *The Young Ones*, playing 'The Savage'. Then the kid begins to gurn and grind like Jimmy Page, in a manner that Hank B. Marvin would never have dreamed of. The kid is taking the sound wherever he wants it to go, beyond the Shadows. He plays the cricket bat with his teeth like Hendrix. He falls to his knees like Townshend. And, just then, his mum sticks her head around the door to tell him that his tea's ready. She sees this unhinged performance and is wide-eyed with shock. The inference – that she might have caught him doing something else – is left hanging.

'We sold a hundred thousand cricket bats last week,' joked Hank. 'No records, but lots of cricket bats.'

Notably, there were no vocals on the Shadows' *20 Golden Greats* at all, not even the recent hit 'Let Me Be the One'; there was nothing later than 1967's 'Maroc 7'. It was a subtle re-writing, but wiping Marvin, Welch and Farrar from the group's history unavoidably meant wiping 'Saturday Dance' and 'Don't Make My Baby Blue' as well. This is what the Shadows *really* were, the album told us.

While the album was at number three in the chart and rising, Hank was interviewed by the *NME*'s Mick Farren. He clearly had little idea of what the album's success would mean for both his past and his future. Bruce did; he would occasionally appear in the interview and say things like 'I can't wait to go out and spend the money'. Farren noted how different the two men were: Hank was wiry, thoughtful, with his hands in perpetual motion, while Bruce was 'heavier, bigger and far more solid. If ever he got short of a few bob, he could easily make a living playing one of Regan's heavy mob in *The Sweeney*.'

Hank was also altogether less sure than Bruce about what the success of *20 Golden Greats* really meant.

He talked to Farren about using the money he made from commercial hits to subsidise the kind of music he wanted to play, without specifying what that was. He talked about Alec Galloway, an alter ego he had devised, as if his previous alter ego – Hank B. Marvin – was now beyond his control, owned by the audience, subsumed by the expectations of fans, of Bruce, of EMI. Alec Galloway apparently had a 'calm ferocity' and a 'robust fragility'.

'Alec Galloway, folks. Alec Galloway. You heard it here first. Alec Galloway is going to be a monster.'

It was as if Marvin, Welch and Farrar's relative failure had caused Hank shame and embarrassment; these demons will often emerge as black humour. 'When you do something different in front of an audience that's not ready for it,' he explained, 'you take a big gamble. Not only with what you're doing, but with what you've done before.'

If he wasn't in the Shadows, if he wasn't even Hank B. Marvin, things would be so much easier, he told Farren. The implication was that *20 Golden Greats* seemed to box him, process him, label him as a thing of the past.

'You can do more extreme things. If I play you a record and tell you it's Alec Galloway, you'll say "Yeah, I like that" or "I don't like it." If I tell you it's the new Hank Marvin, you'll have pre-conceived ideas about it, that it'll have a Shadows feel, or you might be prejudiced anyway and say "He's trying to do a Jeff Beck" or "He's trying to do an Isaac Hayes. Why doesn't he stick to the Shads?" If it's under an assumed name, there's more chance of you accepting it – or not.'

Farren might have felt churlish pointing out that the Shadows' erstwhile frontman had just broken through in the US with a top-five hit and no one in Kalamazoo gave two hoots about the twenty years of baggage he was carrying around. It could equally happen tomorrow in the States for Cliff Richard, for the Shadows or for Alec Galloway.

There was another, more positive way of looking at the success of *20 Golden Greats*: the Shadows were loved. The artwork was cool and clean, their image untainted by missteps like 'Rhythm and Greens', or flubs at Eurovision. Just that clear, ringing sound that had pierced the early '60s airwaves like a siren.

The album also sold to a new, younger generation who were already familiar with 'Apache', and possibly with 'FBI' and 'Wonderful Land' too, but to whom the past was essentially a foreign country waiting to be explored. This was a generation who goggled at the fierce fuzz on 'Stingray' or marvelled at the panoramic power of 'Theme for Young Lovers', tracks the older, fair-weather fans might have only vaguely recalled. This was a generation who would understand that the Shadows had been innovators, the inspiration for so much that came after them. Unlike Lonnie Donegan's scratchy skiffle – which may as well have been George Formby for all the resonance it had in the music of 1977 – the Shadows' music sounded fresh and adventurous, the gateway to avenues that still hadn't been trodden.

*

20 Golden Greats was released just before T. Dan Smith, Newcastle's other great moderniser. He'd had, inevitably, to both deal with dubious companies and iffy contracts and turn a blind eye to get the Brasilia of the north built. He had pleaded guilty to bribery in 1974. Dan hadn't kept up certain standards of conduct in public life and he had to pay. Innovators, modernisers, they'll always take the hit.

He had hustled contracts from local councils for John Poulson, a particularly unpleasant – and unqualified – architect from Yorkshire who had been doing similar on a nationwide scale. To make things happen, Smith reckoned, you needed those ten people, the ones who can make your vision a reality. But rather than Norrie Paramor, he had John Poulson. Dan was a visionary, but his flaw had been working with people who didn't care about his vision, who only wanted to make money for themselves, and he was dragged down with them. T. Dan Smith was sentenced to six years in prison.

He was released after three years and quickly started to campaign for penal reform and pensioners' rights. Occasionally, he even had something to say about municipal housing. He moved into one of the Cruddas Park flats that he'd been responsible for, from which he had a great view of the formerly soot-filthy city he had helped to transform. Dan's sad story showed how quickly and easily radical notions could be hijacked and corrupted – the forces of power, greed and reaction would always be standing in your way and you'd have to try to navigate them. He was a utopian, a modernist, a hero to many, but T. Dan Smith had lost his way.

'Long after I'm gone and dead and forgotten,' Dan told the BBC in 1974, 'I think there will be somebody, somewhere, who will perhaps write a couple of lines and say that the people of the north were slightly better off for things that I did. No matter if I did some things that were wrong. The things that I did right, in the end, will prove to be of more value than any harm that was done.'

*

The 20 Golden Dates tour that followed in 1977 was like an extended encore, a final farewell and a thank-you. The acknowledgment for what the Shadows had achieved was overpowering. In fact, they enjoyed the standing ovations so much that they booked another series of shows, with Cliff on board, at the London Palladium in March 1978, which were recorded for a live album called *Thank You Very Much*. That really felt like closure.

Cliff had had his own triumphant circuit of the track with a TV-advertised album. Making it to number one in 1977, a few months after the Shadows, *40 Golden Greats* still didn't have a long-enough tracklisting to find room for Cliff and the Shadows hits like 'A Voice in the Wilderness', 'I'm the Lonely One' and 'Time Drags By'; it even missed out a number one in 'I Love You'. But – chronologically ordered – the album ended on a high with new single 'My Kinda Life', a Bruce Welch-produced, subtly raised V-sign to anyone who had ever questioned Cliff's judgement or direction. The album that then toppled *40 Golden Greats* from the number-one spot was *Never Mind the Bollocks... Here's the Sex Pistols,* a more obvious 'fuck you' that would harness and inspire the next generation.

A little more than twenty years since Hank and Bruce had appeared on *Six-Five Special* singing 'Teenage Love', they were on Granada's *Get It Together* performing 'Love Deluxe'. They shared the stage with power-pop act the Pleasers, who were gamely resurrecting the Merseybeat sound, and Tommy and the Hot Rocks, a Newcastle group trying to revive the spirit of Gene Vincent. All our yesterdays passed before us, until the Shads came on to play 'Love Deluxe', on which their guitars were barely audible under the synth swooshes and syn-drums. They were attuned to the times, all right; in fact, they sounded more like 1981 had arrived a few years early. But it didn't matter. It wasn't what people wanted from the Shadows and it didn't chart. It was their last vocal A-side.

The Shadows' work was done. The Sex Pistols could take it from here.

EPILOGUE

The success of *20 Golden Greats* would lead the newly reformed Shadows to trust their instincts, head to the studio in March 1977 and hastily make a new record; the result was the rather patchy *Tasty*. The opening track was 'Cricket Bat Boogie', a nod to the by now all-important TV advert; it was 'Guitar Boogie Shuffle' with a tweak. The album also included the adventurous, multipart 'Bermuda Triangle', likely inspired by 10cc's 'I'm Mandy Fly Me' or John Miles' 'Music', which had both been top-ten hits in 1976. The first part was ethereal and left you wondering about the many unexplored areas, places the Shadows' catalogue might have gone; they could have taught Pink Floyd a thing or two about drifty soundscapes. But there had always been another cabaret season in Batley, another summer season in Blackpool, another Stockton panto. It was inevitable that Peter Green, David Gilmour, Pete Townshend or Brian May was going to pick up the baton while it was resting on the bedside table, as you tried to catch a few hours' kip in a Bradford B&B.

They would rarely be this adventurous again and *Tasty* was filled out with a woozy 'Goodbye Yellow Brick Road', a swagger-free 'Honky Tonk Women' and a pasty 'The Most Beautiful Girl'. Here, there was something almost comical about a guitar dutifully following the vocal melody. It added nothing and subtracted a lot when the original singer had been someone as expressive as Charlie Rich.

Much more interesting was a new Hank project, an attempt to create a guitar orchestra, called *The Hank Marvin Guitar Syndicate*. The album opened with the six-minute-plus 'New Earth Parts 1 & 2', a hypnotic, repetitive, spacious track that moved into a tight, almost prog-like second part that sounded gently apocalyptic. The rest of the album was mostly covers (including a gorgeously nimble run through Stevie Wonder's 'Bird of Beauty'), but the airy funk of 'Syndicated' was another superb original, a musical glide over the Chilterns.

Hank gathered nine other guitarists for the album, including 'James Bond Theme'-player Vic Flick, Colin Green from Georgie Fame's Blue Flames and Kevin Peek. Herbie Flowers was recalled on bass after his *Shades of Rock* Shadows cameo and former Tornado Clem Cattini was on drums, and the whole thing had a feeling of lightness and liberation. The long shadow of the Shadows, in the form of a world-swallowing compilation, would soon draw Hank back whether he wanted to return or not.

Nineteen seventy-eight would be a good year for Brian. He recorded library music that would end up on the soundtracks of hit TV series *Dallas* and *Knots Landing*, while his keyboard-playing lad Warren started a band at school. Before he knew it, Brian was back to being driver and roadie, as if he was still in the Krew Kats. Warren's band Glass Ties signed to EMI in 1982 and would release a brace of singles, including the splendid synthpop 'You You You'. He would graduate to recording library music for Bruton, just like his dad, before joining Hank's band and eventually the Shads. Also in 1978, new members Alan Jones (bass) and Cliff Hall (keyboards) joined in time for another tour. *20 Golden Greats* turned out to be the launchpad for a whole new era.

Hank was invited to play on Tim Rice and Andrew Lloyd Webber's *Evita* album in 1977, which became a commercial success and led to the launch of the stage show later that year. One song Hank didn't play on was 'Don't Cry for Me Argentina', but he loved it and put a version together – complete with mock crowd noise, just as Joe Meek might have done – the following year. Bruce wasn't on the record, but with the Shadows' name alive again, Hank wasn't ever going to release it as a solo single.

The Shadows' fate for the next decade was set when 'Don't Cry for Me Argentina' became a shock top-ten hit in 1978. The follow-up, 'Cavatina' – written by British soundtrack composer Stanley Myers and used as the theme for *The Deer Hunter* – gave them another top-ten hit in 1979. It was the first time they'd had consecutive top-ten hits in sixteen years. Sensing that what Shadows fans really wanted at the turn of the '80s was Shadow-fied versions of contemporary hits, they recorded *String of Hits*.

String of Hits would become another TV-advertised number-one album with versions of 'Bright Eyes', a rainy, private-eye take on 'Baker Street' and an interpretation of Blondie's 'Heart of Glass' that suggested it had originally been written for a John Ford movie. The best track by a distance was the album's only original, 'Song for Duke'. It worked equally well as a tribute to Jerry Lordan, twenty years after he turned their world around with 'Apache'; there were suggestions of both 'Wonderful Land' and 'Atlantis', that familiar strain of melancholy. But elsewhere were things like 'Bridge Over Troubled Water' that sounded as engaging as hold music.

It was undeniably safe, but *String of Hits* sold in huge numbers, eventually reaching number one in 1980 making it harder for the progressive wing of the group to win arguments with the more commercially minded. It was followed into the charts by *Another String of Hot Hits* in 1980 and *Hits Right Up Your Street* in 1981. Given a licence to print money, the Shadows would continue to turn out these albums annually until they called it a day with *Reflection* in 1990. Any hit from the '80s that you ever wanted to hear (or never wanted to hear) rendered as a guitar instrumental – 'Flashdance', 'Africa', 'Careless Whisper', 'The Lady in Red', 'Up Where We Belong', 'We Don't Need Another Hero', 'Nothing's Gonna Stop Us Now' – you can guarantee the Shadows did it.

There was the occasional attempt to create new music, original titles, notably on 1984's return to form, *Guardian Angel*. But while 1986's *Moonlight Shadows* would reach number six with its tepid versions of 'Every Breath You Take', 'Hello' and' I Just Called to Say I Love You', *Guardian Angel* topped out at number ninety-eight. Were they a band or were they a business? What were they still in it for? Towards the end, the track listings on TV-advertised albums like *Simply Shadows* and *Steppin' to the Shadows* would be partly decided by a committee rather than just the band.

'I think 1977 was the year that the Shadows became businessmen first and foremost,' said Bruce Welch.

*

In 1980, their twenty-year contract with EMI was up. Other EMI acts had renegotiated royalty rates, kept the rights to their recordings and licensed them back to EMI. The Shadows wanted nothing more than this; they weren't being greedy. But EMI said no. Hadn't the Shadows made them a fortune? Hadn't they always toed the party line? Been absolutely professional and risk-averse? They just wanted a bit of the action. They just wanted to do what everyone else was doing. No, said EMI. So they left.

After signing with Polygram, the group did re-records so that EMI would make less from their back catalogue. 'A lot of fans liked the way we'd revisited them,' said a diplomatic Hank to the Arts Desk, 'but some thought we shouldn't have. I'd be the same. I had a Little Feat album with "Rock 'n' Roll Doctor" on, the original with a terrific slide guitar solo by Lowell George, very simple, very well-constructed, a cracking record. I lost it or it got nicked. I discovered the song a few years later on another album but it's a re-recording. It's not the same. It lost the groove, a shame.'

He yearned to do 'tunes that allowed me to get some creative expression in rather than copy the original with my guitar becoming the voice. That's what we sadly did towards the end of the Shadows' career, which I never really liked doing.'

Progressive versus conservative. The two factions that had been warring in the group since 1958 came to an uneasy truce in the '80s and this would hold until raw boredom on the part of Hank and Brian led to their eventual breaking up. From the perspective of this writer, the departure of John Farrar and his positive influence in 1977, soon followed by losing the influence of Alan Tarney, marked the end of the Shadows' golden era. There are great tracks to be found on the later albums – 'Song for Duke', Brian Bennett's eerie 'Look Back on Love' from *Guardian Angel*, Hank and Brian's 'Our Albert' from the same album – but the momentum and sense of adventure were gone.

For his thirtieth anniversary in the music business, Cliff Richard organised an event – modestly called The Event – at Wembley Stadium in the summer of 1989. In a particularly thrilling moment, Jet and Tony both joined Cliff on stage to perform 'Move It'. 'To me he's almost St Cliff,' Jet wept. 'He's such a special person.' Talking about the Carol Costa affair, he made light of it, saying that they had all been children back then. Hank and Bruce, for their own reasons, declined to join Cliff for this section of the show.

But there would be more anniversaries.

The group reformed for one last tour in 2004. 'It'll be a nice way to go out,' laughed Bruce. 'Forty-five years of too many guitar instrumentals.' They recorded Jerry Lordan's epic 'Life Story', which became the title track of a compilation. It felt appropriate to close the book with another Lordan song. The fifth Shadow had died in July 1995 in Shropshire, near the small town of Bishop's Castle where a blue plaque now hangs outside his favourite pub, the Three Tuns.

Marvin, Welch and Bennett were together for one last time, joined on keyboards by Cliff Hall and on bass by Mark Griffiths. The tour proved successful enough for the Shads to extended the tour into Europe in 2005; this time, Warren Bennett, the next-generation protector of their legacy, finally joined the group on keyboards. The only time they have all played together since – and almost certainly the final, *final* bow – was when Cliff Richard persuaded them to play The

Final Reunion at the O2 in London in 2009, to celebrate their fiftieth anniversary (give or take a few months). They made a new album of re-recordings called *Reunited* to mark the occasion. On stage at the O2, Cliff looked genuinely thrilled to have the Shadows back on stage with him, one last time. The show opened with a dynamic 'We Say Yeah' and, after it, looking out at wild hordes of sixty-something fans, Cliff said, 'Please sit down, you'll only get tired.'

Tony Meehan had left the music industry in the 1990s to become a professional psychologist, a subject he had always been deeply interested in. He worked as a lecturer at a college in London, which he was still doing in 2005 when he had a fall in his Maida Vale flat and died as a result of head injuries. He was just sixty-two years old.

Jet had been sober for Cliff's The Event and would remain so. No one had thought he could do it, but after many attempts, he finally kicked the booze. He would play shows, backed by instro group the Rapiers, and proudly tell crowds from the stage how long he had been sober. He moved to Bembridge on the Isle of Wight, his favourite bolt-hole, where he grew weed and hoped no one would notice (they didn't). He recorded an album in 2007 called *The Journey*, which included the majestic, moving 'Song for Tony', something Jerry Lordan would have been proud of and could have made Tony Meehan blush. After a long battle, Jet Harris died of cancer in 2011.

Licorice Locking had played harmonica with Jet at his last-ever show in Fareham in Hampshire, in February 2011. Though he had only been in the group for little more than a year, Licorice would feel like a former Shadow for the rest of his life. He remained a devoted Jehovah's Witness, but had hit hard times in the late '60s before moving in with his friends Denis and Pat George. Somehow, Licorice stayed under the radar of almost everyone in the Shadows world, even though for years he was playing every weekend at a pub in Bromley. The Georges moved from Streatham to north Wales in 1980, taking Licorice with them. He ended up working there as a window cleaner and a potato roundsman, as well as helping out at a veterinary surgery and in a home for people with special needs.

It wasn't until 1997 that he found a way back into the Shadows' extended family when he received a phone call from John Brown, head of the Fender Club: would Licorice would like to become an honorary member? Of course he would. At a Fender trade show, he met Barry Gibson who worked for Burns; Gibson told Licorice that he was putting a band together for a show in France, with Jet Harris on bass and Clem Cattini on drums. They were calling themselves Local Heroes. Would Licorice like to join them? Of course he would. During the French reunion show, Bruce Welch came on stage to play 'Shadoogie' and, from that point on, Licorice would be a regular at Shadows conventions and fan events until he passed away in 2020.

Bruce would be the primary force behind Shadowmania, an annual get-together of fans and former Shads that he started in 1998 at the Lakeside Country Club in Frimley Green, Surrey. People missed them and here was a chance for former Shadows to get together without any of the aggro, potential acrimony or personal politics that would be involved in a full band reunion. Jet appeared at the very first one and felt the love, receiving a standing ovation for two minutes. Tony Meehan turned up for a couple in the years just before he died. Licorice Locking was a regular attendee; in 2010, backed by a Swiss tribute band, he played bass and harmonica, sang in French and took the roof off with an impassioned 'My Prayer'. At another Shadows convention, the Rapiers' Colin Pryce-Jones remembered the boy Locking wondering why the fans in one of the rooms at the convention centre looked a bit downhearted. Licorice strode into the room and decided to cheer them up with his 'chicken walk', before someone gently pointed out that they weren't Shadows fans; it was a funeral party that just happened to be in the same building.

In 2021, Bruce told the fans 'I have decided that this year's [Shadowmania] will be the last one, due to various health reasons. If you were thinking of coming but haven't booked yet, think again; it will be great to say goodbye to you in person. My very best to all of you, and thanks for your loyalty for all these years...' Through the years, Bruce had always been incredibly generous with the Shadows' worldwide fanbase and this must have been a huge wrench for him.

*

Back in 1992, Neil Young had released his acclaimed *Harvest Moon* album, which went on to rival the sales of his best-loved '70s albums. It included the track 'From Hank to Hendrix', an acknowledgment of the part Hank Marvin had played in Young's journey from bug-eyed kid at the back of the class to international guitar hero. When Cliff and the Shadows played that fiftieth anniversary show at the O2 in 2009, Neil Young and his friend Randy Bachman were invited over. They met Hank during the soundcheck and he handed them the legendary red Strat; Randy got his Vox AC 30 signed by Hank, Bruce and Brian.

At heart they were still – like Pete Townshend, Brian May and Peter Green – just kids, Shadows fans, understanding how the sounds of 'FBI', 'Kon-Tiki' and 'Wonderful Land' had been the key, the one that could open worlds upon worlds of possibilities.

BIBLIOGRAPHY

Beyond published books and contemporary music papers, I found much useful information from forebears who had happily prepared some of the ground for me. I owe a debt of gratitude to the following writers and articles.

Chris Colverson's wonderful online fan memoir *Me and My Shadows*, which really gave me an idea of what it was like to live through the Shadows' first golden age.

The wonderful *Pipeline* magazine, the long-running magazine on instrumental music, provided several invaluable articles and interviews, including ones on Pete Chester, Jerry Lordan and the mid-'60s Jet Harris Group.

I was also kept on my toes by David 'Ghosty' Wills highly entertaining Cliff and the Shadows podcast *We Say Yeah!*. Kindred spirits were found in J.P. Robinson's superb 2016 essay 'The Fate of Sir Cliff Richard' and Marcello Carlin's insightful and inspiring pieces on Cliff and the Shadows on his Then Play Long blog.

Other sources of obscure facts as well as helpful quotes and anecdotes on Jet's immediate post-Shadows career came from Terry Webster's Webstars site; Dick Weindling and Marianne Colloms' piece on Tony for their History of Kilburn and West Hampstead blog;

Jane Graham's interview with Hank in the *Big Issue* in 2017; Thomas H. Green's interview with Hank for the Arts Desk in 2014; articles about Tony on Mike Dolbear's drummers' website; and Andrew Hickey's deeply impressive *A History of Rock Music in 500 Songs* podcast.

Blake, Mark, *Us and Them: The Authorised Story of Hipgnosis* (Nine Eight, 2025)

Bradford, Rob, *Funny Old World: The Life and Music of John Henry Rostill* (Apple Print, 2024)

Bragg, Billy, *Roots, Radicals and Rockers: How Skiffle Changed the World* (Faber & Faber, 2017)

Brewster, Bill; Broughton, Frank, *The Record Players: DJ Revolutionaries* (DJ History, 2010)

Campbell, Malcolm, *A Pocket Guide to Shadow Music* (Idmon Publications, 2006)

Cavanagh, David, *Good Night and Good Riddance: How Thirty-Five Years of John Peel Helped to Shape Modern Life* (Faber and Faber, 2015)

Ellis, Royston, *The Shadows by Themselves* (Consul, 1961)

Everett, Peter, *You'll Never Be 16 Again* (BBC Publications, 1986)

Foster, Mo, *Seventeen Watts? The First 20 Years of British Rock Guitar, the Musicians and Their Stories* (Sanctuary Publishing, 1997)

Frame, Pete, *The Restless Generation: How Rock Music Changed the Face of 1950s Britain* (Omnibus, 2007)

Haines, Luke, *Freaks Out!* (Nine Eight, 2024)

Hawkshaw, Alan, *The Champ: (The Hawk Talks)* (Anchor Print Group, 2011)

Horn, Adrian, *Juke Box Britain: Americanisation and Youth Culture 1945–60* (Manchester University Press, 2009)

Jopling, Norman, *Shake It Up Baby!: Notes from a Pop Music Reporter 1961–1972* (RockHistory, 2015)

Lewisohn, Mark, *The Beatles – All These Years: Volume One: Tune In* (Little, Brown, 2015)

Matthew, Brian, *This Is Where I Came In* (Constable and Company, 1991)

Newton-John, Olivia, *Don't Stop Believin'* (Simon and Schuster, 2018)

Nicolson, Dave, *Jet Harris: In Spite of Everything* (Music Mentor Books, 2011)

Oldham, Andrew Loog, *Stoned* (Vintage, 2001)

Read, Mike, *The Story of the Shadows* (Elm Tree Books, 1983)

Read, Mike; Goodall, Nigel; Lewry, Peter, *Cliff Richard: The Complete Chronicle* (Hamlyn, 1993)

Richard, Cliff, *Me and My Shadows* (Daily Mirror, 1961)

Richard, Cliff, *The Dreamer* (Ebury Press, 2020)

Rust, Victor, *The Shadows Recording Catalogue* (Lulu, 2011)

Schroeder, John, *Sex and Violins: My Affair with Life, Love and Music* (Pen Press, 2009)

Smith, Clive; Wetherell, Bip, *Clem Cattini: My Life Through the Eye of a Tornado* (Mango Books, 2019)

Rivers, Tony, *I'm Nearly Famous: The Tales of a Likely Lad* (Douglas A. Thompson, 2015)

Welch, Bruce, *Rock 'n' Roll I Gave You the Best Years of My Life* (Viking, 1989)

Wilson, Babs, *Me and My Shadow* (New Generation Publishing, 2022)

Wooding, Dan, *I Thought Terry Dene Was Dead* (Coverdale House, 1974)

ACKNOWLEDGEMENTS

First of all, I want to thank Hank Marvin, Bruce Welch, Brian Bennett, Jet Harris, Tony Meehan and Cliff Richard for giving us all so many years of pleasure – it's been a lifelong love – and for giving up their time to talk to me. I was fortunate enough to chat with both Jet and Tony for a feature in *Mojo* magazine in 2004, and luckily had the foresight to keep the recordings of both interviews with these charming, much-missed men.

Many thanks to Alan Tarney, with whom I spent a memorable afternoon in the bar at Queen's Club, and to John Farrar who was kind enough to engage in several transatlantic phone calls.

Huge thanks also to Warren Bennett, holder of the Shads torch, who was most helpful and insightful, and spent two lengthy tea-drinking sessions with me at Cecil Sharp House in north London, filling in gaps and answering my most oblique queries.

And to Terry Britten for his encouragement and succinct quotes.

I am also greatly indebted to:

My agents, David and Sebastian Godwin, and everybody at New Modern. Especially Pete Selby, who I've been chatting to about this book for over a decade, and who knows more about Cliff B-sides than is probably good for him.

Brian Ward, for showing me round Newcastle when I began to write this book, helping me to locate the streets where Hank and Bruce grew up.

Martin Kelly, who knows more about the history of guitars and amps than anybody else I've ever met and gave me my treasured copy of *The Shadows by Themselves* many years ago.

Claudine Lordan, who was a wonderful, chatty host, took me to Jerry Lordan's favourite pub in Shropshire and made me feel bad for not trying harder in French at school.

Juliette Iaciofano at Leo's Den, the shop for all your Cliff and the Shadows needs, who has been incredibly supportive and helpful with contacts and must have thought this book would never come out.

The late Rob Bradford for his years of research, in particular on John Rostill, and to Di Bradford for publishing Rob's detailed updated biography, *Funny Old World*.

Alan Taylor, who was happy to dig out any relevant back issues of his excellent *Pipeline* magazine for me – more power to it and the instro scene.

Mark Williams and his magical shop in Keighley. Thanks to Mark for turning up all manner of Shads clippings and tour programmes, as well as pretty much every issue of *Now Dig This* that I could ever need.

Bernard O'Hara and George Geddes, both kind-hearted Shadows devotees who were always happy to get back to any peculiarly precise questions I had.

Andrew Lewis, for very generously sending me a stack of clippings and ephemera on John Farrar and Olivia Newton-John.

Mark Lewisohn, for helping me to get to the bottom of the connection between Tony Meehan and the Beatles.

Kieron Tyler, for the excellent sleeve notes to Brian Bennett's *Aim High* compilation, and for many happy hours spent over a cold drink talking about the early days of British rock 'n' roll.

Richard Hawley, for his Shads love and good chats about Duane Eddy.

For being great people, passing on records and anecdotes, and helping me out over the years, I'd also like to thank Mike Alway, Jeff Barrett, Gus Bousfield, Nan Brimble, James Brown, Liz Buckley, Derek Burbidge, Ian Catt, Alex Conway, Sarah Cracknell, Alan Dobrin, Travis Elborough, Tom Ewing, Lora Findlay, Jo Forshaw, Mark Goodall, Martin Green, Jerry Jaffe, Ben Jones, Paul Kelly, Alasdair McLellan, Anneliese Midgley, Michael Mulligan, Andrew Oldham, Pete Paphides, Rob Prior, Darren Reed, Andrew Sandoval, Daniel Scott, Roger Spiers, Chris Taylor, Liam Watson, Geoffrey Weiss, Pete Wiggs, Harvey Williams, Debsey Wykes and Andy Zax.

Special thanks go to Tess and Len, who have been incredibly patient with me as I was writing this book and playing 'Man of Mystery' on repeat in the car. Len feels slightly guilty for wiping out the tombola at the Scarborough Shadows convention in 2024.

And lastly to my wonderful dad, who gave me his original copies of 'F.B.I.' and 'Dynamite' ('not "Travellin' Light", the other side!') when I was barely old enough to walk and got the ball rolling.

The team at New Modern would like to thank the following individuals:

Nige Tassell for copy-editing
Jane Henshall for proofreading
Marie Doherty for typesetting
Paul Palmer-Edwards for cover design
Dusty Miller for publicity
Marie Lecouturier, Charlotte Rose, Andreina Brezzo and the team at Simon & Schuster UK for sales and distribution